THEORY AND PROCESSES
OF HISTORY

Biographical Note

FREDERICK JOHN TEGGART was born in Belfast, Ireland, May 9, 1870. He attended Methodist College, Belfast, and Trinity College, Dublin, and received the B.A. degree from Stanford University in 1894 following his move to the United States in 1888. He worked for several years in library administration and taught courses in history and political science at the University of California at Berkeley until, in 1919, he founded there the Department of Social Institutions, which he chaired until his retirement in 1940. In 1925 he attained the professorship in Social Institutions, in 1935 he was named Faculty Research Lecturer, and in 1943 the University awarded him the honorary degree of Doctor of Laws. He was actively engaged in research until shortly before his death on October 12, 1946.

Theory and Processes of History

By FREDERICK J. TEGGART

With a Preface by Kenneth Bock

UNIVERSITY OF CALIFORNIA PRESS

Berkeley, Los Angeles, London

University of California Press
Berkeley, California

University of California Press, Ltd.
London, England

Theory of History, Copyright, 1925, by
Yale University Press

The Processes of History, Copyright, 1918, by
Yale University Press

The two books as here presented in one volume,
Copyright, 1941, by
Frederick J. Teggart

First Paperback Edition, 1960
Second Paperback Edition, 1977

© 1977 by
The Regents of the University of California
ISBN: 0–520–03176–8
Printed in the United States of America

1 2 3 4 5 6 7 8 9

Preface to the 1977 Edition

THIS FOURTH PRINTING of Frederick J. Teggart's *Theory of History* and *Processes of History* comes at a time as opportune as that of their first appearance, for the major problems in humanistic inquiry to which he addressed himself in the first quarter of the twentieth century now confront us in aggravated form at the beginning of its fourth quarter.

The current revival of an explicit evolutionism in sociology and anthropology is attended by little recognition of the serious implications of that complex doctrine which Teggart sought to elucidate. The confusion of what was essentially an eighteenth-century concept of development with the Darwinian theory of organic evolution persists. It has become apparent that the shallow arguments that had presumably laid nineteenth-century notions of social and cultural evolution to rest did not get to the root of the matter. In these circumstances we can profit from reexamination of Teggart's penetrating analysis of the intellectual foundations of the idea of progress that have produced a separation, as he saw it, between the studies of history and evolution.

The related, although quite distinct, resurgence of efforts to explain human social and cultural life in biological terms can also be read more clearly when they are illuminated by Teggart's observations (in 1918) on the consequences that have followed the tendency of "humanists in all branches of the study of man . . . to base their discussions upon what they conceive to be the conclusions of modern biology," to "describe and interpret social relations in terms of a pseudo-biological symbolism," and to compare "man and brute" instead of different cultures. Teggart's decision to take man "as given" was the prevailing scholarly view of his time, and it is worthwhile to be reminded that this judgment was based, not on some stubborn behaviorism, but on a consideration, first, that biologists did not have much to offer the humanist, second, that explanations from human nature did not really explain the social and cultural, and, above all, that cultural differences could be explained in biological terms only by eventual resort to racial theories which had proved both insupportable in fact and a serious obstacle to an open comparison of histories and open relations among peoples.

The breadth of Teggart's view is manifested in his sense of a need to define a broad problem in the study of man, a problem that can bring unity and direction to the myriad legitimate inquiries and puzzles that have engaged the attention of scholars since the time of Hesiod, a problem that can provide a point of focus for the separate humanistic disciplines within the university.

The problem of cultural differences is the central concern of both of the books presented in this volume. It was by a clear statement of this problem and an argument for its importance that Teggart hoped to influence the course of humanistic study and of human affairs. Candid recognition of the variety of life experiences among distinct groups of people in specific areas at specific historical times involved a pluralistic view of history and an abandonment of the traditional quest for cultural similarities or some common denominator of culture lodged in human nature or the system of Culture as such. Acceptance of the plurality of history established a basis for that comparison of histories (not just structures or conditions) which he considered indispensable for a discernment of processes that could account for "how things have come to be as they are." Much of the argument throughout is pointed at demonstrating the preferability of this orientation to differences over the common view which saw them as stages in a universal movement and led to efforts, of either an historical or evolutionary character, to depict an ideal series of epochs in the development of Society or Culture or Civilization. Put another way, the pluralistic view of history called for the plotting of spatial and temporal distributions of classes of events in various human life activities as a way of delineating problems that called for solutions. It is this course that Teggart followed in his *Rome and China*, and it is the procedure that has been used by his most notable successor in this tradition, Margaret T. Hodgen, in her *Change and History*.

Arnold J. Toynbee's acknowledged debt to Teggart is clear even though the substantive works of the two men are quite different and Teggart was not sparing in his criticism of *A Study of History*. The ecumenical outlook, the conception of history as plural, the comparison of histories, the primary concern with cultural differences, the avoidance of traditional forms of historical narration, and the basic problem of accounting for change are common to their theories and methodologies. Teggart offers us no concept of "challenge and response"—he had small capacity or inclination for couching his ideas in catchy phrases, and none of Toynbee's willingness to draw on myths for insights into historical processes—but the *kind* of explanation of cultural innovation that he offered was similar. The closest that Teggart came to expansive speculation on conditions of change was in his picture of concentric circles from universe to human individual through which events (intrusions) had their impact. Toynbee's idea that a people is roused to efforts leading to civilization only upon a disruption of the ordinary course of life is of the same genre.

Teggart's hopes for a spreading influence of the ideas he espoused and reformulated have not been realized in anything like full measure, but recent dissatisfaction among sociologists and anthropologists with the confining atmosphere of structural and functional analysis should foster a climate in which a theoretical foundation for an historical study of social and cultural processes will be sought. The present situation is reminiscent of the mid-nineteenth-century reaction against an abstract and timeless utilitarianism and the call for adoption of an historical perspective in the study of human affairs. That reaction took the form of a return to an eighteenth-century idea of progress and a flood of literature on social and cultural "evolution." As mentioned above, the signs of a similar response today are clear. The implications of evolutionism as they are traced by Teggart, and the alternative approach to the study of processes he suggested, are particularly worthy of our attention at this time if we are not to contribute in our turn to the dreary recycling of social theory that has been characteristic of Western intellectual history.

Kenneth Bock

Preface

O F THE TWO BOOKS included in this volume, the first, entitled *Theory of History*, was originally published by the Yale University Press in 1925; the second, *The Processes of History*, was likewise issued by the Yale University Press, but in 1918. The two are now reprinted without changes other than occasional revisions of phraseology and alterations of punctuation and the elimination of a few references to what were, at the respective dates of writing, current events.

The connection of the two books calls for a word of explanation. In 1916, the University of California Press published, under the title *Prolegomena to History*, a critical inquiry into "the relation of history to literature, philosophy, and science." The investigation thus initiated was continued in the *Theory of History* and, in this later exposition, was extended to other fields of humanistic interest. The consideration which led to these publications was the belief that conditions in the world called imperatively for knowledge of a sort which could be derived only from an exacting inquiry into the actualities of human experience and, further, that the materials required for such a study were available in historical documents. The belief referred to at once raised the question of how it had come about that the knowledge suggested was not now in existence, seeing that the study of history had already reached a high development in the fifth century B.C. To this question the *Prolegomena* and *Theory* provide an answer. Historians have maintained a prescriptive right to utilize the data of human experience in accordance with the traditions of history writing, in other words, for the construction of narratives devoted primarily to the vindication and enhancement of national pride. Social scientists, on the other hand, have essayed to give a 'true' rendering of human history by describing, without reference to dated historical events, what they suppose to be the 'natural' course of change, or have employed historical data to provide factual illustrations for *a priori* theories of 'progress,' 'evolution,' and 'stages of development.' It follows, as a consequence of the reliance placed on these procedures, that the records of human experience have never been examined with the object of determining 'how things actually work' in a world where the lives of men are dominated by the activities of political organizations, or with the aim of elucidating 'how things have come to be as they are' today in all the various parts of the world.

In itself, however, criticism of established procedures can lead to no constructive result. The acquisition of new knowledge must await the formulation of definite proposals for new undertakings. Hence the earlier *Prolegomena to History* (1916) was followed closely by *The Processes of History* (1918), in which an effort was made to bring into relation historical problems which separately had been touched upon by many writers, but which had at no time been systematically surveyed. The brief outline of 1918 was written under conditions which were adverse to sustained deliberation and to the search for more ample materials and documentation than fell within the writer's immediate control. It is to be regarded, indeed, not as an embodiment of new and independent investigations, but as a product of acquaintance with the literature of different fields of scholarship, actuated by a desire to discover an orderly approach to the study of 'how things have come to be as they are.' The new element in the book consists in the coördination of judgments and opinions of scholars which had been expressed sporadically over a long period of time and hitherto had remained widely scattered throughout the literature of humanistic inquiry.

The Processes of History was designed to exhibit a program of research, and after the publication of the *Theory of History* the need became insistent for furtherance of this program through the investigation on new lines of some particular historical problem. A significant topic referred to in the *Processes* was therefore taken for intensive study, and a first statement of the results of this inquiry appeared in *Rome and China, a Study of Correlations in Historical Events,* published by the University of California Press in 1939. In this book the investigation of a given class of events through a comparison of occurrences in the principal regions of the Old World disclosed the existence (during the period investigated) of close correspondences in events throughout the continent of Eurasia, and thus brought to light relations in the histories of widely separated areas which had not previously been suspected.

The critical analysis presented in the *Theory of History* constitutes a preliminary and necessary step toward promoting an awareness of the difficulties which impede the utilization of historical materials for the purpose of understanding the complexities and disasters in which men now find themselves everywhere involved. The program of investigation presented in *The Processes of History* represents a mode of approach to the study of these difficulties which has proved capable of leading to entirely new results within the field of history as conventionally defined. Broadly considered, the most important outcome of these inquiries is the revelation of the interdependence of peoples throughout the world, and the demonstration that a comprehension of the course of events in any one country requires a knowledge of what has been going on 'in all the corners of the earth.'

F. J. T.

Contents

THEORY OF HISTORY

THE PROCESSES OF HISTORY

THEORY OF HISTORY

Introduction

IN 1918 the British Labor Party pronounced its belief in the necessity for increased study, scientific investigation, and deliberate organization of research "in the still undeveloped science of society." "If law," it declared, "is the mother of freedom, science must be the parent of law." In 1795 a similar view was expressed by the National Convention of France, on the occasion of the foundation of the Institut National. So, too, in the twentieth century, Bryce, Wells, Wallas, Gardner, Dewey, and many others have reëchoed the judgments of Vico, Montesquieu, Turgot, Diderot, and Condorcet, of David Hume, Adam Smith, and Jeremy Bentham, in the eighteenth century, in urging the importance of a scientific study of 'man' or of 'society.'

Notwithstanding the aspirations of two centuries, there is apparent, at the present moment, a widespread unrest and dissatisfaction with the character of the studies spoken of familiarly as the 'social sciences.' The evidence of this intellectual disquiet appears, not only in outspoken criticisms of current activities in the study of society, but also in repeated attempts to define anew the relationships of the various disciplines in which the phenomena of human existence are made the object of inquiry, as well as in persistent efforts to improve and strengthen each separate discipline by means of a critical examination and reformulation of its particular problems and modes of procedure.

There can be no question that a strong determination manifests itself at the present time to find a sound basis for the study of man or of society, and this is a most hopeful sign. Yet it must be confessed that the discussions in which the present situation finds expression have led to little more than the elaboration of logical arguments drawn from the distinguishing features of the activities that are pursued in the recognized branches of humanistic study. It is remarkable, indeed, that the fact should not have impressed itself more generally on the minds of contemporary scholars that when established modes of procedure have brought to the surface irreconcilable views on method and aim of inquiry in any field, the time has come for a far-reaching inquiry into the theoretical foundations of the subject in question.

Instead, therefore, of attempting to mitigate our present discontents by seeking to reach, by mutual agreement, a demarcation of existing studies, it would seem imperative that we should endeavor to understand the conditions in thought which have given rise to the present symptoms of disquiet and unrest. If this course be pursued, the fact cannot well be ignored that, in one vital aspect, the discussion in regard to the social sciences has taken its rise (in the United States), not in the universities, but in the schools. In recent years there has been a well-defined movement directed toward the introduction of 'social studies' into the curriculum of the high school. As this movement has progressed, it has become apparent that time could not be found, in the school program, for each of the separate social science disciplines represented in the university. Hence the question has arisen, how the essentials or foundations of the higher studies could be presented in elementary form. What the schools have asked, in principle, is a definition of the common ground from which the special branches of the social sciences have become differentiated. So, in the endeavor to reach back to the 'simple' form, to the logical beginnings of the social sciences, the schools have raised questions of the most fundamental description, questions which cannot be answered without consideration of the conceptual basis upon which these inquiries rest.

The difficulty of the situation which has thus been precipitated lies in the fact that the university studies which are grouped under the head of 'social sciences' recognize no common basis in theory or method. Even a cursory examination of the aims and ideals of the social sciences will reveal the fact that, while extramural humanists have been urging the need of a 'science of society,' the academic exponents of history, economics, anthropology, and sociology have been insisting that the work of each of these branches was in the strictest sense 'scientific.' Under these conditions, the prospect of arriving at a solution of the difficulties which have presented themselves would be encouraging, provided the representatives of each of these subjects were in agreement on the signification of the term 'science.' Inquiry, however, discloses the anomalous complication that while each branch of the social sciences lays claim to the distinction of being 'scientific,' each one follows what, to all appearance, is a distinct and independent 'method.' We are driven, therefore, to the conclusion that it is hopeless to continue the discussion of the relationship of the different social sciences until light has been thrown upon the differences in modes of procedure which characterize the existing studies concerned with the investigation of the activities of men.

The only systematic effort to elucidate the complex situation in regard to method which exists in the field of the humanities has been made by certain philosophers in Germany. The essential feature of this effort has been the acceptance, as given, of the existing differences in method; and the procedure followed has been to set up, at whatever pains, arguments of a logical order to justify the established usages. The method employed in any subject, it is held, is determined by the particular object which the student has in view, so that, to these philosophers, there is nothing incongruous in the notion of there being as many types of 'scientific method' as there are 'scientific' investigators. Whatever the validity of this contention, it will be evident that this effort can contribute nothing to the elucidation of the present complexity in the methodology of the social sciences.

The problem with which we are confronted is set by the fact that while publicists urge the need of a science of society in the name of the general welfare, and while teachers urge the need of instruction in the elements of 'social science' in the interest of the intelligence of the people, the higher learning of the universities, in response to these demands, offers only a series of uncoördinated opinions on the relationship of certain academic subjects, each of which pursues particular and separatist aims, by the employment of exclusive modes of investigation. In attempting to face the difficulty thus presented, it must be recognized that the responsibility for the reëxamination and elucidation of the theoretical bases of the humanistic disciplines cannot be devolved, by the present generation of university scholars, upon its successors or upon the representatives of other types of inquiry. The view has long been expressed that the historian, for example, is not concerned with such problems as the relation of history to science and to philosophy, that his business is simply 'to teach history.' Unhappily, the circumstances in which we are now placed have barred this way of escape from the embarrassing necessity of taking stock of the presuppositions and theories which the present generation has taken over perfunctorily from its predecessors.

Assuming, therefore, that a science of man or of society is a desideratum, and accepting the fact that the persistent efforts to attain this end which have been made during the last two centuries have resulted in failure, it must be assumed either that a scientific study of society is impossible, or that the procedure followed in the conduct of these inquiries has been at fault. The view taken in the present book is that the want of success which has hitherto attended the effort to bring the phenomena of human existence within the purview of science has been due to the presence of definite obstacles, represented primarily by modes of procedure and methodological conceptions inherited from earlier stages of humanistic study.

It is argued, in the second part of the discussion, that the differences in aim and method which particularize the work of the different 'social sciences' today are a result of the efforts put forward two centuries ago by physiocrats and moral philosophers looking to the establishment of a Science of Man (as it was called) upon a strictly scientific basis, as 'scientific method' was then understood. In the eighteenth century, the present social sciences existed as undifferentiated elements in the study of moral philosophy. It was not until after the turmoil of the Revolutionary era that certain aspects of moral philosophy obtained recognition as independent subjects of inquiry and of university teaching, and that 'political economy,' 'sociology,' and 'anthropology' started upon their modern academic careers. It is of the highest importance to observe that this separation of interests involved no change in method. The economics of today goes back to Adam Smith and the physiocrats; the sociology of Auguste Comte and the anthropology of E. B. Tylor carry on eighteenth-century traditions. If this be so, it follows that one of the obstacles which must be surmounted, before we may hope to arrive at a 'social science,' is the influence of eighteenth-century conceptions of science.

The way in which these conceptions continue to affect the intellectual interests of the twentieth century is strikingly illustrated in the relationship existing between history, on the one hand, and economics, sociology, and anthropology, on the other. When philosophers discover today that history cannot become a 'natural science,' because it deals only with particular facts, they are simply bringing to light, by means of logical analysis, the conscious methodological assumptions on which history was excluded from the eighteenth-century 'science of man.' Owing to the influence of the philosophy of Descartes, it was assumed that if moral or social science is to become 'scientific,' it must abstract from the particularity of historical events, just as physics abstracts from the particularity of physical occurrences. As a consequence, the social scientists of the eighteenth century made it their aim to get away from the 'accidental' character of historical happenings, in order to discover the 'normal' or 'natural' course of change. Hence they set up that concept of 'hypothetical,' 'theoretical,' or 'ideal' history which has proved so effective a stumbling block to the expositors of the work of Rousseau, Condorcet, and Comte. In short, the followers of Descartes introduced into the very heart of humanistic study a cleavage between history and the 'scientific' aspects of social inquiry which has not yet been repaired, and which remains to exert an obscure but all-pervading influence upon the humanistic scholarship of the present day.

It will be seen, then, that the eighteenth century, while it imposed its conceptions of scientific method upon the newer studies of economics, sociology, and anthropology, left history free to pursue its own course. Now, it may be taken for granted, despite the views of the men of the Enlightenment, that there can be no 'science of man' which does not take into account the facts of human experience in the past. History deals specifically with these facts, unembarrassed by the Cartesian inheritance of its associates; hence the possibility lay before it of inaugurating a study of man which would be in the closest harmony with the scientific movement of recent times. It is of great interest, therefore, to notice that the historians of the nineteenth century have persistently maintained that their work was in the strictest sense 'scientific.' This assertion, however, leads to a new difficulty, for the historical work of the last century gives no evidence of leading to a science of man or of society. If, then, the work of historians in the nineteenth century has actually been scientific in character, and if this scientific work has not led to the establishment of a science of society, it must be admitted that the present situation of the social sciences becomes one of great difficulty. It has, therefore, seemed necessary (in the first part of this discussion) to inquire closely into the presuppositions and procedure of history, as represented currently in academic work.

The critical aspect of the present inquiry has its outcome in finding, first, that history, so far from being scientific, has remained satisfied with its traditional function of constructing narratives of happenings in the past, and, second, that economics, sociology, and anthropology have maintained an unbroken adherence to conceptions of scientific method which are not in consonance with scientific procedure in more recent times.

This conclusion renders it necessary that we should turn (in the third part) to consider whether it is possible to bring history, on the one hand, and the eighteenth-century group of studies, on the other, into such relation as will afford a basis for scientific investigation in the field of the humanities.

In this book the discussion is wholly theoretical. It may possibly be felt that any judgment in regard to the validity of the type of inquiry described, as an alternative to the types of inquiry now being pursued, must be reserved until such time as the author has ventured to show, by actual examples, how this mode of procedure actually works. It must, however, be evident that the difficulties with which the social sciences are struggling at the present time are difficulties in regard to the theoretical foundations upon which these studies rest. Hence, what we require, in advance of new constructions, is to lay bare the sources of the difficulties which have impeded the acquisition of new knowledge.

PART ONE

THE STUDY OF EVENTS

Chapter 1

The Activities of the Historian

THE FIRST, and most deeply rooted, of the obstacles which lie in the way of a scientific approach to the study of man consists in the traditional practice by which the utilization of the results of historical investigation has been restricted to the construction of historical narratives. Whatever the aim of the inquiry may be, historical investigation presupposes the employment of a critical technique. It is not, therefore, the improvement and refinement of critical procedure in dealing with documentary evidence that has continued to be an obstacle to the attainment of scientific results, but the notion that the proper aim of historical investigation is to provide materials for history writing. The continued adherence to this idea has not only proved a bar to scientific inquiry; it has led the historian into maintaining contradictory positions in theory and in practice, and has involved him in problems which are wholly removed from his sphere of interest and study.

The historian concerns himself, on the one hand, with documents, and, on the other, with happenings or events which have taken place in the past. Historical work involves, first, the critical examination of documentary sources of information, and, second, history writing or historiography. The historian works with documents, and this activity consists in the application of criticism to the contents of written statements which have come down to us from earlier times. As a result of critical inquiry, statements are elicited from documentary materials, and these statements are the 'facts' of history. Out of these facts the historian composes narratives, with the object, as he sees it, of telling 'what it was that actually happened.'

This dual aspect has been characteristic of history from the time of Herodotus down to the present. In the hands of the academic historian of today history retains all the distinguishing features which it acquired in the classical period. Even in the present generation history has made no break with the past. The modern academic historian does not assume that, under his guidance, history has changed its nature. He does not question that the narratives of earlier writers are 'history'; they are simply unacceptable as being judged uncritical or untrue.

Nevertheless it must be observed that the modern historian is of the opinion that his work represents both a new departure in the study of documents and a far-reaching improvement in historical writing. Up to 1850, it is affirmed, history was a branch of literature; since that time it has become a science.[1] Beginning with Grote, it is said, a reform was introduced, and this reform consisted in the elimination of all literary ornaments and of statements without proof. As used by historians, however, the word 'scientific' signifies merely the use of a critical technique, and applies only to the mode of procedure fol-

---

[1] C. V. Langlois & C. Seignobos, *Introduction to the Study of History*, tr. by G. G. Berry (New York, 1903), pp. 302, 310.

On the debate on whether history is a 'science,' compare Carl Becker, "Detachment and the Writing of History," *Atlantic Monthly*, 106 (1910), p. 524: "If it is not science, it is nothing," with Elie Faure, *History of Art: Ancient Art*, tr. by Walter Pach (New York, 1921), p. xl: "The historian who calls himself a scientist simply utters a piece of folly." For other examples of this diversity of opinion, see: William Stubbs, *Seventeen Lectures on the Study of Medieval and Modern History* (Oxford, 1887), p. 85. Albert Sorel, *Nouveaux essais d'histoire et de critique* (Paris, 1898), p. 11. J. B. Bury, *An Inaugural Lecture* (Cambridge, 1903), p. 42. C. H. Firth, *A Plea for the Historical Teaching of History* (2d ed., Oxford, 1905), p. 8. Pasquale Villari, *Studies, Historical and Critical* (New York, 1907), p. 108. Camille Jullian, *Extraits des historiens français du xix* siècle (6* éd., Paris, 1910), p. cxxviii. Gabriel Monod, "Histoire," in *De la méthode dans les sciences* (2* éd., Paris, 1910), pp. 371–372. G. Desdevises du Dezert & L. Bréhier, *Le travail historique* (Paris, 1913), pp. 5, 17. G. M. Trevelyan, *Clio, a Muse; and Other Essays* (London, 1913), p. 30. Viscount Haldane, *The Meaning of Truth in History* (London, 1914), p. 34. W. R. Thayer, "History—Quick or Dead?" *Atlantic Monthly*, 122 (1918), p. 638; "Fallacies in History," *American Historical Review*, 25 (1920), p. 181. J. T. Shotwell, *An Introduction to the History of History* (New York, 1922), pp. 8–9, J. W. Swain, "What Is History?" *Journal of Philosophy*, 20 (1923), pp. 281, 348.

lowed in the establishment of particular facts; it does not suggest research directed to the solution of scientific problems, or imply the adoption of the 'method of science' as understood in other fields of inquiry. It is unquestionable that the technique of historical investigation has been improved in recent generations, and that the technique of history writing has been modified in deference to new standards of literary taste; but these improvements and modifications cannot be taken to represent any marked discontinuity with the practice of historians in the past.

What is of interest in the claims put forward by modern academic historians is that the attitude of superiority which they adopt toward their predecessors is a marked characteristic of historical writers in all generations. It may be said, in the words of Polybius, that each later historian "makes such a parade of minute accuracy, and inveighs so bitterly when refuting others, that people come to imagine that all other historians have been mere dreamers, and have spoken at random in describing the world; and that he is the only man who has made accurate investigations, and unravelled every history with intelligence."[2] The judgment that earlier accounts are untrue, or at best inaccurate, is common to historians in all periods. The remarks of Thucydides on Herodotus, of Polybius on Timaeus, of Lucian on Ctesias, are typical of ancient historiography.[3] In modern times the same attitude has been maintained. Macaulay and Froude are the butt of every novice. Round calls Freeman "a superseded fossil." Arbois de Jubainville requires a volume to expose the faults of Fustel de Coulanges. "The modern French historian . . . reproaches Stubbs for his insularity, his simple faith in liberty, his conviction of the unique character of the English constitution, and . . . for the invincible prejudice which made him unable to see the

[2] Polybius xii. 26, tr. by E. S. Shuckburgh.

[3] Bernadotte Perrin, "The Ethics and Amenities of Greek Historiography," *American Journal of Philology*, 18 (1897), pp. 255–274. Cf. A. J. Toynbee, *Greek Historical Thought from Homer to the Age of Heraclius* (London, 1924), pp. 33, 41, 43, 48, 54, 66, 75, 206, 215, 220, 223, 229, 236, etc.

full value of French scholarship, and the true lessons of French medieval history."[4] So, in devoting themselves to the truthful statement of what has happened, ancient as well as modern historians have uniformly found the writings of their predecessors to be devoid of critical insight.

The conclusion just stated is substantiated by a further consideration. With his attention fixed upon his own efforts, the academic historian of today dates the beginning of 'history' from the middle of the nineteenth century. Singularly enough, however, the investigator who has turned his attention to the examination of history writing in almost any period before the present would have 'history' begin with the activities represented in the particular period to which he has devoted his inquiries. Gooch believes that "for the liberty of thought and expression, the insight into different ages and the judicial temper on which historical science depends, the world had to wait till the nineteenth century"[5]—the period of which he writes. Grant would have it that the writing of history, in the present meaning of the word, began in England in the eighteenth century.[6] Lord Acton thought that it was in the Renaissance, when the art of exposing falsehood dawned upon keen Italian minds, that history, in the modern sense, began to be understood.[7] Freeman regarded William of Malmesbury, in the twelfth century, as the first of critical historians.[8] Bury is of the opinion that the Greeks originated history because they were the first to apply criticism to historical materials.[9]

---

[4] T. F. Tout, *Chapters in the Administrative History of Medieval England,* vol. 1 (Manchester, 1920), pp. 7–8.

[5] G. P. Gooch, *History and Historians in the Nineteenth Century* (London, 1913), p. 13. That the twentieth century has arrived at the point of criticizing the nineteenth may be seen from the remarks of Henri Pirenne, "De l'influence allemande sur le mouvement historique contemporaine," *Scientia,* 34 (1923), p. 174.

[6] A. J. Grant, *English Historians* (London, 1906), p. xxiv.

[7] Lord Acton, *A Lecture on the Study of History* (London, 1896), p. 11.

[8] E. A. Freeman, *The History of the Norman Conquest of England,* vol. 5 (Oxford, 1876), p. 578.

[9] J. B. Bury, *The Ancient Greek Historians* (New York, 1909), pp. 1–2. J. T. Shotwell, *An Introduction to the History of History* (New York, 1922), p. 6.

In any age the activity of the historian arises from the perception that, judged by his standards, the histories previously written are unreliable and misinformed. The background of historical inquiry is, therefore, the existence of these earlier accounts, and, with implied reference to this background, the historian defines his purpose as being to set forth what it was that actually occurred. The decision to tell the truth about what had taken place in the past was not arrived at for the first time in the nineteenth century. Ranke was not the first historian to make up his mind to tell 'exactly what happened.' In the sixth century B.C., Hecataeus, having before him, not the novels of Sir Walter Scott,[10] but the traditional stories of the Greeks, proceeded to revise what had been told and to state the truth as it appeared to him.[11] Generation after generation, historians have assumed the responsibility of setting forth "without prejudices, depravations, or sinister items" the record of the past.[12]

If we are to understand the insistence of each later generation upon its exclusive apprehension of the truth of what had happened in former times, it will be necessary to observe that ancient and modern historians have been affected equally by an influence of which neither the one nor the other has been fully conscious. As Goethe remarked, "History must from time to time be rewritten, not because many new facts have been discovered, but because new aspects come into view, because the participant in the progress of an age is led to standpoints from which the past can be regarded and judged in a novel manner."[13] Every generation, Mark Pattison said, requires the facts to be recast in its own mold, and demands that history be rewritten from its own point of view. This is not because

---

[10] On Ranke and Scott, cf. G. P. Gooch, as cited, p. 78.

[11] J. B. Bury, as cited, p. 13.

[12] Edmund Bolton, *Hypercritica* (1618?), in J. E. Spingarn, *Critical Essays of the Seventeenth Century*, vol. 1 (Oxford, 1908), p. 93. Cf. the statement of Polydore Vergil, quoted in Cardinal Gasquet, *Monastic Life in the Middle Ages* (London, 1922), p. 191.

[13] Quoted in J. T. Merz, *A History of European Thought in the Nineteenth Century*, vol. 1 (Edinburgh, 1896), p. 7.

the facts are continually accumulating, because criticism is growing more rigid, or even because style varies. The reason is that ideas change, and that the whole mode and manner of looking at things alters in every age.[14] Hence it is that "most of the great historians whom our age has produced will, centuries hence, probably be more interesting as exhibiting special methods of research, special views on political, social, and literary progress, than as faithful and reliable chroniclers of events; and the objectivity on which some of them pride themselves will be looked upon not as freedom from but as unconsciousness on their part of the preconceived notions which have governed them."[15]

The characteristics of history have not changed since the beginnings of historiography among the Greeks. Historical inquiry is carried on at present, as formerly, for the purpose of providing the factual materials required in history writing. It follows, therefore, that any critical examination of the activities of historians must concern itself primarily with the form in which the results of historical investigation are presented.

It is of some importance to observe that this is not the mode of approach adopted in modern 'introductions' to historical study. The common element in these methodological guides lies in the fact that the dominant interest of each and all is in describing the successive steps followed in the preparation of materials for the use of the historical writer; the major emphasis falls upon the description of the operations incidental to work with documents. In these technical manuals, then, the traditional procedure of historians is assumed, and the discussion of method in history takes the form of a series of categorical statements of what should be done in the technical preparation of a history, ignoring inquiry into the significance of what a history actually represents.

[14] Mark Pattison, *Essays*, vol. 1 (Oxford, 1874), p. 2. F. H. Bradley, *The Presuppositions of Critical History* (Oxford, 1874), p. 15. Sir Charles Oman, "The Modern Historian and His Difficulties," in his *The Unfortunate Colonel Despard, and Other Studies* (London, 1922), p. 210.

[15] J. T. Merz, as cited, p. 7. W. G. Sumner, *Folkways* (Boston, 1907), pp. 635–636.

If, on the other hand, we are to comprehend the nature of history as an intellectual enterprise, it will be necessary to forget for the moment the pronouncements of introductions to 'historical method.' It will be necessary to examine the relation in which historiography stands to the life of communities and nations, to consider the specific interest which has gained for it an abiding recognition in all cultured societies, and to determine the elements which characterize it as a permanent type of literature.

Chapter 2

The Characteristics of Historical Narrative

Hᴵꜱᴛᴏʀʏ is the narrative statement of happenings in the past. No annalist, and no historian, attempts to set down all that has taken place. Not everything that has happened is known to the historian, however well informed. As Wace, in the twelfth century, remarked, "no person can know everything, or hear everything, or see everything." However near the event, any statement is incomplete, and of necessity varies with the opportunities of the narrator for observation and with his relation to the occurrences which he undertakes to describe.

Again, it is a point borne in upon us by the events of the last few decades that history is concerned, not with the everyday life of individuals, but with happenings which affect the welfare of communities in a higher sense than the vicissitudes of men's private fortunes. Hence it is inevitable that histories should chronicle wars and ignore the routine existence of peoples. In the broadest view, everything that has occurred in the past is, or may be, material for history, but it is commonly appreciated that not all happenings within a country from day to day are of 'historical' importance. The subject matter of history consists of occurrences which are unusual and out of the common, of events which for one reason or another compel the attention of men, and which are held worthy of being kept in remembrance.

Historical narrative, then, represents only a selection from what is known to have taken place. The contemporary historian does not include every detail which may have come to his knowledge; he presents only such matters as, from his point of view, are of importance. The modern historian, in turn, is limited in his selection to the restricted content of the original statements or other contemporary documents.

When we turn to consider what 'importance' means with reference to events, it becomes evident that this represents a complex and difficult problem, and one which occupies a prominent place in all modern discussions of the place and value of history as a form of knowledge. In considering this problem, it must be remembered that, as Descartes said, "even the most accurate of histories, if they do not exactly misrepresent or exaggerate the value of things in order to render them more worthy of being read, at least omit in them all the circumstances which are basest and least notable; and from this fact it follows that what is retained is not portrayed as it really is."[1] It must also be recognized that any judgment of the importance of what has happened, in times recent or times remote, is relative to the time, place, position, and ideas of the writer. Every age has its own criteria for distinguishing between the usual and the unusual, and the conception of what is remarkable and worthy of record is a function of the whole body of ideas current in any generation. What the writer sets down is dictated, not merely by his private judgment, but by that of the community of which he forms a part. Furthermore, history is a long-established form of literature, and the selection of facts to be included in any history is influenced by the spirit and the conventions of traditional historiography.

History is the narrative statement of happenings which concern the fortunes and the existence of a particular people or nation. The inspiration of this narrative will, in the first place, be the fact of some crucial struggle. Consequently, historic art, as Hirn says, "has everywhere reached its highest state of development amongst nations who have had to hold their own *vi et armis* against neighboring tribes, or in the midst of which

---

[1] René Descartes, "Discourse on the Method" (1637), in his *Philosophical Works,* tr. by E. S. Haldane & G. R. Ross, vol. 1 (Cambridge, 1911), pp. 84–85.

antagonistic families have fought for supremacy."[2] "Most of
the old German heroic poetry," Ker remarks, "is clearly to be
traced, as far as its subjects are concerned, to the most exciting
periods in early German history, between the fourth and sixth
centuries."[3] "Speaking broadly," Bernadotte Perrin observes,
"it has always required some great spectacular struggle—the
Trojan war, the Persian wars, the Peloponnesian war, the duel
between Sparta and Thebes, the Hellenic conquest of Asia—to
elicit, as it were, a great historian."[4] In France the best historical writing of the medieval period was stimulated by the
Crusades.[5] Similarly, in the fifteenth century, "it was the early
success of the French war which gave the stimulus that was
needed to produce the first-fruit of a national historical literature" in England;[6] while, not to multiply instances unnecessarily, it is a commonplace that European historiography in
the nineteenth century was born of war. *Les grands historiens
naissent pour les grands événements.*[7] (Yet the war of 1914–18
inspired no great historian; it was followed, as Mr. Wells says,
by "an almost universal intellectual and moral lassitude.")

The inspiration of history writing accounts, in large measure, for the spirit in which it is written. This spirit may best
be appreciated by a consideration of the earlier forms in which
historical occurrences are described. Heroic poetry, for example, begins in descriptions of notable events. A perfect example
of this type of narrative is the Old English poem on the battle
of Maldon. The Anglo-Saxon Chronicle records the incident
to which the poem relates (A.D. 991): "This year was Ipswich
plundered; and very soon afterwards was Alderman Britnoth

[2] Yrjö Hirn, *The Origins of Art* (London, 1900), p. 179.

[3] W. P. Ker, *Epic and Romance* (London, 1897), p. 24.

[4] Bernadotte Perrin, "History," in *Greek Literature, a Series of Lectures Delivered at Columbia University* (New York, 1912), p. 152.

[5] W. H. Schofield, *English Literature from the Norman Conquest to Chaucer*
(New York, 1906), p. 125.

[6] C. L. Kingsford, *English Historical Literature in the Fifteenth Century* (Oxford, 1913), p. 8.

[7] Gabriel Hanotaux, "De l'histoire et des historiens," *Revue des deux mondes*,
6ᵉ pér., 17 (1913), p. 482.

slain at Maldon." The poem is epic in quality, and its tone may be caught from Professor Ker's translation of a fine passage:

Byrhtwold spoke and grasped his shield—he was an old companion—he shook his ashen spear, and taught courage to them that fought:—"Thought shall be the harder, heart the keener, mood shall be the more, as our might lessens. Here our prince lies low, they have hewn him to death! Grief and sorrow forever on the man that leaves this war-play! I am old of years, but hence I will not go; I think to lay me down by the side of my lord, by the side of the man I cherished."[8]

The speech is the poet's, but it embodies the spirit of the time and glories in the heroic deed, even though it ended in disaster, and prizes the virtues of loyalty to the chieftain and unflinching courage in the face of defeat. Heroic poetry owes its origin to contemporary compositions which glorify the hero's exploit immediately after the event. The chief object which the characters of the heroic age set before themselves was to 'win glory,' to have their fame celebrated for all time; and such glory was to be won by brave deeds.[9] "Let him who can," is the sentiment of *Beowulf*, "win for himself glory before he dies; that is the best thing which can come to a warrior in after times, when he is no more."

In the heroic age the deeds celebrated and the glory attained were alike personal, and the hero neither hesitated to boast of his own prowess nor to reward others for singing his praises.[10] "The great works of commemoration," Hirn says, "are all monuments of boasting. By the grandiloquent hieroglyphics on palaces and pyramids and by the extolling hymns that he orders to be sung in his praise, the exultant hero endeavors to win from future admirers a meed of praise which shall quench his unsatisfied thirst for glorification. Even in this case, therefore, history, in its psychological sense—that is, the concentration of attention upon times other than the present—has been born of pride. By relying on this emotionalistic interpreta-

[8] W. P. Ker, as cited, p. 63.

[9] H. M. Chadwick, *The Heroic Age* (Cambridge, 1912), pp. 87, 88, 325 ff., 339.

[10] W. P. Ker, *The Dark Ages* (New York, 1904), p. 77.

tion," he proceeds, "we can explain the otherwise extraordinary development of commemorative art amongst tribes on relatively low stages of intellectual development. The same explanation also accounts for the artistic value of primitive records. The intensely emotional element of exultation, pride, and boasting that pervades so many of the commemorative poems and dramas makes this kind of history an art in the proper sense of the word."[11]

The relation of the historian's statement to the event which it describes is brought out strikingly by Sir Ian Hamilton: "When once the fight has been fairly lost or won," he says, "it is the tendency of all ranks to combine and recast the story of their achievement into a shape which shall satisfy the susceptibilities of national and regimental vainglory. It is then already too late for the painstaking historian to set to work. . . . On the actual day of battle naked truths may be picked up for the asking; by the following morning they have already begun to get into their uniforms."[12] It is evident, then, that historiography is not a colorless record, but is a rendering of what has happened in terms of the emotions awakened by the result.

The historian is confronted with a situation, the outcome or climax of unusual and important happenings which have deeply affected the welfare and fortunes of the group to which he belongs. The typical theme of the historian is the series of happenings which has led up to this situation.

When we come to consider the manner in which the historian deals with the theme he has taken up, we are reminded of the tragedies of the Athenian dramatists. In the construction of these tragedies the Greek poets drew upon histories or legends the outcome of which was predetermined and known to everyone. By consecrated usage the tragedians were restricted in their choice of subjects to a circle of stories the main outlines of which were already fixed. The details utilized in the telling

---

[11] Yrjö Hirn, as cited, p. 181.

[12] Sir Ian Hamilton, *A Staff Officer's Scrap-book during the Russo-Japanese War*, vol. 1 (5th impr., London, 1907), p. v.

of the story might vary, but the final issue was a thing given; and in drama the end necessarily dominates the structure of the whole. In Greek tragedy the end of the story was the dramatist's starting point, and from this he worked back to a beginning. The invention of the author was concerned, not with displaying the consequences that would follow if a given character were placed in a certain initial situation, but with presenting such a character as would make the known outcome appear rational and inevitable, in terms of the highest possibilities of human nature as revealed in the stress of unwonted circumstances.

From the time of Herodotus to the present day, historians have devoted themselves to an undertaking which resembles closely that exemplified in Greek tragedy. They have described great and serious occurrences in the light of their outcome, and have sought to make the deeds of heroes and great men intelligible by the imaginative reconstruction of character. "It is in the realizing of grand character," Stubbs held, "that the strength of historical genius chiefly displays itself."[13] In this important particular, therefore, historiography is indistinguishable from imaginative literature. "The artist's power of thought is properly shown not in the direct enunciation of ideas but in mastery over motive."[14]

It must, however, be pointed out that the type of unity in historiography differs in an important particular from that of tragedy—more particularly since it has been said that tragedy succeeded epic.[15] In early heroic poetry the 'action' is simple, being concerned with the deeds of individual heroes. In the Homeric epic, however, the scope of the narrative has significantly widened. "The story and the deeds of those who pass across its wide canvas are linked with the larger movement of which the men themselves are but a part. The particular action

---

[13] William Stubbs, *Seventeen Lectures on the Study of Medieval and Modern History* (Oxford, 1887), pp. 112–113.

[14] Theodore Watts-Dunton, "Poetry," in *Encyclopædia Britannica* (9th ed.), vol. 19, p. 268.

[15] Aristotle *Poetics* iv. 10.

rests upon forces outside itself. The hero is swept into the tide of events. The hairbreadth escapes, the surprises, the episodes, the marvelous incidents of epic story, only partly depend on the spontaneous energy of the hero."[16] The epic poem, in short, relates a great and complete action which attaches itself to the fortunes of a people, or to the destiny of mankind. Tragedy, on the other hand, represents the destiny of the individual man. In tragic drama it is but seldom that outward circumstances are entirely dominant over the forces of the human spirit. Obviously, then, tragedy, in succeeding to epic, does not carry over the notable outlook in which the fate of the individual appears subordinated to the fortunes of a group.

In the wonderful creative outburst that followed the Persian war, drama and history, springing from the same root in epic, so completely developed their special types of appeal that they appear to us, as to Polybius (ii. 56), to be widely opposed to each other. Tragedy, even at the beginning, assumed the point of view which takes the fate of the individual to be the essential interest in all drama. History, in a wholly different spirit, laid emphasis upon the fate of the nation or the group. The dramatist displays the individual struggling in the self-woven toils of destiny; the historian presents the common fortunes of the group as affected by the motives and passions of specific persons. It is not the fate of individuals with which history is concerned, but the fate of nations. Yet, inasmuch as the group is only to be seen in the named individuals who represent it, there is an instant tendency on the part of historians to follow the traditions of drama. The tendency is obvious in classical historiography owing to the convention, inherited from epic poetry, that permitted the introduction of speeches; but the admiration of modern scholars for Thucydides (in whom the dramatic attitude was pronounced), the persistent emphasis on 'character drawing,' and the far-reaching attraction of historical romance show the danger in which the art of Herodotus ever stands from the rival art of Aeschylus and Sophocles.

[16] S. H. Butcher, *Aristotle's Theory of Poetry and Fine Art* (3d ed., London, 1902), p. 353.

Usage in language makes a clear distinction between the terms 'annals' and 'history.' By 'annals' is meant a record or register of events taken just as they come in the order of time, and hence including in juxtaposition matters separate and disconnected in themselves. In 'history,' on the other hand, there must be unity and logical coherence of the parts. History displays an 'action' (in the dramatic sense) with a beginning, middle, and end. Annals are not history, precisely because they lack unity, coherence, and internal development. In historiography, as in tragedy, the first consideration is the 'action,' and the problem confronting every historian is how to bring the heterogeneous materials at his disposal within the compass of a unity.

The characteristic 'action' in historiography presents the issue of a crucial struggle between different groups, societies, or nations. This distinctive interest appears fully developed, at the beginning of prose historiography, in Herodotus. In its first form, the work of the 'Father of History' consisted merely of the story of the Persian invasion, now comprised in the last three books.[17] The author thus began with the narrative of a single war which was to him recent history. This was a story, simple in action, conceived in the old heroic spirit, of a victory won against overwhelming odds. The account was one that redounded to the glory of Athens and flattered Athenian pride. Herodotus represented the Athenians as "truly the saviors of Greece"; but he did more: he gave currency and authority to a story which embodied Athenian tradition and justified Athenian empire. "If the story is true," Bury remarks, "that the Athenians bestowed on him ten talents in recognition of the merits of his work, it was a small remuneration for the service he rendered to the renown of their city."[18]

At some point later in his career, Herodotus came to have a new vision of the war, seeing in it the culmination of different converging series of events; it is in this later form that his his-

[17] Herodotus, IV–VI, ed. by R. W. Macan, vol. 1 (London, 1895), p. xcii.
[18] J. B. Bury, *The Ancient Greek Historians* (New York, 1909), pp. 62, 65.

tory has won the undying admiration of men. It is this wide outlook that constitutes the work of Herodotus a masterpiece of historical writing and gives unity to the whole narrative.[19] The view which he takes of the movement of events is inseparable from the emotion in the light of which it is beheld. Whether the Persians retired unbeaten, having effected their object, or whether the honor of their repulse should be accorded to the arms of Sparta, is, in this connection, immaterial; what matters is that Athens was remade, intellectually reborn, as a result of the war. The first form of the work may well be set down as the expression of a pardonable vainglory; the enlargement, on the other hand, reflects not merely pride in achievement, but, what is of the highest significance, the ambition born of victory (the inspiration of which, for the moment, made all things seem possible), the dream that led Athens to defeat and Alexander to conquest.

The work of Herodotus is of the type of history that narrates the details of a recent event, with a prefatory account of the circumstances that led up to it. In such works the focus is the denouement as it appears to the author; the unity is inspired by the outcome. Furthermore, it is characteristic of this type that in proportion as the event is felt to be decisive will there be a marked tendency to look upon the present outcome as determining the future. Of this type Polybius, especially in view of his self-conscious explanation, is another interesting example:

Now in times preceding this period [he says], the events of the world's history may be said to have happened in a state of isolation, because each action, both in its inception and in its development, was disconnected with all others by time or place. But from this period we find that the history has become an organic whole, and the affairs of Italy and Lybia are bound up with those of Asia and Greece, and the general current of events sets to one fixed point. The distinctive feature of our work [he goes on to say] corresponds with the marvellous characteristic of our times; for as Fortune has swayed almost all the affairs of the world to one centre, and com-

[19] Henri Ouvré, *Les formes littéraires de la pensée grecque* (Paris, 1900), pp. 307–308.

pelled every force to set in one and the same direction, so we would by means of our History bring under a common view, for the benefit of our readers, the operations which Fortune has employed for the completion of a combined system of the world. Indeed it was this above all that incited and urged us to attempt the writing of history.[20]

The theme of Roman conquest unified the work of Polybius; at the same time the far-reaching success of the Republic led him to look toward the future, for, he remarks (iii. 4), "it seemed agreed and forced on the conviction of all men, that all that remained to the world is to submit to the Romans, and to perform whatever they shall enjoin."

The extension of the power of Rome had a further influence on historiography, since it may be said to have forced upon men a second type of history, namely, that in which the past of a single nation is seen as a self-contained whole. This type, of which the great example in classical antiquity is the work of Livy, and which to us, owing to its cultivation in the nineteenth century, may seem even the natural and proper form of history writing, was not only late in emerging, but, even after its appearance, suffered a long eclipse in the Middle Ages.

In Herodotus everything leads up to the crisis of the Persian invasion, and the happenings antecedent to this event fall within the 'action' of the drama he presents, setting, as it were, the characters upon the stage and introducing the 'complication.' In Livy the stimulus is also a crisis in the affairs of a people, but of a different kind. The author is not stirred to write by the outcome of a single war, nor is there a dramatic climax in his presentation. The crisis is, one may say, 'unresolved'; it is present to the minds of Livy and his auditors rather than depicted in his work. Livy's view is concentrated upon the internal history of the Roman people; he looks back from the height to which a long series of achievements has brought the Roman people, and sees at every step victory won by Roman piety, constancy, and discipline. The spirit in which

[20] Polybius i. 3–4, tr. by J. L. Strachan-Davidson.

he writes is not, however, that of exultation in victory, even though his theme is the ever-increasing glory of Rome; it is pride, certainly, but the pride of assured position, of conscious superiority. His pride is also of a contemplative sort: a mingling of regret for the noble virtues of an earlier generation, of distrust in the present, and—far from an ambitious daring—an actual foreboding of the future.

It is apparent, then, that history, viewed in retrospect, is not a merely judicial statement of what has taken place in the past. The selection of materials by the historian and the mode in which he presents his theme are determined by the conscious or unconscious desire to glorify the actions of the group to which he belongs, and of which, for the moment, he is the spokesman. Histories proceed out of the life of nations, and reflect the emotions consequent upon the outcome of events.

In the modern period, history has not changed its nature. Concurrently with the rise of the spirit of nationality during the last century, historiography became self-conscious of its function as the literary expression of the consciousness of national existence. "Only through history," Schopenhauer said in 1818, "does a nation become completely conscious of itself."[21] Indeed, the potency of the type of statement which we call 'history' for inducing unity of sentiment and action is one of the notable discoveries of the nineteenth century.[22] History provides a body of ideas which serves to unify the attitude of the individuals of a nation toward their common country; the feeling of nationality is due primarily to a common pride in past events. *Le véritable patriotisme n'est pas l'amour du sol, c'est l'amour du passé, c'est le respect pour les générations qui nous ont précédés.*[23] Everyone is familiar with the part played

---

[21] Arthur Schopenhauer, *The World As Will and Idea*, tr. by R. B. Haldane & J. Kemp, vol. 3 (London, 1886), p. 228.

[22] The discovery, as is well known, was that of Baron von Stein. See Sir J. R. Seeley, *Life and Times of Stein*, vol. 3 (Cambridge, 1878), p. 499. G. P. Gooch, *History and Historians in the Nineteenth Century* (London, 1913), p. 65. G. S. Ford, *Stein and the Era of Reform in Prussia* (Princeton, 1922), pp. 322–326.

[23] Fustel de Coulanges, *Questions historiques* (Paris, 1893), p. 6. Cf. Ernest Renan, "Qu'est-ce qu'une nation," in his *Discours et conférences* (Paris, 1887).

by historical writings in arousing the dormant spirit of nationality during the last century. In the hands of the masters
of historiography, history has stirred peoples great and small
to self-assertion and to action.[24] During the last hundred years
we have had in every country a guild of professional scholars
devoted to creating and keeping alive national aspirations—
and national antagonisms. In every land, to use the words of
John Morley, the historian has been the hearth at which the
soul of the country has been kept alive.[25] It is obvious, indeed,
that *l'histoire travaille d'une manière secrète et sûre à la grandeur de la Patrie.*[26] Not only has history writing awakened
peoples to a consciousness of nationality; it has prompted them
to action by inciting hopes for the future. Success, as in the
case of Athens, leads on ambition; and the historian, like Herodotus, justifies the forward policy. Through recounting or
representing the exploits of earlier generations, Hirn says, the
descendants acquire that healthy feeling of pride which is the
most important factor of success in the struggle for national
existence.[27]

Historical narrative is bound up with recollections of national achievement in the past, and with hopes and aspirations
for national greatness in the future. As a form of literature,
history has an exceptional and highly important place in the
life of civilized peoples. On the other hand, it must be evident
that this form of literature is at the opposite pole from the type
of knowledge which we associate with the word 'science.'

---

[24] Lord Acton, "Nationality" (1862), in his *History of Freedom, and Other Essays* (London, 1907), pp. 270–300. H. M. Stephens, "Modern Historians and Their Influence on Small Nationalities," *Contemporary Review*, 52 (1887), pp. 107–121; "Nationality and History," *American Historical Review*, 21 (1916), pp. 225–236.

[25] Viscount Morley, *Notes on Politics and History* (New York, 1914), p. 66.

[26] Gabriel Monod, "Introduction," *Revue historique*, 1 (1876), p. 38. Cf. Camille Jullian, "L'érudition allemande," in Gabriel Petit & Maurice Leudet, *Les Allemands et la science* (Paris, 1916), p. 230.

[27] Yrjö Hirn, as cited, p. 179.

Chapter 3

The Aims of the Academic Historian

HAVING considered briefly the relation of history to national life, it is necessary to recur to the activities of the modern academic historian, more particularly in view of the reiterated assertion that his work is 'scientific.'

It has been stated above that the typical point of departure in historiography is a given situation (for example, the defeat of the Persians by the Greeks), and that, with this as a beginning, the historian proceeds to set forth what, in his judgment, have been the antecedent happenings and actions through which this situation has arisen. Now, in practice, the academic historian does not begin with a situation which calls for explanation, but with a document which calls for critical examination and analysis. His initial assumption is that "the historian works with documents,"[1] and that, where these fail, his occupation comes to an end. With the adoption of this mode of approach, he conceives of his work as the determination, by inference from the documents, of what has happened in the past, and, subsequently, the setting down of his findings without reference to any predetermined idea or interest.

---

[1] C. V. Langlois & C. Seignobos, *Introduction to the Study of History*, tr. by G. G. Berry (New York, 1903), p. 17. This work (first published in 1898) has been used for illustrative purposes as being the most important 'introduction' available to students in the English language; in respect to the views cited, it is fully representative of opinion among historical scholars. Other introductions are: Ernst Bernheim, *Lehrbuch der historischen Methode* (Leipzig, 1889; 5. Aufl., 1908); Charles & Victor Mortet, *La science de l'histoire* (Paris, 1894); Charles Seignobos, *La méthode historique appliquée aux sciences sociales* (Paris, 1901); Ernst Bernheim, *Einleitung in die Geschichtswissenschaft* (Leipzig, 1905); Aloys Meister, ed., *Grundriss der Geschichtswissenschaft* (Leipzig, 1906 ff.); Gustav Wolff, *Einführung in das Studium der Neueren Geschichte* (Berlin, 1910); G. N. Desdevises du Dezert & Louis Bréhier, *Le travail historique* (Paris, 1913).

The 'facts' with which the historian deals are statements made by individuals in regard to the actions of other individuals. At all stages in his inquiry the historian is occupied with testimony of a character that would seldom or never be accepted in a court. He admits that any decision with respect to what actually happened must turn upon the existence of different statements made by individuals having independent knowledge of the happenings in question, but he also admits that for important periods of history this requirement cannot be met. The unsupported affirmations of one man concerning the actions and motives of an opponent would not be accepted in the ordinary affairs of life, yet historians all retain the habit of stating facts on the authority of Thucydides or of Caesar, and end by admitting any statement which does not happen to be contradicted by another accessible document.[2] Needless to say, even under the most advantageous conditions a large measure of uncertainty must attach to inquiries focused upon the actions of men, reported by persons whose relation to the actions we can only surmise, described in language which does not permit us to reproduce the mental images which were present in the mind of the observer.[3]

Historical inquiry is concerned with statements about actions and occurrences. As evidence for the happenings to which they refer, these statements are incomplete and of doubtful validity. Moreover, for any time earlier than the most 'modern' history, the statements which have been preserved are mere fragmentary allusions to what has happened. The historian is dependent upon documents, and, in this dependence, he is at the mercy of accident and of changing modes of thought. Fortuitous conditions alone have brought to the shore of the present the flotsam which constitutes existing memorials of the past.[4] The activities of the historical investigator in attempting to determine what it was that actually happened from the evidence of documents are thus restricted within narrow limits.

---

[2] Langlois & Seignobos, as cited, p. 197.

[3] *Ibid.*, p. 221.   [4] *Ibid.*, p. 203.

He cannot observe ancient happenings for himself; he cannot arrive at any fuller information of what occurred than is contained in the documents which have survived. The imperfections of the record cannot now be repaired; all that might have been known is not now ascertainable. Furthermore, since what men observe in any age is determined by current interests and ideas, it is evident that no record made in past times could possibly satisfy the needs of the thought of today.

Historical criticism yields only isolated 'facts.'[5] The academic historian pursues his inquiries "in the faith that a complete assemblage of the smallest facts of human history will tell in the end; the labour is performed for posterity."[6] The facts having been arrived at, it follows that something must be done with them; and, in point of fact, the academic historian, without further questioning, casts the results of his investigations in the mold of traditional historiography.[7]

With his acceptance of traditional modes of presentation or exposition, the historian finds himself in difficulties. He finds that the critical study of documents is one thing, the statement of the results of such inquiry another. Preoccupation with original documents brings with it a sense of security, a conviction that work based upon primary materials must necessarily be sound and enduring. Hence the academic historian holds to the belief that, having discovered the facts, all that remains to be done is to state what he has found without prejudice or bias. It is not to be wondered at that, having adopted this view, he should be nonplussed, and eventually irritated, when it is pointed out that the end of all this effort is the composition of a narrative marked by partisanship and emotion. Nevertheless, in adopting narrative as the form for the statement of his results, the modern historian is simply maintaining the traditions of history writing, and his dilemma arises from his inability to see that in following traditional historiography he

---

[5] Langlois & Seignobos, as cited, p. 211.

[6] J. B. Bury, *An Inaugural Lecture* (Cambridge, 1903), p. 31.

[7] C. & V. Mortet, as cited, p. 60. G. N. Desdevises du Dezert & L. Bréhier, as cited, p. 8.

cannot escape the inherent qualities and characteristics of this particular form of art.

The difficulties which have resulted from the adoption of traditional historiography as a type-form for the statement of the results of historical investigation come to light in every 'introduction to historical study.' It is said, for example, that "men whose information is all that could be desired, whose monographs intended for specialists are full of merit, show themselves capable, when they write for the public, of grave offences against scientific method [i.e., the ideals of academic history]. . . . The reason is that these authors, when they address the public, wish to produce an effect upon it. Their desire to make a strong impression leads them to a certain relaxation of scientific rigour, and to the old rejected habits of ancient historiography. These men, scrupulous and minute as they are when they are engaged in establishing details, abandon themselves, in their exposition of general questions, to their natural impulses, like the common run of men. They take sides, they censure, they extol; they colour, they embellish; they allow themselves to be influenced by personal, patriotic, moral, or metaphysical considerations. And, over and above all this, they apply themselves, with their several degrees of talent, to the task of producing works of art."[8] What this defection from academic precepts means is that, in writing a sustained narrative, the academic historian follows the established precedents of historiography; it is the writer on 'historical method' who has failed to recognize the fundamental characteristics of historical narration.

The difficulties in which the historian finds himself are inseparable from the mode of procedure which he has adopted. In the first place, he begins with the study of a body of documents, and proceeds to the presentation of the results of his investigations in the form of a historical narrative. In the second place, he has taken over this form of statement without consideration of the source of inspiration and of the charac-

---

[8] Langlois & Seignobos, as cited, p. 314.

teristics of history writing. Third, in the effort to eliminate the emotional and aesthetic features of the older historiography, he has set up an ideal of detachment and impartiality which admittedly is applicable only to detailed monographic studies addressed to other historical scholars.

Nevertheless the modern historian cannot avoid the necessity of making extended surveys of historical events, if only for the purposes of academic instruction. This activity he regards, not as the construction of a history, but as the making of a 'synthesis.' In one sense, there is reason for this differentiation. It has been pointed out that the nonacademic historian of earlier times began with a given situation, the outcome of crucial events in the life of a nation, and proceeded to explain this situation in terms of the sequence of events leading up to it. It has been shown, too, that the academic historian sets out from a body of documents, and arrives at a group of isolated 'facts,' of which, naturally, he desires to make some use. We may see, then, that whereas the older historian was considering a present situation in the light of its antecedents, the academic historian considers a series of happenings in and for itself. The documents give only isolated particulars, which fall into a chronological order; the academic historian is obliged to invent for himself an 'action' into which as a framework he may dispose the uncoördinated elements provided by antecedent inquiry.[9] It is evident, then, that the modern historian has succeeded, in one respect, in dissociating his work from historiography in its traditional form; but, in doing so, he has only increased his own difficulties.

To make a synthesis, to build up the separate elements, provided by investigation, into a connected narrative, requires that a series of events must be envisaged 'as a whole.' The 'whole' which the historian envisages is not a totality corresponding to all that has taken place; usually, it is not even the sum of the particulars which have been ascertained. It is a selection from the available data so arranged as to convey to the

[9] Langlois & Seignobos, as cited, p. 224.

reader, not the actual complexity of happenings, but such happenings as the historian considers of importance in a period of time or in a series of occurrences. The 'synthesis' of the modern historian is, then, as much a personal presentation of what has happened as the narrative of the earlier historian; the academic historian, no less than his predecessor, is engaged in the construction of a work of art.

We are now in a position to recognize the justice of Mr. Balfour's remark that, in the writing of history, "there is always an artist to be reckoned with. It may be Thucydides. It may be Dr. Dryasdust. . . . But there is always somebody; and though that somebody might repudiate the notion that his narrative was a work of art, yet he cannot evade responsibility for selection, for emphasis, and for colour. We may think him a bad artist, but, even in his own despite, an artist he is;—an artist whose material is not marble or stone, but brute fact."[10] *L'art seul et non la science peut finalement nous donner des images d'ensemble.*[11]

Furthermore, when we perceive that the academic historian of today is simply the latest representative of the long line of historical writers which stretches back to Hecataeus and Herodotus, the significance of his efforts to tell the truth will be better appreciated. "What has in the main caused history to be written, and when written to be eagerly read, is neither its scientific value nor its practical utility, but its aesthetic interest. Men love to contemplate the performances of their fellows, and whatever enables them to do so, whether we belittle it as gossip or exalt it as history, will find admirers in abundance. . . . Directly it appears [however] that the governing preoccupation of an historian is to be picturesque, his narrative becomes intolerable. This is because the interest—I mean the aesthetic interest—of history largely depends upon its accuracy; or (more strictly) upon its supposed accuracy. . . . Fact has an

---

[10] A. J. Balfour, *Theism and Humanism* (London, 1915), pp. 85–86.

[11] Harald Höffding, *La pensée humaine,* tr. par Jacques de Coussage (Paris, 1911), p. 293.

interest, because it is fact; because it actually happened; because actual people who really lived and really suffered and really rejoiced caused it to happen, or were affected by its happening. And on this interest the charm of history essentially depends."[12] The documentary scholar is thus justified in his endeavors. Through his efforts assurance is given to the public that the statements embodied in the most recent history are really true. Without such assurance the emotion associated with historical literature would be inhibited by the presence of doubt. It is this assurance, on the other hand, which has made history the important instrument of propaganda which it has become.

The aim of the academic historian to state his results with 'impartiality' likewise finds its explanation in the aesthetic requirements of historiography. The experience of Edward Gibbon affords an illustration. The reader of Gibbon's autobiographies will recollect that, from youth upward, he had "aspired to the character of an historian." Before deciding to write the *Decline and Fall of the Roman Empire*, he had spent years in search of a suitable subject. Thus he had been much occupied with the thought of writing upon some period of English history: Richard the First attracted him, as did the Wars of the Barons, the exploits of the Black Prince, and the lives of Sir Philip Sydney and Sir Walter Raleigh.[13] As his ideas matured, however, Gibbon eliminated the English subjects from consideration. In July, 1762, he wrote in his diary: "I am afraid of being reduced to drop my Hero [Raleigh]. . . . Could I even surmount these obstacles [which he has detailed], I should shrink with terror from the modern history of England, where every character is a problem, and every reader a friend or an enemy; where a writer is supposed to hoist a flag of party,

[12] A. J. Balfour, as cited, pp. 82–83. Cf. G. M. Trevelyan, "History and Literature," *History*, n.s., 9 (1924), p. 91: "Truth is the criterion of historical study; but its impelling motive is poetic. Its poetry consists in its being true. There we find the synthesis of the scientific and literary views of history."

[13] *The Autobiographies of Edward Gibbon*, ed. by John Murray (2d ed., London, 1897), pp. 258–259; cf. pp. 193–197, 275–278, 301–302, 407–409.

and is devoted to damnation by the adverse faction." "I must," he concluded, "embrace a safer and more extensive theme." The history of the origin and establishment of the liberty of the Swiss next engaged his attention, Switzerland having become for him a second home. This "glorious theme" proved so attractive that Gibbon actually wrote a "first book," which was badly received and so abandoned. He was conscious, he said, that he had not attained "the genuine style, the middle tone, of that species of writing."[14] So, after years of study and deliberation, he decided against writing the history of either of the countries to which he was emotionally attached. That is, Gibbon discovered that the characteristic interest or emotion of national history stood in the way of the production of a work of art: on the one hand, he could not achieve the "middle tone," and, on the other, his audience could not, in reading, overcome their political feelings. "It was at Rome," he stated, "on the fifteenth of October, 1764, as I sat musing amidst the ruins of the Capitol, while the barefooted fryars were singing Vespers in the temple of Jupiter, that the idea of writing the decline and fall of the City first started to my mind."[15]

It is evident, then, that Gibbon's success as a historian was not due, as has frequently been suggested, to some fortunate accident which gave him a great subject, nor yet to the brilliance of his style or his accuracy of statement; it was due to the deliberation with which he approached the writing of history, and to the care which he took to rule out, as far as was humanly possible, every element of failure. His experience deserves the closest study from historical writers; here, however, one or two points only need be noted. In the first place, it will be observed that Gibbon's initial attempts followed the mode of procedure of the modern academic historian; he considered certain episodes or movements in the past from the point of view of chronological order. His later effort was determined by his recognition of a present situation (barefooted friars in

[14] *Ibid.*, pp. 195–196, 276, 408.
[15] *Ibid.*, p. 302; cf. pp. 405–406.

the temple of Jupiter), and from this as a point of departure he went back to a beginning and followed out the steps through which the present situation had come into existence. In this way he envisaged a complete 'action' of what may be described as the classical type.

Even more interesting, however, is Gibbon's recognition of the fact that an impartial attitude is impossible for the historian in dealing with a subject which enlists political sympathy or passion. When political questions are the subject of discussion, passion is inevitably aroused, and "every reader is a friend or an enemy." Loyalty to a cause may, indeed, be said even to forbid the inhibition, the restraint, of such feelings. What is felt to be misrepresentation of one's country stirs indignant protest, though the circumstances may be a century old and hidden in obscurity. As Mommsen said, "those who have lived through historical events . . . begin to see that history is neither written nor made without love or hate."[16] What Gibbon saw was that partisanship and patriotism are destructive of that exteriorized, 'distanced' view which is the very core of aesthetic presentation. What the modern historian aims at in advocating 'impartiality' is identical with the 'genuine style, the middle tone,' which Gibbon strove so earnestly to attain. The demand for 'impartiality' is just the unconscious recognition of the need for 'distance' in history writing.[17]

We may see, then, that the truthfulness, objectivity, and impartiality on which the academic historian bases his claim to a scientific presentation of fact are, in themselves, simply requirements of historiographic art.

History is not the mere statement of 'what has actually happened.' The historian, whether he sets out to explain a given present in the light of its antecedents or to create a synthesis of what has happened from the materials provided by docu-

---

[16] Quoted in G. P. Gooch, *History and Historians in the Nineteenth Century* (London, 1913), p. 458.

[17] See Edward Bullough, " 'Psychical Distance' As a Factor in Art and As an Æsthetic Principle," *British Journal of Psychology*, 5 (1912), pp. 87–118.

ments, is engaged in making a construction, and his performance is conditioned by the records which have been preserved,
by the ideas and interests of the present in which the historian
lives, by the exigencies and requirements of a form of art. With
whatever care the facts are sifted, with whatever sincerity they
are subsequently presented, narrative statement remains art,
and, as such, is not science. The ambition and desire of historians, in the last half-century, to achieve scientific results is
only an additional evidence of the influence of the demand for
scientific knowledge in regard to the affairs of men to which
attention was directed at the outset. This hope or desire of
historians can, however, be realized only when they have come
to appreciate that, in adopting the mode of presentation for
their results which is characteristic of traditional historiography, they have cut themselves off from any possibility of the
attainment of scientific results.

Chapter 4

National History and World History

THE ADHERENCE of the modern historian to traditional historiography has had a wider influence, as an obstacle
to the extension of the method of science to the study of man,
than that of restricting the activities of historical scholars to
the practice of the art of history writing.

Up to the present, academic history has not succeeded in
liberating itself from the influence of the Romantic period,
during which, in every country of Europe, the spirit of nationality demanded the rewriting of history in terms of a new
sense of national existence and a new enthusiasm for national
achievements in the past. In all essentials it has remained un-
affected by the scientific movement of the second half of the
nineteenth century. When, from time to time, individuals influenced by this latter movement of thought have questioned
the validity of history as an academic discipline, historians have
defended their position with vigor and aggressiveness. They
have asserted that their intentions were misunderstood,[1] that
their work is 'scientific,' that their real aim is the determination
of the 'truth,' and, in the last analysis, that history is identical with philosophy. Notwithstanding this defense, it must be
urged that the devotion of modern historians to old practice
in historical composition has fostered the expression of patriotic emotions, and has awakened ambitions which have led
to disastrous results in the modern world; it has limited the
outlook of men by confining their view of the past within narrow particularist bounds; it has promoted the incorporation in

[1] J. H. Round, "Historical Research," *Nineteenth Century*, 44 (1898), p. 1005.
G. L. Burr, "The Freedom of History," *American Historical Review*, 22 (1917),
p. 265.

histories of philosophies based upon superficial hypotheses and untenable analogies; it has led to the exploitation of history in the so-called 'idealistic reaction' against science; it has perpetuated naïve concepts of causation, and has effectually prevented the systematic study of the factors and processes which have influenced human activities and hence have affected in a high degree the welfare of men. It will now be necessary to consider some of these points in detail.

The scientific study of man must take into consideration the facts that are available in regard to mankind without limitation in respect to time or place. Academic history, on the other hand, finds its characteristic interest in national history.[2] In this the emotional appeal is strongest, the type of unity is simplest, and the linguistic difficulties inseparable from the use of documents are most readily overcome. At the same time, nationalistic history fixes the attention of the investigator, no less than of the reader, upon one country, and so limits the possibility of any wide outlook upon the activities of other peoples. It creates an interest, indeed, which is inimical to a balanced judgment in regard to events, for, of necessity, it magnifies the role of some one unit in the conduct of affairs.

The particularist influence of academic history is evident from an examination of its relation to geographical areas. National history involves a restriction of attention to the affairs of some one land, great or small. History, as taught in the centers of Western civilization, limits the areas which it includes within its scope to certain lands which have come to be regarded as being of special significance and importance. Academic history confines its view of the past to the geographical areas of the Mediterranean basin and of western Europe. The division of history, for teaching purposes, into 'ancient,' 'medieval,' and 'modern' obscures the fact that these terms have reference, not to the world at large, but to a relatively small part of the earth's surface.

[2] C. V. Langlois & C. Seignobos, *Introduction to the Study of History*, tr. by G. G. Berry (New York, 1903), p. 311.

Within the area selected for consideration, attention is further restricted to certain types of activity. The focus of interest is the dominant political authority of the country, and the principal matters dealt with are the relations of the central government to other such governments, the maintenance and the succession of governmental power, and the relations of the central government to special groups within the community. It is true that, from time to time, protests have been made against this narrowing of interest, but, in spite of questionings persistently renewed, the conventional limitation of history to political affairs maintains its prestige and its sway.

The restrictions imposed upon historical study and historical writing will be recognized at once if we consider any such phrase as 'the history of England.' Here, at first sight, the word 'England' appears to be a geographical term, and the inference would seem to follow that a work designated 'History of England' would concern itself with actions and events of every description which have taken place within this particular part of the British Isles. In reality, however, the word 'England,' in this connection, is the name of a politico-geographical unit, a state; and the subject matter of a 'history of England' will be the affairs of the central government which, in the course of time, has succeeded in extending its influence over England, Wales, Scotland, and Ireland. For other phases of the activities of the inhabitants of Great Britain we must look to other sources of information: histories of literature, philosophy, and science; histories of agriculture, industry, and commerce. The term 'political history of England' (which is occasionally used) would be at once more accurate and more desirable; and if the title 'History of English Polity,' 'Politics,' or 'Government' were employed for conventional nationalistic histories, the relation in which these works stand to the histories of other activities of the English people would be apparent. With this differentiation, the 'history of England' would not be taken as representing the totality or 'whole' of English achievement in the past.

Furthermore, to gain a knowledge of what has actually happened in the British Islands it would be necessary, not only to consider the activities of Englishmen which lie outside the operations of the central government, but to supplement the history of England with histories of Wales, Scotland, and Ireland, and with histories of counties, cities, boroughs, and other local units. With any one of these lesser units as a focus, we may again have a series of specialized histories of intellectual and industrial activities.

Now, if we look at this descending series of histories, it will be apparent that 'the history of England' is not a synthesis created out of the materials of 'local' histories. The history of any national unit is something other than the sum of activities of the minor political units of which the nation may be said to be composed. It is a synthesis of happenings on another level, and with another interest or 'unity' than that of local histories. We are thus brought to see that any historical synthesis has reference to some particular geographical area, that ultimately there must be as many histories as there are geographical regions, and as many histories as there are groupings and interests in communities. It follows that every history is particular, for every history is a story unified by a specific interest in the mind of the historian.

The type of synthesis dominant in the nineteenth century is a product of the movement, in political discussion, which has concentrated attention upon the idea of the State. Nationalistic history and the Theory of the State are products of one and the same set of conditions. They are alike particularistic, and alike result in a narrowing of sympathy and of attention. The wealth of materials available for the study of the past of a country cannot be brought within the scope of any 'central government' synthesis. Nationalistic historiography can never do justice to the content of the past.

If the aim of history be to state 'what has actually happened,' there can be no escape from the conclusion that the final test of traditional historiography must lie in its ability to formulate a synthesis of the history of mankind.

What we are given in undertaking a consideration of 'world' history is a vast series of histories of localities, great and small, without any apparent focus or element of coördination. In dealing with the affairs of one country, the concept of the nation as constituting a political entity, placed in opposition to all other members of the same class, permits a synthesis with a clearly defined interest or focus. It scarcely requires to be pointed out that there is no corresponding entity which includes all the political units and peoples of the world. In dealing with 'world' history, therefore, we are left in the predicament aptly described by Professor Bury: "To write the history of Greece," he says, "at almost any period without dissipating the interest is a task of immense difficulty, as any one knows who has tried, because there is no constant unity or fixed centre to which the actions and aims of the numerous states can be subordinated or related."[3] There is no unity in Greek history such as Polybius discovered in the history of the Mediterranean lands when Rome had once achieved an ascendancy in the ancient world. There is no unity in Greek history such as has been given to that of the British Islands through the slow subjugation of Wales, Scotland, and Ireland by England, that is, by their aggregation under the English crown. The history of the world is an exaggerated case of the history of ancient Greece; the historian is left without a focus of the type he has been accustomed to employ in nationalistic historiography.

Nevertheless the historian does attempt to write the history of man in conformity with the pattern of the history of a state or nation. He takes it for granted, apparently, that there are different levels of generality in history writing, and that world history stands in some such relation to national histories as that in which national history stands to local histories. But how is this envisagement of world history as a whole to be accomplished? How, for example, is the continuous history of China to be brought into relation with the history of Europe since the foundation of the city of Rome? In point of fact, the syn-

---

[3] J. B. Bury, *The Ancient Greek Historians* (New York, 1909), p. 23.

theses of 'world' history and 'national' history are not on the
same footing. National history has unity of time sequence,
unity of place, and unity of personality (i.e., the nation). World
history must deal with an assemblage of time sequences, of
places, and of personalities. To bring these elements within the
compass of a narrative, the historian is driven to assume a unitary time series, to shift, with every scene, from place to place,
to substitute for the personality of the nation some general
concept or 'philosophy of history.'

In world history the unity which the historian seeks to impose upon the facts is, in the first place, chronological. The inference is that since events take place in time, and since there
is only one order or direction in time, therefore all events must
fit into one time series. The presupposition of world history
seems to be that the histories of all the different areas of the
world, or at least what is essential or 'important' in those histories, may be brought within the compass of one chronological
sequence. As we have seen, however, all histories have reference to specific areas. Time and activity are not extinguished
in one area when happenings in another part of the world claim
the interest and attention of the historian. Greece does not disappear from the earth when Rome becomes the center of the
historical narrative. The assumption that all histories may be
reduced to one history is, therefore, simply an expedient which
the historian has adopted in the attempt to overcome the infinite particularity and multiplicity of events. In actuality, all
histories are parallel in time and run concurrently. History is
not unitary, but pluralistic. There is not one history of man,
but a vast series of histories of particular groups, which includes pictures of darkness and failure no less than pictures of
'success' and 'progress.'

With this irreconcilable diversity of interests before him, the
historian, from the writer of the Book of Daniel down to the
present, has assumed that at any given moment in the past some
one power or state has occupied such a position of dominance
in the world that it might be taken as the center of the narra-

tive. World history thus becomes the account of the succession of empire. Hence the task of the historian would appear to consist in the identification of this succession of dominant or significant units, and in the narration of world events in terms of the 'national' history of each successive power as it comes into prominence. World history is thus a narrative of happenings selected from the incidents given in certain histories, the historian adding one episode after another like beads upon a string; the synthesis consists in the selection of situations from the history of one national unit after another. The order of succession of these different histories is well defined only so far as the history of Rome occupies the central or critical point in the development of the story. The effort to construct a synthesis on these lines is directed by the concept of Rome as a world power; and we can scarcely avoid the conclusion that the assumption of one dominant state at each moment of the world's history is forced upon the historian by the absence of a 'world state' to give unity to the history of man.

The history of Rome may well be regarded as giving unity to European history; but this emphasis on the place of Rome in the history of the world merely brings out the fact that we write world history as Europeans. If the history of Rome is to occupy the center of the world stage at the beginning of the Christian era, where are we to find a place for the Chinese empire under the Han dynasty? The European center for world history is even more unsatisfactory when we consider the Middle Ages. Everyone is familiar with the story of the 'medieval siege of Europe,' which is depicted as a sustained defense of Western lands against successive inundations of barbarians. Other views of the scene may, however, be taken; and this fact has been illustrated by a Mohammedan writer of the present day. In A.D. 712, says Ameer Ali, Mûsa crossed into France. "Standing on the Pyrenees, the dauntless Viceroy conceived the project of conquering the whole of Europe. . . . The cautious and hesitating policy of the Damascene Court lost the glorious opportunity, with the consequence that Europe remained enveloped in intellectual darkness for the next eight centuries.'"[4] Furthermore, it somewhat clarifies our ideas of world history to observe that a historian, writing on the history of Asia, and referring to the invasion of Europe by the Mongols in the thirteenth century, remarks that, in this singular 'barbarian' invasion, the real barbarians were not the Oriental invaders, but the Europeans who were attacked.[5]

We may see, then, that the world history which we write is not an account of the total activities of mankind, but a selection of these activities as affecting, and as observed by, the inhabitants of western Europe. Within the time series which we set up, an artificial focus is introduced by writing the story in terms of the national history of one political unit after another. Any order which is introduced into the march of events is conditioned by the geographical standpoint of the author. With all our efforts to attain complete objectivity, we cannot divest ourselves of the outlook imposed upon us by life and education in a particular country.

The unity of any history is the creation of an artist, and is arrived at through the selection from given data or materials of such facts as are in harmony with the artist's conception or purpose. In attempting to deal with one thing of which there is no other instance, with a class of which there is only one member (such as the universe, or world history), we encounter difficulty, even in the simplest effort to formulate a description of it. Sooner or later we are forced into the position of saying that this one thing is like something else with which we are more familiar, and so we have recourse to analogy.

In national history, for example, what gives force and vitality to the narrative is the envisagement of the 'whole' in terms of the nation conceived as a living entity or personality. *Dans ces jours mémorables,* Michelet said, *une grande lumière se fit, et j'aperçus la France.*

In world history what we may speak of as the form of the

---

[4] Ameer Ali, *A Short History of the Saracens* (London, 1899), p. 111.

[5] Léon Cahun, *Introduction à l'histoire de l'Asie* (Paris, 1896), p. 355.

sequence of events has been envisaged as a cycle, as a drama, and as a progress. The Greeks thought of history as an endless succession of identical cycles of events. In this view, the cosmical process consisted of exactly recurring cycles, in which the minutest occurrences were punctually repeated. We do not remember them; if we did, they would not be the same.[6] The establishment of Christianity gave to the world another vision of history, which represented it as a drama contained within the limits of Creation and the Day of Judgment, and divided into acts by the supernatural interventions recorded in sacred history. Since the Enlightenment of the eighteenth century, the philosophy of history of Christian theology has been superseded, in great measure, by a succession of theories representing world history as the working out of some implicit principle or idea. Indeed, "all kinds of baseless and worthless speculations—even the merest dreams and vagaries—have been confidently presented as philosophy [of history]. The most unsubstantial and fantastic hypotheses which metaphysics or theology, analogy or imagination, could supply or suggest, have been pretentiously maintained to explain the course and meaning of human development."[7] Philosophy of history, it has been said, consists in choosing among contemporary doctrines any striking idea whatever, and in making of this idea, or its negation, the pivot of a historical narrative.[8]

It will be apparent, then, that any attempt to formulate a concept of world history as a single series of events in time leads at once to a teleological explanation, and involves a judgment in regard to the future no less than in regard to the present and the past. Thus, concretely, Professor Bury views the whole sequence of history as an interminable procession, in the van of which all the epochs of the past are nothing more than

[6] On the Greek theory of cycles, cf. J. B. Bury, *The Ancient Greek Historians* (New York, 1909), pp. 205, 248, 254; *The Idea of Progress* (London, 1920), pp. 10–13, 354. Theodor Gomperz, *Greek Thinkers*, vol. 1, tr. by Laurie Magnus (New York, 1901), p. 141.

[7] Robert Flint, *Historical Philosophy in France* (New York, 1894), p. 18.

[8] Arbois de Jubainville, *Deux manières d'écrire l'histoire* (Paris, 1896), p. 5.

a few of the front carriages. Modern history he represents as "the field in which we may hope to charm from human history [as a whole] the secret of its rational movement, . . . and win a glimpse of a fragment of the pattern on a carpet, of which probably much the greater part is still unwoven."[9] The picture varies from writer to writer, but perhaps the most widely adopted type has been that arrived at by instituting an analogy between the life cycle of the individual and the entire existence of humanity.[10] The most recent example of this mode of thought is not without interest. "The germ of Western society," says Arnold Toynbee, "first developed in the body of Greek society, like a child in the womb. The Roman Empire was the period of pregnancy during which the new life was sheltered and nurtured by the old. The 'Dark Age' was the crisis of birth, in which the child broke away from its parent and emerged as a separate, though naked and helpless, individual. The Middle Ages were the period of childhood, in which the new creature, though immature, found itself able to live and grow independently. The fourteenth and fifteenth centuries, with their marked characteristics of transition, may stand for puberty, and the centuries since the year 1500 for our prime."[11] What is to be observed, in all such attempts, is that the completion of the design, or the realization of the development, must be conceived as falling in a remote future.

The infinite variety of the theories advanced, in the effort to arrive at a basis for a synthesis of world history, leads to recognition of the fact that our concept of the 'whole' of history must proceed out of our own philosophy of life. Whatever the nature of these highly personalized philosophies, the essential matter is that, by his acceptance of the principle that such philosophies are necessary, the historian admits that the significance of the historical past is to be judged, not on the

[9] J. B. Bury, "The Place of Modern History in the Perspective of Knowledge," *Congress of Arts and Science, St. Louis, 1904*, vol. 2 (Boston, 1906), p. 152.

[10] Cf. ch. 8, below.

[11] Arnold Toynbee, "History," in *The Legacy of Greece,* ed. by R. W. Livingstone (Oxford, 1922), p. 290.

evidence of 'what has actually happened,' but, ultimately, on the basis of our personal speculations upon the future and destiny of the human race. This, it is to be understood, is the unavoidable result of the adoption of traditional historiography as the sole form for the statement of the results of historical investigation.

Chapter 5

The Logical Implications of Historical Narrative

THE ACADEMIC HISTORIAN has accepted traditional historiography without critical examination of its implications, and this acceptance has led him away from the activity which we speak of as 'science' into a world of speculation, designated 'philosophy of history,' which thus appears as the final aim of his endeavors. This, however, is not the only result of his adoption of the practices of earlier historical writers, for his acceptance has led him, further, into the midst of disputing philosophers, and has made him a party to debates with which, as a historian, he has no proper concern. The historian may, indeed, feel a sense of elation when he comes upon the statement, however justified, that "History is Philosophy and Philosophy History"; yet, supposing the statement to be true, he must be aware that the result so expressed is not the outcome of his own conscious efforts, but is a consequence of his devotion to the traditional form of historiography.

The interest of modern philosophy in history has its origin in the avowal of the historian that his aim is to formulate a synthesis, and to arrive at the 'meaning' or significance of the 'whole' of human history, by setting down 'what it was that actually happened.' With such an aim, it would really seem as if the philosopher and the historian were engaged upon different phases of the same task. Each in his own way, apparently, is endeavoring to elicit from the world of phenomena the meaning or significance of things. The philosopher, after contemplation, arrives at a 'philosophy'; the historian sets out with a philosophy, and finds exemplification of it in the world of events. Logically, then, their activities would appear to be complementary and interdependent.

The mind of a thinking being is largely occupied in making constructions; impressions come to us, and we fit them into our own schemes of thought. Our constructions, conscious or unconscious, are framed for the purpose of setting up an intelligent conception of the world we live in; philosophy and science are the two methods available for the attainment of this object. The philosopher may be said to look upon the universe as a work of art, and he adopts the view that the significance of any part depends upon the meaning of the whole. For him it is made up of details, but is not a mere aggregate; it is a whole or unity in which the details acquire a significance that does not attach to them taken separately. In a work of art, and in the universe as the philosopher views it, the whole is something more than the sum of all its parts; and this conception finds expression in the doctrine that analysis always falsifies, because the parts of a complex whole as contained in that whole are different from what they would otherwise be.

In opposition to this conception, science maintains that any view of the whole must be in conformity with what is known of the parts, and so, putting off the entire question of 'meaning,' devotes its endeavors to the arduous undertaking of dissecting and sorting the objects of experience. In either case, it should be observed, the result arrived at is a hypothesis; but, whereas the hypotheses of science relate to strands or factors of which more than one example is to be found in the world, those of philosophy relate to a unique thing, the universe itself, so that verification by comparison is here impossible. It follows that, while the constructions of science may be tested by reference to objective actualities, those of philosophy can be criticized only in respect to their self-consistency in thought. Philosophy, as Kant remarked, is constructed out of the resources of reason.

"The essence of philosophy," in the judgment of Bernard Bosanquet, "lies in the connected vision of the totality of things, maintaining in every point the subordination of every element and factor as conditioned by the totality. It may be compared to the best theory of impressionism. You may perfect your detail and finish as much as you please, but there is one inexorable condition. Lose subordination to the whole and all is lost. You must never violate the singleness of the impression."[1] Now it is with this eye of the impressionist that the philosopher turns to survey history. He says, for example, that "a series of historical events is a true individual. A mere succession of events in time is by no means adequate to form an historical sequence; a thread of connection, a relating principle must run through all the particular events and give them a unity in the light of which alone the particular event can have any significance. History deals always with the progress or decadence of a unitary being which persists as an individual in spite of changes; it never deals with a collection of sequent but unrelated events. Unless this were the case, any fact would be of equal importance to the historian with every other fact; selection can take place only with reference to a universal."[2]

The historian is also an impressionist, and he expresses his aim in terms which have a close correspondence with those employed by the philosopher. Thus a contemporary writer finds himself confronted with the problem of the relationship of history to the specialized histories of art, law, religion, and so forth. Is history merely a residuum left after these subjects have become independent studies, and is this residuum destined to be still further reduced by some secession of tomorrow? The answer given might have been drawn from any introduction to philosophy. The vital phenomena of human life cannot, Professor Robinson says, be exhausted by any number of monographs on special subjects. Man is more than the sum of his scientifically classifiable operations. The whole is something more than the sum of its parts; "these may be

---

[1] Bernard Bosanquet, "Science and Philosophy," *Proceedings of the Aristotelian Society*, n.s., 15 (1914–15), p. 13.

[2] G. H. Sabine, "Hume's Contribution to the Historical Method," *Philosophical Review*, 15 (1906), p. 17.

studied, each by itself, with advantage, but specialization would lead to the most absurd results if there were not some one to study the process as a whole, and that some one is the historian."[3] Obviously, then, the philosopher contemplates the 'universe' as a work of art; the historian creates a work of art out of the materials available for the study of the past; the philosopher assumes that the 'whole' which the historian presents corresponds with a 'whole' existent in events.

It is pertinent to ask, "In what does this whole consist?" The historian, as has been seen, is not informed of all that has happened in the past; actually, his materials are fragmentary in the highest degree. In undertaking to grasp the 'whole,' he is forced to admit his lack of acquaintance with by far the greater part of the details necessary for such a purpose. He may, however, argue that, in order to recognize the design woven into a carpet, it is not necessary to examine every thread and fiber which has gone to its making. One might describe the pattern while remaining in ignorance of the style, type, source, or purpose of an Oriental rug. A design is something more than, and is different from, the parts (materials) in which it is represented. The design, poorly or adequately, stands for an idea; and the 'whole' is this idea. But, we may well ask, "What evidence is there for thinking that the course of events has a pattern, or that it represents an idea?" Clearly this is an assumption. We are driven, then, to ask whence is derived the design which the historian seeks to identify. Professor Bury assumes that the design is inherent in the events; in practice, however, the design or idea of the 'whole' takes form in the mind of the historian. As we have seen, the historian 'abstracts from' the available information in regard to the past to construct a 'whole'; in short, he imposes his own idea upon the facts with which he deals. The pattern which the historian reads into the facts is his own creation; the 'whole' which he sets forth does not inhere in the happenings of time, but takes form in his imagination.

[3] J. H. Robinson, *The New History* (New York, 1912), pp. 65–68.

Academic historians insist that their aim is to get at the facts, to disclose, by means of documentary inquiry, what has actually happened. In this conception, truth in history means that the statements made by the historiographer have documentary support. On the other hand, facts are not 'true' in themselves, but in relation to some statement or proposition. It follows that, in history writing, 'truth' is of the type that characterizes art, and is entirely removed from that which characterizes science. "What, then," asks Viscount Haldane, "is to be the standard of truth for the historian? The analogy of the artist who paints a portrait may prove not without significance for the answer to this question. The great artist does not put on canvas a simple reproduction of the appearance of his subject at a particular moment; that is the work of the photographer. Art, in the highest sense, has to disentangle the significance of the whole from its details and to reproduce it. The truth of art is a truth that must thus be born again of the artist's mind. No mere narration of details will give the whole that at once dominates these details and yet does not exist apart from them."[4] Research in itself, the same authority points out, can never arrive at truth in the field of history. "The knowledge of the historian is only partially derived from research." History founded on merely scientific methods would be a mockery.[5] The materials afforded by state papers and other historical documents must be used "by a man who possesses the gifts requisite for presenting the narrative as that of an organic whole, and that organic whole must in its expression be born afresh in his mind."[6] "Art alone can adequately make the idea of the whole shine forth in the particulars in which it is immanent."[7]

Whatever the reason for the correspondence between the point of view of the philosopher and that of the historian, the nature of the effect upon the position of the latter is beyond

[4] Viscount Haldane, *The Meaning of Truth in History* (London, 1914), p. 7.

[5] *Ibid.*, pp. 31, 32.

[6] *Ibid.*, p. 2[1].

[7] *Ibid.*, p. 22. Cf. David Morrison, "The Treatment of History by Philosophers," *Proceedings of the Aristotelian Society*, n.s., 14 (1914), p. 295.

question. This effect has been expressed, sympathetically, by Professor Bury. In supporting the thesis that "history is a science, no less and no more," he argues (correctly) that the philosophical interpretation of history is the only hypothesis on which the postulate of 'history for its own sake' can be justified as valid. "This principle of 'history for its own sake,' " he continues, "might be described as the motto or watchword of the great movement of historical research which has gone on increasing in volume and power since the beginning of the last century. But," he asks, "has this principle a theoretical justification? It seems to me," he says, "that our decision of this question must fall out according to the view we take of the relation of man's historical development to the whole of reality. We are brought face to face with a philosophical problem. Our apprehension of history and our reason for studying it must ultimately be determined by the view we entertain of the *moles et machina mundi* as a whole."[8] So, in bringing his discussion to a close, Bury says that "the answer to the question, 'What is the position of modern history in the domain of universal knowledge?' depends in the first instance on our view of the fundamental question at issue between idealism and naturalism."[9] Again, Windelband, adopting fully the point of view of the historian, finds that "the theory of knowledge of historical science must be sought in ethics," taking ethics as practical philosophy in its entirety. "The ultimate problems of ethics," however, "bring us back to the metaphysical problems in which is discussed what meaning the temporal course of events has in relation to the timeless reality as the genuine being," only to discover, at the end, that "no metaphysical theory helps us in regard to this fundamental antithesis of the temporal and timeless."[10]

So, by adopting without consideration the practice of traditional historiography, the academic historian obligates himself,

---

[8] J. B. Bury, "The Place of Modern History," as cited, pp. 143–144.

[9] *Ibid.*, p. 152.

[10] Wilhelm Windelband, *An Introduction to Philosophy*, tr. by Joseph McCabe (London, 1921), pp. 279, 299.

as a preliminary to the writing of history, to a decision upon the most vexed and difficult problems of philosophical thought.

It is necessary to point out that the modern philosopher occupies himself with criticism rather than with construction, and that he regards as his special activity the criticism of the methods as well as the analysis of the fundamental concepts and assumptions of the sciences. In other words, the scientist is intent upon his own enterprises; "the philosopher comes into being as one who is interested in observing what it is that the scientist is so intently doing."[11] Here, again, philosophy follows science; and it is of the utmost importance to observe, in the present connection, that, while it investigates methodology, philosophy does not devise methods for men of science to follow. As the sciences progress in actual insight, they must complete, improve, refine, and extend their methods;[12] the philosopher simply analyzes the methods employed by the sciences at a given time. As Rashdall says, "It is not the business of the logician to lay down rules for the guidance of scientific men. In so far as logic is concerned with the actual methods of particular sciences, the logician must rather analyse the methods actually employed in those sciences up to the present than to attempt to prescribe *a priori* the methods they must follow."[13] Logic does not justify, it describes method; it accepts the actual procedure of the sciences.

In the course of his examination of the procedure followed in different intellectual activities, the logician considers the nature of history. In this pursuit he has been much perturbed at the obvious differences between history and science. Until recently, philosophy has asserted that history is not science. The distinction goes back to Aristotle, who regarded science as knowledge of the universal, history as knowledge of the particular. The contrast is explicit in European thought since the

[11] R. B. Perry, *The Approach to Philosophy* (London, 1905), p. 119.

[12] Wilhelm Windelband, in *Encyclopædia of the Philosophical Sciences*, tr. by B. E. Meyer, vol. 1 (London, 1913), p. 43.

[13] Hastings Rashdall, *Proceedings of the Aristotelian Society*, n.s., 6 (1905–06), p. 1.

Renaissance, but for long the opposition was maintained as between history and philosophy. Bacon and Hobbes thought that history is properly concerned with individuals circumscribed by time and place, whereas philosophy discards individuals and deals only with abstract notions. In the nineteenth century the argument shifts so as to bring the antithesis between history and science. Schopenhauer asserted that history is not a science because it deals with the particular and individual, whereas the sciences are systems of conceptions; and he insisted that, while the sciences speak of what always is, history knows only that which is once and then is no more. A more recent form of the contrast has been that the sciences deal with facts that recur, history with what has once happened and can never be reproduced. The antithesis has lent itself to a wealth of expression: Nature deals with the typical in the manifold, History separates the manifold from the typical; Nature is the realm of necessity, History is the realm of freedom; Natural Science systematizes and classifies, History individualizes and narrates; Natural Science deals with the abstract and conceptual, History with the actual and concrete.

In current discussion the antithesis is based on the views expressed by historians during the nineteenth century, and, more specifically, on the formula of Ranke that the office of the historian is simply to state what it was that actually happened.[14] While historians, heedless of the outcome, were occupying themselves in describing the succession of such particular events as could be detailed from available documents, logicians were observing their activities with the object of determining the principles of historical procedure. What they discovered was that 'history' is identical with 'historiography'; that it is the narrative of certain exceptional happenings particularized by names and dates, selected by an individual as of value or worth in relation to a given set of ideas. History, meaning 'the past,' is thus envisaged as an after-one-another procession of occurrences, each one emerging somehow from what has gone

---

[14] L. von Ranke, *Sämmtliche Werke* (3. Aufl., Leipzig, 1877), Bd. 33, p. vii.

before, and every occurrence is regarded as individual and un-repeated. In support of this view, it is urged that in the world of everyday life, that is, in the concrete world of experience, in the world of action and of men, there is nothing but the actuality of deeds done that may not be undone, of words uttered that may not be recalled. Among the myriad possibilities of a given moment a single choice is made, and the entire future is dominated thereby; among the ways open but one is followed, and this way can never be retraced. In relation to this world of unrepeated fact, it is argued that 'history' stands out as the record of a unique series of events that has happened once for all. Hence the logician finds that 'history' with its statements of unique happenings differs from the sciences, which he describes as concerned with recurrent uniformities and with the discovery of 'laws.'

In considering this view of history, it must be pointed out that, while philosophy takes as its province the criticism of method in the sciences, this analysis has not remained disin-terested. Indeed, in this discussion the philosopher, carrying into his writings all the importunity of life,[15] has come to regard science with hostility, and, curiously enough, to accept history as an ally. We cannot, therefore, adopt the views of logicians on these subjects without scrutiny.[16]

---

[15] R. B. Perry, *Present Philosophical Tendencies* (New York, 1912), p. 38.

[16] The more notable exponents of the ideas here referred to are: Wilhelm Dilthey, *Einleitung in die Geisteswissenschaften* (Leipzig, 1883). Georg Simmel, *Die Probleme der Geschichtsphilosophie* (Leipzig, 1892; 3. Aufl., 1907). Wilhelm Windelband, *Geschichte und Naturwissenschaft* (Strassburg, 1894), in his *Präludien* (2. Aufl., Tübingen, 1903; 5. Aufl., 1915); *Einleitung in die Philosophie* (Tübingen, 1914), *An Introduction to Philosophy*, tr. by Joseph McCabe (London, [1921]). Heinrich Rickert, *Die Grenzen der naturwissenschaftlichen Begriffs-bildung* (Freiburg i. B., Tübingen, 1896–1902; 2 Aufl., Tübingen, 1913); *Kultur-wissenschaft und Naturwissenschaft* (Freiburg i. B., 1899; 2. Aufl., Tübingen, 1910); "Geschichtsphilosophie," in Wilhelm Windelband, ed., *Die Philosophie im Beginn des zwanzigsten Jahrhunderts*, 2. Bd. (Heidelberg, 1905), pp. 51–135. For a general presentation of the point of view in logic, see Ernst Troeltsch, "Historiography," in James Hastings, *Encyclopædia of Religion and Ethics*, vol. 6 (New York, 1914), pp. 716–723. For critical studies of Windelband and Rickert, see: Antonio Aliotta, *The Idealistic Reaction against Science*, tr. by Agnes Mc-Caskill (London, 1914), pp. 196–273. Ernst Troeltsch, "Ueber den Begriff einer

It is commonly stated in philosophical literature that science is the more perfect the farther removed it is from what is individual and concrete; that science dissects, and can never return to the actual object from which it set out. The instant, it is said, we attempt to explain reality by means of science, that which is truly real will elude our grasp. Now the fact is that such statements have reference, not to the procedure of science, but to what the philosopher considers science to be. In direct opposition to this view, we may contend that science is interested in the data of experience in a much fuller sense than is the exponent of logical theory.

The philosopher accepts a landscape, and is interested in the 'value,' 'meaning,' or 'significance' of what he finds. Henceforth he considers the 'whole' which he has selected from or read into the concrete totality presented in experience. His way of looking at the landscape may be compared to 'the best theory of impressionism.' The scientist, on the other hand, does not accept what is given just as it presents itself. He is conscious that we look at an object, not with our eyes, but with our interests. He is aware that an infinity of detail lies behind any datum of experience, and he goes below or behind the surface as presented to examine into the way in which things work. So the geologist and the physiographer see the actual landscape with other eyes than does the artist; the physiologist and the physician have a fuller awareness of the human body than the most anxious mother. The scientist has occasion to know that the human eye has a very limited range of sight, and he endeavors to extend this range by the use of instruments; but he also extends the limits of human vision by pointing out that this contour is the result of the action of water in times past,

historischen Dialektik. Windelband-Rickert und Hegel," *Historische Zeitschrift*, 119 (1919), pp. 373–426. Erich Becher, *Geisteswissenschaften und Naturwissenschaften* (München, 1921). The most adequate discussion of the general problem appears in the symposium by R. G. Collingwood, A. E. Taylor, and F. C. S. Schiller on the question, "Are History and Science Different Kinds of Knowledge?" *Mind*, 31 (1922), pp. 442–466. Cf. also M. R. Cohen, "The Insurgence against Reason," *Journal of Philosophy*, 22 (1925), pp. 120–123.

that this groove in the rock is the result of ancient glacial action. Furthermore, in dealing with an evolution the scientist does not merely recite history, he shows that the 'new' is the product of the working of natural processes in the course of time. The theory of Natural Selection may not be a correct description of the way in which the biologically 'new' emerges, but at least it gives a fuller content and more profound interest to the concrete facts of life in the world. At bottom, the difference between philosophy and history, on the one hand, and science, on the other, is the difference between aesthetic 'appreciation' and knowledge, between emotional realization of a scene or situation and painstaking investigation. The philosopher, the artist, and the historian set out from the concrete, and arrive at some conception of a 'whole.' In doing this they leave behind them the totality of what is 'given' in all its fullness, and never return to it again. The scientist, on the other hand, is forced by the very nature of his inquiries to remain in immediate contact with the actual; his every theory is tested by reference back to the concrete reality; and, furthermore, he looks out, daily and hourly, upon a world informed and enriched by the knowledge gained in his inquiries.[17]

It is neither desirable in this discussion, nor is it essential to the purpose in view, to inquire into the source of the antagonism between idealism and science. The idealist has taken history as an ally because he has discovered in it a form of knowledge, miscalled 'science,' which he may place in opposition to 'natural science.' This opposition has been so emphasized that it has become the central feature in the 'idealistic reaction' which "has tended to degrade science into a false form of knowledge and to find the true form in history."[18] The steps of the argument appear to be: the real is always individual and unique; history concerns itself only with the individual and

---

[17] Cf. Hugo Münsterberg, *Psychology and Life* (Boston, 1899), pp. 187–191. A. E. Taylor, *Elements of Metaphysics* (London, 1903), p. 55. Antonio Aliotta, as cited, p. 216. R. G. Collingwood, *Mind*, 31 (1922), pp. 447–448.

[18] R. G. Collingwood, as cited, p. 445.

unique; therefore history is the knowledge or 'science' of reality. It follows that "history, like philosophy, is the knowledge
of the one real world," or, in short, that "history and philosophy are the same thing."[19]

The focal point in the discussion lies in the statement that
history deals with facts which are individual, rare, characteristic, exceptional, unique. Now, unquestionably, the totality
of things and events is unique. So, too, every concrete experience in its totality is unique; it cannot be duplicated. On the
other hand, historical narrative does not even pretend to describe the totality of what has happened; historiography utilizes
only a selection from all that has actually occurred. What, then,
is the relation of this selection to the sum total of actual events?
In the argument under consideration, the unique in history is
defined by the statement of its opposite, namely, that which is
common, constant, or which repeats itself. The definition of the
unique by reference to its opposite assumes, obviously, that
the historian divides the unique totality from which he sets
out into two classes: the unique and the nonunique or common. He abstracts from the totality to get the unique. Abstraction, as everyone is aware, sets free some factor so that it may
be used. In employing abstraction, the historian follows, in
part, the procedure of the natural scientist; but, whereas the
latter utilizes abstraction for the purpose of illuminating reality (the actual), and for the purpose of extending our knowledge of the world, the historian utilizes it, in the manner of the
artist, for the purpose of constructing a synthesis, of creating
a unique 'whole,' of producing a work of art.

The nature of the contention made by those who insist that
'history' is the 'science' of the unique and the particular may
be made clear by an illustration. If we write a narrative of the
history of landholding in England, we select such facts as are
of importance for the impression we desire to convey—let us
say, the necessity or the injustice of 'enclosures.' This narrative
will be a record of facts which appear to the historian to be

<hr>

[19] R. G. Collingwood, *Religion and Philosophy* (London, 1916), p. 51.

individual and unique, and, it is maintained, will be a true history. If, on the other hand, we desire, as a preliminary step, to understand the problem of landholding in England, and, as a means to this end, compare the historical facts of landholding in different countries, examining the factors or elements which have affected landholding in a great variety of places, this, according to the view expressed, will *not* be history. Yet it would appear to the uninitiated that the latter type of study would be essential if a history of landholding in England is to be written, and, more particularly, if we are to discover what was 'unique' in that history. However, if we accept the standpoint of the landscape artist, it will be recognized that what the particular scene before us has in common with other scenes is of less than no moment; what is of importance is the scene as it presents itself, with its own interest for the painter, its own significance, its own meaning. The painter 'appreciates' the landscape, and depicts it in the light of his appreciation. In the judgment of the philosopher, the historian views the past as the painter views the landscape, and gives his personal rendering of what has happened in terms of its significance, meaning, and value.

The notion that history deals only with facts which are unique finds its fullest expression in the thought of certain writers who regard it as the knowledge of the individual or particular, in contradistinction to the natural sciences, which, they say, are concerned with the discovery of 'laws.'

The word 'individual' comes to us charged with a wealth of significance, derived, in no small part, from personal associations. "I myself am an individual" is, in general, our substitute for a definition of individuality. When we come to ask, "What is the principle that individuates the world?" Josiah Royce thinks "we are fain to conceal our uncertainty behind a mere repetition of the assertion that individuals are facts."[20] Royce's examination of the problem led him to the conclusion that the process of individualizing consists in setting up a class with one

---

[20] Josiah Royce, *The Conception of God* (New York, 1897), p. 220.

member and no more, and that this class is constructed with reference to an exclusive interest.[21] An individual is the object of an exclusive interest; conversely, any organizing interest leads to individualization. Thus the "unique individuals with which the historian works are not necessarily persons nor are they single events; they may be the life of a people, the evolution of European society, the evolution of world society, the evolution of the visible universe." Obviously an organizing interest, such as that represented here by the concept of 'evolution,' is required to give individuality or unity to the mass of detail which constitutes the life of a people or that of the visible universe. This interest, however, dominates the details which are included in the picture, and we reach the conclusion that the individuality of past events or facts emerges when these interest us because of their importance for a particular narrative composition. Whether a given historical fact is of value for historiography, we are told, depends upon its importance for a given synthesis.

It will be seen, then, that in accepting history as the 'science' of the 'individual' we have not progressed beyond the point of affirming that, in order to construct a synthesis, the historian must begin with some 'philosophy of history.' From whatever point we approach the consideration of traditional historiography, we find ourselves in the presence of the same set of problems. The historian sets out to create a 'whole,' and this 'whole' is of necessity the organization of a body of fact from the standpoint of some *a priori* interest.

When it is said that an 'individual' is simply the object of an exclusive interest, one may take exception on the ground that the definition fails to do justice to the feeling which attaches to 'individuality' as manifested in concrete instances. However the term may be defined, we feel that an 'individual' has personality; that what is individual has a worth, a value, in and for itself. In our everyday way of looking at things, we recognize an opposition between what is 'individual' and what is common

---

[21] Josiah Royce, as cited, p. 264.

and ordinary. When we say that a work of art has 'individual-ity,' we mean that it stands out, that it makes an enduring impression, that it is unforgettable. History is the memory of persons and situations which men will not surrender to oblivion. This interest of men in the unforgettable happenings of the past, modern logic has recognized as of the very essence of historiography. Not content, however, to accept history as a story worth telling because of its emotional appeal to human kind, the logician has faced the questions: "By what standards does the historian judge of the events of the past?" "What is it we value when we select or single out something from the past for record and preservation?" In proposing these questions, the logician has rendered a service to history which it is difficult to overestimate. This service does not consist in any 'justification' of the historian's procedure, but in revealing the implications of that procedure by pressing home the inquiry into the bases of the historian's activity.

The problem of 'value' in historiography has been investigated by various philosophers, notably by Heinrich Rickert. History, Rickert points out, does not conform to the method of science; it is a *Wissenschaft* of a particular kind and with a particular aim. The historian concerns himself with documentary inquiry, but he considers the facts elicited by investigation with the object of selecting data for a synthesis. In other words, the historian passes judgment upon the facts; he reaches a decision on their intellectual, moral, and aesthetic worth. The importance of Rickert's work lies in the demonstration that these judgments of the historian are formulated in the light of "transcendental ideal standards of value." "The individual elements of history can be combined into a higher unity only by referring to a universal value. . . . If we would distinguish the essential from the non-essential in the world of experience, in a way which is universally valid, we must have a criterion of selection, an ideal norm which will enable us to eliminate everything which is not of importance to the attainment of that universal end, and to arrange the most important moments of historical development in a hierarchical scale of values."[22]

It does not concern the present argument to describe the characteristics of Rickert's system of transcendental idealism, with its curious postulate that nothing exists unless it is judged to do so, that facts are such only so far as they are recognized. We are not concerned with the doctrine that the transcendent Ought is an object of knowledge, nor even with the 'philosophy of history' which regards the cosmic process as the progressive historic actualization of the ideal. What is germane in Rickert's philosophy is simply the proof it affords that traditional historiography requires for its 'justification' the recognition that its implicit judgments are of a transcendental character.

[22] Antonio Aliotta, as cited, p. 210.

Chapter 6

The Concept of Cause in History Writing

THE PHILOSOPHERS who have undertaken to construct systems based upon the concept of 'history' as the knowledge of the ultimately real have assumed that the historian embodied in his narrative 'just what it was that actually happened.' The historian does not, as a matter of fact, simply state what it was that happened. It is his acknowledged endeavor to 'explain' events, to reveal 'causes,' and the typical procedure followed in this effort consists in the introduction, in the narrative, of speculations concerning personal motives. "Motives," it has been said, "constitute the ultimate stuff of history."[1]

The initial suggestion of the idea which takes personal motive as the basis of historical 'causation' comes from the habit of regarding history as concerned exclusively with 'deeds' and 'events.' When something happens, somebody must be 'at the bottom of it,' and we begin to speculate on the motives which could have prompted some person to commit the deed. This procedure is followed by everyone in daily life, and by all historians in accounting for the actions of historical characters. It is of importance to note that this exercise of the imagination is regarded by academic historians as the final test of competent scholarship. It may be well to present evidence on this point.

Of Bishop Stubbs it was said by an intimate: "His historical insight was such as to enable him not only to judge of men and of the course of events, but to make him capable of predicting with remarkable precision how a man would act in certain cir-

[1] W. R. Thayer, "History—Quick or Dead?" *Atlantic Monthly*, 122 (1918), p. 638.

cumstances."[2] Stubbs himself wrote: "It is almost a matter of necessity for the student of history to work out for himself some definite idea of the characters of the great men of the period he is employed upon. History cannot be well read as a chess problem, and the man who tries to read it so is not worthy to read it at all. Its scenes cannot be realized, its lessons cannot be learned, if the actors are looked upon merely as puppets."[3]

"The historian," Henry Nettleship said, "is not merely a lover of truth, not only a chronicler of events. These, indeed, he must be at his peril, but how much more! Insight into human nature—and this implies the rarest knowledge and finest sympathy of which man is capable; the power of tracing the delicate relation between deed and motive, and the pressure of action upon circumstance and circumstance upon action; knowledge of the world, in short, in the highest sense of that expression."[4]

Firth is of the opinion that a contemporary "who undertook to write a history of the seventeenth century could put together a pretty full account of what happened, but it must be necessarily rather superficial and general. He could not go below the surface and explain either the causes of events or the motives of the actors."[5]

We are moderns, but Dionysius of Halicarnassus wrote of Theopompus: "There remains his crowning and most characteristic quality, . . . the gift of seeing and stating in each case not only what is obvious to the multitude, but of examining even the hidden motives of actions and actors and the feelings of the soul (things not easily discerned by the crowd), and laying bare all the mysteries of seeming virtue and undiscovered vice. Indeed, I can well believe that the fabled examination,

---

[2] W. H. Hutton, *William Stubbs, Bishop of Oxford* (London, 1906), p. 169.

[3] William Stubbs, *Historical Introductions to the Rolls Series*, ed. by Arthur Hassall (London, 1902), p. 89; *Seventeen Lectures on the Study of Medieval and Modern History* (Oxford, 1887), p. 85.

[4] Henry Nettleship, *Lectures and Essays,* 2d series, ed. by F. Haverfield (Oxford, 1895), p. 245.

[5] C. H. Firth, "The Development of the Study of Seventeenth-Century History," *Transactions of the Royal Historical Society,* 3d series, 7 (1913), pp. 28–29.

before the judges in the other world, of souls in Hades when separated from the body is of the same searching kind as that which is conducted by means of the writings of Theopompus."[6]

It seems unnecessary to point out the inherent weakness of any attempt to account for the actions of Alexanders and Attilas on the basis of speculations upon their motives. The ascription of motives, based on the psychology of daily life, is a dubious venture for one who professes to limit his statements to known and documented facts. Furthermore, unchecked as it is by any process of verification, the practice leads on to one still less in keeping with the claims of historical research and still further removed from the type of inquiry denominated 'science'—to ethical judgments upon the conduct of historical characters. So Lord Acton could say: "I exhort you never to debase the moral currency or to lower the standard of rectitude, but to try others by the final maxim that governs your own lives, and to suffer no man and no cause to escape the undying penalty which history has the power to inflict on wrong."[7] It may be well to point out that the masters of ethical theory are the first to utter warnings against the formulation of judgments such as this. "Histories," T. H. Green remarked, "no doubt, would be much shortened, and would be found much duller, if speculations about the motives (as distinct from the intentions) of the chief historical agents were omitted; nor shall we soon cease to criticise the actions of contemporaries on the strength of inferences from act to motive. But in all this we are on very uncertain ground. . . . It is wiser not to make guesses where we can do no more than guess, and to confine ourselves . . . to measuring the value of actions by their effects without reference to the character of the agents."[8]

---

[6] *Letter to Pompeius* vi, in *The Three Literary Letters of Dionysius,* tr. by W. R. Roberts (Cambridge, 1901).

[7] Lord Acton, *A Lecture on the Study of History* (London, 1896), p. 63. On the utilization of history for moral teaching, see D. T. Starnes, "Purpose in the Writing of History," *Modern Philology,* 23 (1922–1923), pp. 281–300.

[8] T. H. Green, *Prolegomena to Ethics,* ed. by A. C. Bradley (Oxford, 1883), pp. 318–319. Cf. C. D. Burns, "History and Philosophy," *Monist,* 32 (1922), p. 363.

One of the great difficulties inherent in the study of causation in history lies in the fact that the materials with which the historian deals suggest in a singularly obvious fashion the elementary form of the concept of cause. As everyone knows, the idea of cause is bound up with that of human volition; "our search for causes is ultimately derived from the search for means to the practical realisation of results in which we are interested."[9] The prime material of the concept is our consciousness of acting. 'Cause' is conceived as an activity which operates to produce an 'effect.' To the historian cause means the existence of will or activity on the part of some person or persons. Now historical investigation yields only isolated facts, and for the purposes of historiography these must be connected. The assumption is that the facts ascertained constitute a series of such an order that between any two of its members other series of inferred happenings may be interpolated. "The hidden motives, desires, and energies which underlie or accompany the external events require to be somehow connected, to present themselves in some order and continuity, before we are able to grasp and record them."[10] Obviously, what is here implied is the idea of 'cause' as a direct personal agency.

In constructing a narrative, every event is 'explained' in terms of some particular antecedent or antecedents, given or imagined. The character of this antecedent is worthy of attention. In the concept of cause as fully developed[11] there are three terms: the antecedent, an intervening process to be determined by investigation, the consequent. In history there are also three terms: the antecedent event, an inferred series of (psychic) happenings, the consequent. The difference between the two series lies in the nature of the middle term—the historian arrives at his causal explanation, not by scientific investigation, but simply by adding imaginatively to the number of terms in the

[9] A. E. Taylor, *Elements of Metaphysics* (London, 1903), pp. 168–169.

[10] J. T. Merz, *A History of European Thought in the Nineteenth Century*, vol. 1 (Edinburgh, 1896), p. 1.

[11] Théodule Ribot, *The Evolution of General Ideas*, tr. by F. A. Welby (Chicago, 1899), p. 180.

chronological series. Since it would appear that the intercala-
tions are regarded by the historian as true in the same sense
as are the facts which he records on the basis of documentary
evidence, it is to be inferred that, in his judgment, there is no
distinction between the factual and the imaginative terms in
the series. What the words 'cause and effect' actually imply in
history is the relation of 'before and after.' It follows necessarily
that causation, as it appears to the historian, is not distinguishable from order in time.[12]

There is still another aspect of the historian's idea of cause
to which reference may be made. In a wider extension, 'cause'
means the ordering of events by divine will or purpose. The
Greeks conceived of this divine ordering as being in accordance with established custom. An earlier type of thought
regained influence, however, with the introduction of Christianity, which admitted the belief that direct interventions of
Providence were attested by extraordinary or unusual happenings. One of the significant developments in historiography
during the last century has been the extrusion of the miraculous from the explanation of events, an achievement which is
referred to in modern discussion as the establishment of the
principle of 'continuity' in history. The elimination of supernatural interventions from the chain of historical causation,
and the establishment of the idea of 'continuity,' have not, however, been followed by the adoption of scientific modes of
inquiry. The reason for this neglect is to be found in the traditional effort of the historian to view history as a 'whole' or
unity, and hence as constituting a unitary 'causal development,'
a single 'causal process.'[13] So, when the practice of the academic
historian is examined with reference to the conception of cause
which is implied in it, the dominating influence of teleology
and idealism becomes apparent. "Only when facts and events
cease to be unconnected, when they appear to us linked to-

[12] J. S. Mill, *A System of Logic*, bk. 3, ch. 24.

[13] J. B. Bury, "Darwinism and History," in A. C. Seward, ed., *Darwinism and Modern Science* (Cambridge, 1909), p. 531.

gether according to some design and purpose, leading us back to some originating cause or forward to some destined end, can we speak of history in the sense which the word has acquired in modern language."[14] If we regard history as constituting a 'whole,' the 'cause' looked for will be the design or purpose which gives determinate form to this unity. Once more, then, the historian, by his adoption of traditional historiography, is led beyond the domain of fact into the realm of unverifiable speculation. Professor Bury's idea of the history of man "as a causal process which contains within itself the explanation of the development of man from his primitive state to the point which he has reached"[15] means simply the acceptance of a philosophical interpretation of history. It means that the 'cause' is some principle immanent or inherent in the whole course of events—the Absolute unfolding itself through the dialectic process. The search for such a cause lies within the province of the philosopher, not within that of the historian.

It may be well to state categorically that the writer is far from seeking to argue that traditional historiography is something to be discountenanced and rejected by thoughtful men. History is one of the great forms of literature, and represents a valid interest of the human spirit. It is not the purpose of this inquiry either to attack or to defend the art of writing history, but to show that, in accepting this traditional form of statement as the end and aim of his activities, the modern 'scientific' historian has placed a most serious obstacle in the way of the development of a scientific study of man or of society.

As we have seen, the academic historian works with documents, and, where these fail his occupation comes to an end. At the second step, the historian presents the results of his inquiries in the form of a narrative. In it he proposes to tell only what it was that actually happened. Historical narrative, however, is not photography; it is not a literal transcript of events. The historian, in point of fact, does not confine himself to

---

[14] J. T. Merz, as cited, p. 1.
[15] J. B. Bury, as cited, p. 531.

the statement of what he finds in the documents; he is not merely an annalist. To the data derived from documentary investigation he adds his own conception of the facts (represented by the selection he makes from what the documents supply), his inferences with respect to the motives of the characters in the drama, his philosophy of history and of life.

The modern historian did not invent narrative or historiography. He found this form of literature in possession of the field, and accepted it without hesitation or critical examination. As a result of this acceptance he has been led into the adoption of practices which, verbally, he condemns. He has not recognized that whereas, as an investigator, he begins with a body of documents, and arrives at a series of isolated statements of fact, as a writer of history he begins with an idea, an intuitive apprehension, which thenceforward gives form and unity to the series of events or deeds which he recounts. In his work as an investigator, the historian follows his sources; in his work as a historiographer, he follows his own predilections. As a consequence, however detached and disinterested the historian may be in conducting his preliminary inquiries, once he turns to present his results in narrative form he becomes an artist, interested primarily in conveying to the reader the picture which has taken form in his own mind. The dominating element in historiography is not 'what actually happened,' but the concept or idea in the light of which the historian views the known facts of the past. Some such concept is necessary if the historian is to rise above the plane of the annalist and construct a synthesis, a unity, a whole. Traditional historiography demands of the historian some view or interpretation of events, but, in making this demand, it leads him beyond the documents, beyond any ascertainable knowledge of the past, beyond the facts altogether, into the realm of 'ends' and of emotionalized speculation.

As we have seen, it has been maintained that logic has 'justified' the established practice of historians. In the first place, logic cannot 'justify,' it describes method. It may, nevertheless, bring to light implications in method of which scholars have themselves been unaware. This has happened for historiography, in which, for special reasons, philosophers have taken a particular interest. In their analysis of the procedure followed, logicians have brought to light the thoroughgoing philosophical tendencies of academic history. The concurrence of history and philosophy arises from the way in which each of these pursuits regards the world; historian and philosopher alike conceive of the universe and of the course of events as constituting a 'whole' or unity. The arguments which have been put forward by logicians in defense of historiography are not a justification of history, but a demonstration that the immediate interest of the philosopher in supporting historians is due to the idea that 'history' represents a type of knowledge which is fundamentally different from that of 'natural science.'

If, then, we are to have a science of man, historical investigation must be freed from its present subordination to the art of history writing.

PART TWO

THE STUDY OF CHANGE

The Aims of Historical and Evolutionary Inquiry

THE SECOND major obstacle to the application of the method of science to the study of man lies in the way in which humanists and scientists alike have approached the study of change in time.

The modern historian, as we have seen, has defined the aim of his work to be the narrative statement of what has actually happened in the past; the modern logician has reached the conclusion that the aim of history is the description of events, of occurrences which are unusual, uncommon, unique. It has been pointed out that the historian subtracts from the totality of things to arrive at the unique events which he undertakes to set forth. Obviously, then, there is another class of facts which remains to be considered, a class which differs in some essential from events, a class which, it is agreed, has the marked characteristic that it admits of the application of the method of science.

The most cursory observation of the world makes us aware of objects, entities, things, as well as of events. Science deals with objects, entities, things, and their relations; history concerns itself with events. Now events, as we say, 'happen'; but things undergo change. Things do not 'undergo' events, though they may be affected by them. It is of importance to notice that our everyday, common-sense judgment associates change with events. On the other hand, extraordinary as it may seem, scientific investigation, during the last two centuries, has maintained the view that the study of change in objects, entities, and things must be carried on independently of the study of events. As a result of this very remarkable theoretical assumption, the study of history and the study of evolution are carried on in different worlds, and without appreciation of their common relation to the study of change in the course of time. As the next step in this inquiry, therefore, it will be necessary to examine the historical facts relating to this separation, which has proved a stumbling block no less to humanistic than to biological investigation.

What we are given in experience is an existent *present,* and the question necessarily arises: "Of what does this present consist?" Two distinct and conflicting views are held by humanistic students with respect to the content of the 'present' which they undertake to explain.

In the first place, the 'present' may be thought of as a given *situation,* as the culmination of a continuous series of actions or deeds. This view leads to typical results, which have been clearly expressed by Professor Becker. "As for myself," he says, "I find the state of man as it now is in Europe intelligible, in so far as it can be made intelligible, chiefly through a study of the concrete doings and sayings of particular Europeans, more especially during the last hundred years or so; and in the endeavor to attain this kind of understanding, the sort of information which I find most useful is that which reveals the conscious motives and purposes that appear to have had a determining influence."[1] A present situation is thus explained by going back to some point in the past, and by carrying down a narrative of happenings from that beginning to the moment of immediate interest or concern. As, however, the bare narration of what is known to have occurred is not in itself considered to be explanatory, the historian adds, at each step, new series of (psychological) events which he himself has discerned by intuition. The intelligibility which the historian thus introduces into the materials which he selects for his composition is of the same order as that provided by the author of a historical novel or drama.

---

[1] Carl Becker, *American Historical Review,* 24 (1918), p. 267.

As has been pointed out earlier, the modern historian comes naturally by this interest in deeds and motives. In the best tradition of romanticism, the academic historian continues to accept the unusual, the strange, the exceptional, as the substance of his story; and he solves the riddles of the past by the imaginative reconstruction of personal character. Furthermore, romanticism in history finds its inspiration in the conception of the history of a nation as the record of a single life, that is, in the doctrine of 'continuity.' This particular interest had its most complete development in Germany, and under German influence became the approved type of history in academic usage—with results which I have endeavored to describe. The historiography of romanticism focuses attention upon a single series of occurrences relating to one people, nation, or state, and considers this series as a unity or whole. The narrative is concerned with deeds and actions, and the 'present' is regarded simply as the latest situation which has emerged from what has gone before.

Nationalistic history of the Romantic period did not, however, wholly supersede the rationalistic historiography of the eighteenth century. This type is characterized by an insistence that the study of history must take cognizance of all races and nations, as well as of all phases of human activity.[2] From the time of Voltaire, indeed, there has been a persistent current of opposition to the view that history should concern itself primarily with national affairs and with the activities of national governments. At the present time this opposition is marked, and there is a pronounced movement of thought which favors a widely inclusive policy in historical study and inquiry. In his presidential address before the International Congress of Historical Studies in 1913, Lord Bryce drew attention to the "immense expansion" which has taken place in the scope of historical studies. "We have now come to regard history," he said, "as a record of every form of human effort and achieve-

[2] Eduard Fueter, *Histoire de l'historiographie moderne*, tr. par Emile Jeanmaire (Paris, 1914), pp. 415–433.

ment, concerned not any more definitely with political events and institutions than with all the other factors that have moulded man and all the other expressions his creative activity has found." As illustrating this enlargement of view, he mentions specifically the interest taken by historians in the study of primitive man, in the study of early Mediterranean civilizations, and in the study of the habits and manners, the religious ideas and rudimentary political institutions, of backward races and tribes. In short, he remarked that "the historian, who in the days of Thucydides needed to look no further than to Susa on the east and Carthage on the west, must now extend his vision to take in the whole earth."[3]

In the second place, then, the 'present' from which we set out may be thought of as a *condition*—the existing condition of mankind. Here we reach a point of crucial importance. If we accept the 'present' as a status or condition to be investigated, attention will be directed not so much to deeds and events as to things that exist—institutions, customs, arts, ideas. The consideration of a *situation* involving action leads directly to the naming of the individuals concerned, to speculations regarding their motives and purposes, to the problem of causation. On the other hand, the consideration of a *condition* leads at once to the concept of existences or entities undergoing change. Instead of the question, "Why did a particular individual do this?" the inquiry will take the form: "How are we to account for the differences in institutions, arts, and forms of knowledge which we encounter among different peoples?" Instead of the concept of events resulting from personal decisions, we have the concept of things changing slowly, *pedetemtim,* as Lucretius expressed it, step by step.

The contrast between the acceptance of the 'present' as a situation, emerging as a result of antecedent actions, and the 'present' as a condition of things, resulting from the operation of changes in the past, reveals the source of all the difficulties and differences of opinion which have arisen in dealing with

[3] Cf. also Eduard Fueter, as cited, pp. 752–758: "Remarques finales."

history as a subject of study and investigation. History as an academic subject deals with situations and happenings, with actions and motives, not with the problem of change and with the processes through which institutions, arts, and ideas have undergone modification in the course of time. As a consequence, academic history ends in narratives which embody, for each generation, the 'human interest' of the past, not in statements of 'how things work' in the world of men. Academic history, as now carried on, leads to historiography, and to problems of aesthetics and philosophy; history conceived as the study of change should lead directly to scientific investigation and research.

There is, however, another way in which this contrast presents itself. The acceptance of the 'present' as a situation has led to the study of history in the usual understanding of the term; the acceptance of the 'present' as a condition has led to the study which we designate 'evolution.' It will appear, in what follows, that just as the study of history has concentrated attention upon events to the ignoring of the study of processes of change, so the study of evolution has concentrated attention upon processes of change to the exclusion of events. We may now turn to inquire how this separation has been brought about.

Chapter 8

The Idea of Progress and the Foundations of the Comparative Method

IN THE PRESENCE of any phenomenon of nature, the early Greek philosophers asked themselves two questions: "Of what elements is it composed?" and "How did it originate?" If we keep to the second question, it will be observed that the form of the inquiry, "How did it originate?" inevitably throws the mind back upon some earlier, and usually remote, happening or situation, from which as a point of departure it turns to retraverse at leisure the whole interval separating that beginning from the present. For the Greeks, and for other peoples, such as the ancient Hebrews, genealogy was the framework into which these explanations were fitted, and events were arranged in a genealogical chain stretching from the imagined ultimate source, of the family or of causation, to the present situation or occurrence which is the immediate object of interest. In relation to this investigation of origins and genealogies, it is of importance to recognize that when we ask, "How did it originate?" we are referring to an explicit something which is before us here and now. It is the form of the question that carries the mind back; the matter to be explained still remains in the present.

A genealogy has three elements: a person present or spoken of; a series of ancestors; and a specific 'first' individual, source, or origin. With this pattern to start from, the Greeks arrived at a convention or type scheme for the explanation of things in general. "The genealogical method was capable of wide extension, and could be applied to other than human or even animal relationships. Hesiod's Theogony is a genealogy of heaven and earth, and all that in them is. According to Aeschylus, gain is bred from gain, slaughter from slaughter, woe from woe.... The ascending lines of ancestry were followed up until they led to a common father of all; every series of outrages was traced through successive reprisals back to an initial crime; and more generally every event was affiliated to a preceding event, until the whole chain had been attached to an ultimate self-existing cause."[1] In the hands of the earlier Greeks, then, the genealogical method provided a form into which could be fitted an explanation either of a situation in the affairs of men or of a condition of things in the world of nature.

We have seen, however, that the procedure of explaining or elucidating a given present by stating its antecedents in time is what constitutes the 'historical method.' "To comprehend the significance of the present," Professor Bury says, "we must be acquainted with the history of the past. This," he continues, "is the main reason (according to our present ideas) why a study of history is desirable, if not indispensable, for the man who undertakes to share in the conduct of public affairs, and is desirable also for the private citizen who votes, and criticises, and contributes to the shaping of public opinion."[2] The 'historical method' involves the recognition of three terms: an existent present; a point of departure or beginning; and a series of occurrences connecting the origin with the present. It is obvious that this formula is the same as the 'genealogical method' of the Greeks, and that the 'historical method' represents the perpetuation of the first means employed in the attempt to deal with the succession of events and changes in the course of time.

The earlier Greeks, to all appearance, made no distinction between the genealogical presentation of a series of events

[1] A. W. Benn, *The Greek Philosophers* (2d ed., London, 1914), p. 49.
[2] J. B. Bury, *The Ancient Greek Historians* (New York, 1909), p. 249.

and the study of change in time. The latter subject came, however, to occupy an important place in philosophical discussions at a subsequent period; in the hands of the philosophers inquiry took the form, not of a scientific investigation of the *modus operandi* of change, but of an analysis of its metaphysical implications.

It has been remarked that, strictly speaking, there are only two periods in the history of Occidental philosophy, the pre-Socratic and the Socratic. The first took external nature as its point of departure. Socrates, by introducing the logical method of definition, discovered a new order of existence, which was subject, not to mechanical, but to teleological laws. The Socratics, still envisaging change under the old genealogical form, brought it into the foreground of discussion in relation to the concept of teleology. Plato and Aristotle utilized the genealogical mode of presentation in their consideration of the different forms of government, but they set up genealogical series for the purpose of developing a teleological argument. Thus Aristotle outlines the genealogy of society from its beginning in the household, through the village, to its latest form in the city-state; the use which he makes of this series, however, is to show that, while the household or family comes first in time, the state is logically prior, since it is the end *(telos)* or complete development of the earlier associations.[3]

In Aristotle's view, teleology is the true mode of approach to the study of nature. The explanation of a thing is reached only when we are able to view it in the light of a purpose. All movement is directed toward some end, and becomes intelligible only when this end has been discovered and defined. Of the special points in Aristotle's philosophy which have continued to influence thought in immediate relation to the study of man, one or two only need be mentioned in the present connection.

[3] A. C. Bradley, "Aristotle's Conception of the State," in *Hellenica, a Collection of Essays*, ed. by Evelyn Abbott (London, 1880), p. 198. W. L. Newman, *The Politics of Aristotle*, vol. 1 (Oxford, 1887), pp. 84–85. W. D. Ross, *Aristotle* (New York, 1924), pp. 236–237.

In the first place, it should be borne in mind that Aristotle regarded the end or purpose of each particular thing to be the realization or actualization of its highest possibilities, and that he identified 'that which is best for each thing' with 'the best it can do.' This doctrine came to exert a profound influence upon ideas of development in the eighteenth century.

Again, it is necessary to point to his idea that only that is natural which takes place of itself, or contains the principle of change in itself. In opposition to that which is natural, or which comes by nature, he recognized that which is accidental, or which comes by chance, in other words, the emergence of results which were not intended. From this it follows that the aim of scientific inquiry is to determine what is natural, or normal, in contradistinction to what has happened by accident or by chance. This doctrine has had a determining influence upon modern conceptions of the purpose or aim of scientific investigation, and represents the greatest single obstacle to the unification of the studies of 'history' and 'evolution.'

Furthermore, it is to be observed that, in considering the problems presented by the existence of different forms of life, Aristotle saw in the organic world "merely a juxtaposition of higher and lower, not a succession, and still less a derivation of the one from the other."[4] It is of particular interest to note that a theory of development appears, in Aristotle's writing, only in connection with his discussion of social organization, of science, and of art. Here, however, we find the recognition of an ascent from lower to higher forms, a progress gradually realized in the course of time. "This movement [he thought] has already reached its goal times without number, and has as often been compelled to ebb back to its starting-point. For secular catastrophes, repeated with immeasurable frequency, have laid the earth waste, destroyed the race of mankind down to a small remnant, and then allowed that race to rise anew and enter upon and retravel its ascending path of civilization

[4] Theodor Gomperz, *Greek Thinkers,* vol. 4, tr. by G. G. Berry (New York, 1912), p. 154.

again and again and again."[5] Clearly, then, Aristotle held the view that human advancement goes through a determined, or natural, series of steps in successive 'cycles.'

In the modern period, it was likewise in relation to the study of man that the problem of progressive change came to attract attention.

The later years of the seventeenth century are marked, in the history of literature, by the famous 'quarrel' over the relative merits of the ancients and moderns.[6] It should be observed that the disputants on the opposing sides of this controversy utilized historical materials, but they did not write histories. What they were concerned with was a comparison of the condition of things, that is, of the arts, sciences, inventions, morals, in ancient and modern times. The result of this activity was the formulation, in relation to the study of man, of certain ideas which have continued to influence the views entertained of progressive change and of evolution down to the present.

Of these conceptions, one of the most influential is the analogy between the development or life cycle of the individual and the progress of the race. In modern, as in ancient, times observation of life has led men to repeated endeavors to introduce some measure of intelligibility into the vicissitudes of fortune by framing for themselves a picture or model of the course of change in the existence of peoples and of humanity. In the reign of Trajan, the historian Florus had asked his readers to consider the Roman people "as if it were one man" passing through the stages of birth, adolescence, maturity, and old age. In the time of Alaric, the Visigoth, St. Augustine ex-

---

[5] Theodor Gomperz, as cited, p. 126.

[6] Hippolyte Rigault, *Histoire de la querelle des anciens et des modernes* (Paris, 1856). Alfred Michiels, "Querelle des anciens et des modernes," in his *Histoire des idées littéraires en France au xixe siècle* (4e éd., Paris, 1863), pp. 32–150. Ferdinand Brunetière, "La formation de l'idée de progrès au xviiie siècle" [1892], in his *Etudes critiques sur l'histoire de la littérature française, 5e série* (6e éd., Paris, 1922), pp. 183–250. Jules Delvaille, *Essai sur l'histoire de l'idée de progrès jusqu'à la fin du xviiie siècle* (Paris, 1910). Hubert Gillot, *La querelle des anciens et des modernes en France* (Paris, 1914). J. B. Bury, *The Idea of Progress: An Inquiry into Its Origin and Growth* (London, 1920).

tended this view, and envisaged the life of humanity, the succession of the generations from Adam to the end of the ages, as the life of a single person. The analogy reappears at the Renaissance, and becomes an integral part of the thought of the seventeenth century. As expressed by Pascal, just as the individual advances from day to day in knowledge, so mankind makes continual progress as the world grows older; hence, he thought, the entire sequence of men, through the ages, should be looked upon as a single individual existing always and learning continually.[7] In this form, the analogy recurs insistently throughout the eighteenth century, and enters significantly into the system of Auguste Comte. In the later nineteenth century, the analogy, again expanded, becomes identified with the "biological view of the universe," so that "the whole scheme of things is regarded as a single organism, advancing methodically through stages of its growth in obedience to inevitable laws of self-expansion."[8]

A second important influence in shaping our modern ideas of progressive change is likewise to be traced back to the author of *The City of God*. Polybius had envisaged the history of the ancient world as unified by the extension of the political power of Rome. St. Augustine gave unity to the history of mankind by conceiving it as subject to the unitary government of God. In opposition to the rationalism of Descartes, Bossuet, in 1681, brought forward anew the thesis of St. Augustine, and in his *Discours sur l'histoire universelle* depicted the events of world history as falling into a series of epochs, following the design of Providence for the accomplishment of a specific purpose. As we shall see, the work of Bossuet became the model for the generalized histories of culture of Turgot, Condorcet, and Auguste Comte.

[7] Blaise Pascal, "Fragment d'un Traité du vide," in his *Pensées et opuscules*, publiés par Léon Brunschvig (5ᵉ éd., Paris, 1909), pp. 80–81.

For examples of the use of the analogy, see Jules Delvaille, as cited, pp. 35, 86, 106, 165, 188, 194, 195, 207, 222, 242, 264, 286, 384, 391, 450, 458, 461, 480, 554, 557, 570, 620, 675.

[8] J. A. Symonds, *Essays Speculative and Suggestive* (3d ed., London, 1907), p. 5.

A third result of the 'quarrel' of the ancients and moderns was the dissemination of conceptions of scientific method derived from the philosophy of Descartes.[9] In the dispute, those who took the side of the moderns were under the necessity of defending their position in the face of able and aggressive opponents. In this situation they availed themselves of an argument based upon the Cartesian axiom of the stability, regularity, permanence, and immutability of the laws of nature.[10] These laws, they contended, are constant; they are the same today as they have been throughout the past. Nature, therefore, produces men of equal ability and genius in every age.[11] It follows, consequently, that the moderns, being in possession of the accumulated experience of preceding generations, have an advantage over antiquity comparable to that of old age over childhood.

The weak spot in this argument, to the disputants of the seventeenth century, was the admitted break in continuity represented by the Middle Ages.[12] If the doctrine of the invariability of the laws or powers of nature was to be maintained, it was necessary to account for the actual breaches of continuity in the past. The explanation given by Perrault and Fontenelle was that, while nature makes the same provision for advancement in every age, barbarian invasions, long wars, and governments which discourage science and art may occasion interruptions of progress, and impose long periods of ignorance and bad taste.[13] Evidently, then, advancement would be continuous, were it not for the discontinuities caused by the misapplied energies of men.

The outcome of the 'quarrel' was that those who took the

---

[9] Jules Delvaille, as cited, see index, p. 744. Cf. Francisque Bouillier, *Histoire de la philosophie cartésienne* (3ᵉ éd., Paris, 1868). Louis Liard, *Descartes* (Paris, 1882). Alfred Fouillée, "Descartes et les doctrines contemporaines," in his *Le mouvement idéaliste et la réaction contre la science positive* (2ᵉ éd., Paris, 1896), pp. 302–318. Gustave Lanson, "L'influence de la philosophie cartésienne sur la littérature française," *Revue de métaphysique et de morale*, 4 (1896), pp. 517–550. Norman Kemp Smith, *Studies in the Cartesian Philosophy* (London, 1902).

[10] J. B. Bury, as cited, pp. 82, 99, 112.   [12] *Ibid.*, pp. 80, 85, 106, 156.

[11] *Ibid.*, pp. 84, 86.   [13] *Ibid.*, pp. 85–86, 106.

side of the moderns were led to formulate the views (1) that advancement in knowledge is natural and necessary, certain and endless; (2) that advancement in knowledge can only proceed slowly, and by insensible degrees; and (3) that knowledge is continually advancing toward perfection.[14] In the earlier part of the eighteenth century, these views were extended, as by the Abbé de Saint-Pierre, to the general progress of man. The conception of civilization progressing slowly but surely toward the goal of human happiness in the future thus became established as a settled conviction.[15]

The matter of importance, in this formulation, is that through it modern thought became committed to the assumption that progress is 'natural' and to be expected. As a consequence, from the end of the seventeenth century men have concerned themselves, not with the investigation of the conditions under which advancement takes place, but with inquiry into the obstacles which are thought to have delayed or interrupted the 'natural course' of development, and with proposals for the removal of these obstacles. A typical expression of this point of view appears, for example, in the statement of Malthus, in 1803, that "in an inquiry concerning the improvement of society, the mode of conducting the subject which naturally presents itself, is: 1. To investigate the causes that have hitherto impeded the progress of mankind toward happiness; and 2. To examine the probability of the total or partial removal of these causes in the future."[16]

The judgment that progressive change is natural carried with it, in the eighteenth century, a world of implication which twentieth-century thought has been too ready to overlook. While, in the earlier period, the 'natural' was perhaps most commonly opposed to the 'miraculous' or to the 'artificial,' particular interest, in the present connection, attaches to the

---

[14] *Ibid.*, pp. 104–105, 109, 112, 126, 171.

[15] *Ibid.*, pp. 136–137, 143.

[16] T. R. Malthus, *An Essay on the Principle of Population* (new ed., London, 1803), p. 1.

opposition of the 'natural' to the 'unusual,'[17] that is, of the
normal to the exceptional, of that which was regarded as frequent to what was thought to be rare. In more recent phraseology, the same concept is expressed in the opposition between
that which is recurrent and that which happens but once. What
gives this distinction its significance is that, in the eighteenth
century, scientific inquiry concerned itself with what was 'natural,' to the exclusion of what was judged to be 'unnatural,'
'monstrous,' 'accidental,' and 'unusual.'

Cartesian philosophy assumed the existence of an established order in the universe, and of a body of laws established
by Nature. These conceptions were so vivid, for eighteenth-
century thought, that more than one attempt was made to set
forth the 'Code of Nature' in detail. The confidence with which
such an enterprise was undertaken was an outgrowth of the
Cartesian view that the true method of science was represented
exclusively in the procedure of geometry; in other words, that
scientific method consisted in logical deduction from 'clear
and simple ideas' accepted as axioms. In conformity with this
method, definite results were the more readily arrived at, in the
study of man, because of the accepted opinion that the System
of Nature was teleological throughout. It was not doubted that
the laws of Nature, like those of Louis XIV, were designed with
reference to predetermined ends. Hence the laws of Nature
came to be thought of as the orderly provisions which Nature makes for the realization of certain specific purposes, these
purposes, discernible by the exercise of reason, being nothing
other than the promotion of the progress and happiness of
mankind.

The System of Nature, it is true, is not immediately apparent
in the seemingly hopeless entanglement and diversity of the
data of experience. In the study of man, however, the belief
was entertained that the system could be determined by the
aid of analogy, and the scientific study of society was envisaged

[17] David Hume, *Essays, Moral, Political, and Literary,* ed. by T. H. Green
and T. H. Grose, vol. 2 (London, 1875), pp. 275–276.

after the pattern of the contemporary study of physiology. Now, if we are to arrive at a knowledge of the 'true' functioning of the human organism, it is evident that we must ignore the peculiarities, abnormalities, and accidental characteristics of any particular 'subject' examined. A physiology will not be a series of descriptions of unusual or pathological cases; it will not even be the description of any actual human body; it will be a description of what is conceived to be *the* human body, in its functional aspects. Evidently, then, physiology, as a science, has for its object a knowledge of what is natural or normal, abstraction being made from the 'accidental' aspects of what is given in experience. It is this conception of the aim of scientific inquiry which dominated the thought of the eighteenth century, and which has continued to exert a pervasive influence in humanistic inquiry down to the present.

Furthermore, it is of importance to recognize that the procedure of physiology was taken as a model for the scientific study of how society undergoes change in the course of time, as well as for the investigation of how society is constituted. Physiology is interested in tracing the course of development of the living being from its embryonic state to its final dissolution, as well as in the functioning of the mature organism. Here, again, its interest is in the 'natural' or normal aspects of growth, in abstraction from the 'accidental' differences which may appear in the life of any particular individual. Leibniz had expressed the view that "each created being is pregnant with its future state, and naturally follows a certain course, if nothing hinders it."[18] The humanists of the eighteenth century, associating this view with Pascal's analogy, assumed that the scientific study of change must have for its aim the determination of the 'natural' or normal course of development of social groups, abstraction being made from the 'accidental' interferences or hindrances occasioned by historical 'events.' In its full realization, they envisaged the scientific study of society as

---

[18] Leibniz, *The Monadology, and Other Philosophical Writings*, tr. by Robert Latta (Oxford, 1898), p. 44, n. 1.

concerned with the discovery of the orderly provisions which
Nature has made for the development or progress of nations
and of mankind.

The results of this reasoning appear, fully developed, in the
work of Adam Smith. The great object of his inquiries, Dugald
Stewart states, was to illustrate the provisions made by Nature
for a gradual and progressive augmentation in the means of
natural wealth, and to demonstrate that the most effectual plan
for advancing a people to greatness is to maintain that order
of things which Nature has pointed out.[19] It is of the highest
importance to observe that if we adopt this point of view, and
undertake the investigation of the provision which Nature has
made for the "natural progress of opulence in a country," historical events will be conceived merely as interferences with
the 'natural order.'[20] Hence inquiry will proceed upon the assumption that "in most cases, it is of more importance to ascer-
tain the progress that is most simple, than the progress that is
most agreeable to fact, for . . . it is certainly true, that the real
progress is not always the most natural. It may have been determined by particular accidents, which are not likely again to
occur, and which cannot be considered as forming any part of
that general provision which nature has made for the improvement of the race."[21]

We are now in a position to see that the 'theoretical,' 'conjec-
tural,'[22] 'hypothetical,'[23] or 'natural'[24] history of the eighteenth
century represents, not some curious aberration of thought,
but a most serious effort to lay the foundations for a strictly
scientific approach to the study of man.

As a consequence, then, of the adoption of Cartesian conceptions, it was assumed that progressive change is natural or

[19] Dugald Stewart, "Account of the Life and Writings of Adam Smith" [1793],
in his *Collected Works*, ed. by Sir William Hamilton, vol. 10 (Edinburgh, 1858),
p. 60.

[20] *Ibid.*, p. 36. [21] *Ibid.*, p. 37. [22] *Ibid.*, p. 34.

[23] J. J. Rousseau, "Discours sur l'inégalité," in his *Political Writings*, ed. by
C. E. Vaughan, vol. 1 (Cambridge, 1915), pp. 139, 141.

[24] David Hume, "The Natural History of Religion," in his *Essays*, as cited,
pp. 309 ff.

normal, that it is always slow and gradual, and that it leads toward a condition of perfection. It was assumed, further, that the laws of nature represent the orderly provision which Nature has made for the attainment of her purposes or ends. With these presuppositions, the purpose of scientific inquiry was understood to be the determination of the natural or normal course of change. What this mode of approach entailed was that the investigator should ignore, or rather eliminate from consideration, the intrusive influences which had interfered with the operations of the 'natural order' in the course of time. The point of view was thus arrived at from which historical events were regarded as unimportant and irrelevant for the purposes of scientific inquiry in the investigation of progress and of evolution.

For an understanding of the later activities of humanists, it is of importance to observe how the investigation of the 'theoretical' or 'hypothetical' history of the eighteenth century was to be carried on.

The debate over the relative merits of the ancients and moderns led to the comparison of the conditions of things—of knowledge, morals, and arts—in classical antiquity and in modern times. In another field, the seventeenth century likewise instituted comparison between (a) the social conditions observed in existing 'savage' groups and (b) the conditions revealed in the earliest historical records of civilized peoples.

Some suggestion of this mode of comparison is to be found in the *Leviathan* of Thomas Hobbes (1651). In "the state of nature," Hobbes thought, men were "in that condition which is called warre." Answering the possible objection that, in the past, there never had been "such a time, nor condition of warre as this," he argued that "there are many places where they live so now."[25] The significance of this statement is that Hobbes accepted information in regard to the present condition of "the savage people in many places in America" as evidence for the condition of European peoples in times past. John Locke

---

[25] Thomas Hobbes, *Leviathan*, ed. by A. R. Waller (Cambridge, 1904), p. 85.

(1690), discussing the early development of the kingship, considered it necessary to "look back as far as history will direct us." Having presented a generalized description of the status of kings in the earliest times, he appealed, in confirmation of his description, to the practices of "the people of America," and justified this appeal on the ground that America "is still a pattern of the first ages in Asia and Europe."[26]

From these beginnings, the practice of comparing the present condition of men in various parts of Asia, Africa, and America with the early condition of men in Europe was widely adopted. Fontenelle, in the seventeenth century, had thought there was *une conformité étonnante* between the myths of the Americans and those of the Greeks.[27] Père Alexandre discovered similarities in the religious ceremonies of the Chinese and those of the Greeks and Romans.[28] Père Lafitau was of the opinion that the natives of America bore a striking resemblance to the Greeks of the time of Homer and to the Hebrews of the time of Moses.[29] Jaucourt, in the *Encyclopédie,* compared the rites of purification practiced by the negroes of the Gold Coast with those of the ancient Hebrews.[30] Adam Ferguson (1767) held that "the inhabitants of Britain, at the time of the first Roman invasions, resembled, in many things, the present

---

[26] John Locke, "Of Civil Government," in his *Works,* vol. 4 (12th ed., London, 1824), pp. 399, 402.

[27] Fontenelle, "Sur l'histoire," in his *Œuvres,* t. 9 (nouvelle éd., Amsterdam, 1764), p. 243.

[28] Noël Alexandre, *Conformité des cérémonies chinoises avec l'idolâtrie grecque et romaine* (Cologne, 1700). Also M. de la Créquinière, *Conformité des coutumes des Indiens orientaux avec celles des Juifs et des autres peuples de l'antiquité* (Bruxelles, 1704).

[29] J. F. Lafitau, *Mœurs des sauvages américains comparées aux mœurs des premiers temps* (Paris, 1724). Cf. Arnold van Gennep, *Religions, mœurs et légendes,* 5ᵉ série (Paris, 1914), pp. 111–133. Gilbert Chinard, *L'Amérique et le rêve exotique dans la littérature française* (Paris, 1913), pp. 315–326. Note Chinard's remark, p. 321, n. 1: "Ces rapprochements avec l'antiquité se retrouvent chez tous les voyageurs qui ont des lettres."

[30] René Hubert, *Les sciences sociales dans l'Encyclopédie* (Paris, 1923), p. 84. Also Charles de Brosses, *Du culte des dieux fétiches, ou Parallèle de l'ancienne religion de l'Egypte avec la religion actuelle de Nigritie* (1760). Cf. Arnold van Gennep, as cited, pp. 161–178.

natives of North America."[31] The views of the author of the *Essay on the History of Civil Society* may, indeed, be taken as typical of the period. He goes on to say that "Thucydides, notwithstanding the prejudice of his country against the name of Barbarian, understood that it was in the customs of barbarous nations he was to study the more ancient manners of Greece. The Romans," he continues, "might have found an image of their own ancestors, in the representations they have given of ours; and if ever an Arab clan shall become a civilized nation, or any American tribe escape the poison which is administered by our traders of Europe, it may be from the relations of the present time, and the descriptions which are now given by travellers, that such a people, in after ages, may best collect the accounts of their origin. It is in their present condition that we are to behold, as in a mirror, the features of our own progenitors. . . . If," he concludes, "in advanced years, we would form a just notion of our progress from the cradle, we must have recourse to the nursery; and from the example of those who are still in the period of life we mean to describe, take our representation of past manners, that cannot, in any other way, be recalled."[32] Finally, it may be observed that William Robertson (1777) thought that "there is nothing wonderful in the similitude between the Americans and the barbarous nations of our continent." The human mind, in his opinion, "holds a course so regular, that in every age and country the dominion of particular passions will be attended with similar effects." Hence, "without supposing any consanguinity between such distant nations, or imagining that their religious ceremonies were conveyed by tradition from the one to the other, we may ascribe this uniformity, which in many instances seems very amazing, to the natural operation of superstition and enthusiasm upon the weakness of the human mind."[33]

[31] Adam Ferguson, *An Essay on the History of Civil Society* (8th ed., Philadelphia, 1819), p. 137.

[32] *Ibid.*, pp. 146–147.

[33] William Robertson, *The History of America*, vol. 1 (London, 1777), pp. 268, 269, 270. Dr. Robertson's remarks will be found to be of particular significance

By the end of the first half of the eighteenth century, two important views had thus been established. It was accepted, first, that the study of European history revealed the fact that there had been a progressive movement of change from ancient to modern times; and, second, that the present condition of 'savage' groups might be taken to represent the early condition of civilized peoples. Now, the great aim of Cartesian science was to discover the major uniformities (such as the laws of motion) which lie behind the explicit differences which are revealed by the senses in the actual world. When, therefore, the men of the eighteenth century began to compare the various states of culture made known by historical study and geographical discovery, the scientific interests of the time led them to devote their attention to the *similarities*[34] which could be detected in these various cultures. As a result of the direction thus given to inquiry, it was found that the states of culture discovered to exist in America, Asia, and Africa were similar to the states of culture known, from historical evidence, to have existed in ancient Palestine, Egypt, Greece, and Rome. Hence the inference was forced upon the observer that these similarities pointed to a uniform series of stages in the development of mankind. The next step, therefore, in the study of man was the attempt to arrive at a synthetic statement of the successive stages in human development.

The thought had already suggested itself to Locke that there was no imaginable condition of human society which might not be found in actual existence somewhere in the world, but he does not appear to have envisaged the possibility of arranging the different societies in a 'progressive' order. It remained for Turgot, in 1750, to initiate the long series of modern attempts (so far as appears, without reference to Hesiod, Aeschylus, or Lucretius) to formulate a scheme of cultural stages. The

---

for the history of anthropology if considered as a reaction against the 'diffusion' theories current in the eighteenth century.

[34] Cf. Karl Marbe, *Die Gleichförmigkeit in der Welt* (München, 1916–1919), Bd. I, chs. 2–7; Bd. II, ch. 2.

immediate stimulus for Turgot's effort was derived from Bossuet's *Discours sur l'histoire universelle* (1681). This exceedingly influential work had presented the history of mankind under the form of twelve epochs, beginning with "Adam, or Creation; the first age of the world," and coming down to "Charlemagne, or the establishment of the New Empire." Turgot, dissatisfied with this 'historical' account, formed the idea of rewriting Bossuet's history in the light of the concept of Progress. Universal history, he thought, should display the successive advances of the human race, and undertake to point out the causes that have contributed to these results. In his *Plan de deux discours sur l'histoire universelle* he describes, not the epochs of Adam, Noah, Abraham, Moses, and the Capture of Troy, but the condition of man in the successive stages of culture: the hunting stage, followed by pastoral life, the rise of agriculture, and the introduction of government.[35]

It is of interest to note that Rousseau, in his *Discours sur l'origine et les fondements de l'inégalité parmi les hommes* (1755), similarly recognized a series of cultural stages in the period anterior to the establishment of civil government.[36] It was not, however, until 1793 that the suggestions of Turgot were carried out, in a way to enlist the sympathy and interest of the public, in Condorcet's *Esquisse d'un tableau historique des progrès de l'esprit humain*. From the appearance of this memorable work, the procedure of delineating the cultural development of mankind in the form of an 'ideal' or generalized series—what Dugald Stewart described as 'theoretical history'—has retained a dominant influence in the study of man, more particularly in sociology and anthropology.

We have seen that Bossuet had envisaged the course of history as a whole or unity, as constituting a unilinear series of 'epochs.' Condorcet imagined the cultural development of

---

[35] Turgot, *Œuvres* [nouvelle éd.], par Gustave Schelle, t. 1 (Paris, 1913), p. 278.

[36] A. O. Lovejoy, "The Supposed Primitivism of Rousseau's Discourse on Inequality," *Modern Philology*, 21 (1923), pp. 165–186. Cf. also Jean Morel, "Recherches sur les sources du Discours de l'inégalité," *Annales de la Société Jean-Jacques Rousseau*, 5 (1909), pp. 119–198. Gilbert Chinard, as cited, pp. 341–365.

mankind as a unilinear series of 'stages.' We have seen that
Pascal represented the advancement of mankind as analogous
to the growth or development of the individual. Condorcet
pictured universal history as the progress of the human race
advancing as an immense whole steadily, though slowly, toward
ultimate perfection—*à une perfection plus grande*. It should
be remembered, further, that Leibniz envisaged the universe
under the aspect of a series of monads or units, continuous,
without break, from the simplest imaginable form up to the
completeness and perfection of the Divine Being. Condorcet
thought that the actual state of the universe exhibited, at one
and the same instant, every nuance of barbarism and civilization, and thus displayed at one view every step taken by the
human mind, every stage through which it had passed, the history of every age.

The combined influence of these conceptions of continuous
series provided a foundation for the opinion that the infinite
variety of human cultural groups might be arranged in an
'ideal' series, representing the 'natural order' of the development of mankind. This 'natural order' was accepted as applicable at once to the progressive stages exhibited in the historical
series and to the differences of culture discoverable in the
present.

Chapter 9

The Sociological Method of Auguste Comte

W ITH THE beginning of the nineteenth century, two distinct movements are to be found dividing the humanistic field. History sets out anew with the determination to confine its attention to 'events,' the facts of the past; the study of man takes for its aim the discovery of the 'natural order' of change in society, the determination of the 'laws of progress.' The impasse at which history has arrived having already been described (Part I), it now becomes necessary to examine the results which have been achieved in the second type of inquiry.

The outstanding figure in the effort to create a scientific study of man, or of society, during the nineteenth century, was Auguste Comte, whose *Cours de philosophie positive* (1830–1842) has exercised a marked influence down to the present time. For an appreciation of Comte's indebtedness to the eighteenth century, and of his influence upon later thought, an exposition of his mode of procedure, which is based throughout upon the employment of deduction and analogy, must be attempted. This, unfortunately, cannot be accomplished with brevity.

All systematic inquiry, Comte explains, is either theoretical or practical; positive philosophy will concern itself only with the theoretical. Theoretical inquiry, again, consists of two parts: (1) sciences which are abstract, general, and law-discovering; and (2) sciences which are concrete, particular, and descriptive. Positive philosophy will concern itself only with the abstract, since the concrete sciences are merely secondary or derived, consisting in the application of the 'laws' previously discovered to the actual existence of different entities.[1] Further, in accordance with the analogy of physics, each of the abstract sciences is subdivided into a statics and a dynamics. In the organic sphere, Comte distinguishes between abstract biology and concrete 'natural history'; the latter is not considered. Abstract biology is divided into (*a*) anatomy or biological statics and (*b*) physiology or biological dynamics. Similarly, he divides social physics (to which he later gave the name of 'sociology') into (*a*) social anatomy or social statics and (*b*) social physiology or social dynamics.

It is necessary to direct attention to some of the characteristic features of Comte's treatment of abstract biology, since this constitutes the background of his formulation of social physics.

In the first place, anatomy or biological statics, in his system, is concerned with the investigation of the 'laws' of the organism. This inquiry involves (1) the study of the structure and composition of the 'tissues' or anatomical elements and (2) the construction of *la grande hiérarchie biologique*. In his discussion of this hierarchy or classification, Comte specifically states that all known or possible organisms must be coördinated in a single series, 'necessarily linear,' in which each species will occupy a 'rigorously determined' place.[2] He conceives of a final arrangement of species in an order such that any given species will be inferior to all those which precede it, and superior to all those which follow it. As against Lamarck,[3] Comte insists upon the doctrine of the fixity of species; he condemns all 'vain speculations' into the origin of the forms of life, and holds, as a great natural law, that all species have a tendency to perpetuate themselves indefinitely, with the same principal characteristics, despite the variation of the exterior conditions of existence.

In the second place, physiology or biological dynamics is concerned with the investigation of the 'laws' of life. It inquires

---

[1] Auguste Comte, *Cours de philosophie positive* (4e éd., Paris, 1877), t. 1, pp. 56–57.

[2] *Ibid.*, t. 3, p. 387.   [3] *Ibid.*, t. 3, xliie leçon, passim.

into the relation of the organism to its environment, and into the functions of organs. It investigates the sensibility and irritability of organisms, and the mechanism of animal movements. It deals with the phenomena of the generation or reproduction, the growth or development, and the deterioration or gradual decline from maturity to death of living bodies.[4] It should be observed particularly that, in Comte's system, 'evolution' is represented, first, by the life cycle of the individual, and second, by the rigidly constituted classificatory series, which represents a life cycle 'perfectly analogous' to the development of the individual. In Comte's view, the investigation of the development of the entire series of the forms of life is to be carried on by an inquiry into the principles of growth as exhibited in the life of the individual.

On turning now to social physics, we find, first, that social anatomy or social statics is described as being concerned with the study of organization; it makes analysis of the conditions of existence of the individual, of the family, and of society; it investigates the actions and reactions of the different parts of the social system. Second, we find that social physiology or social dynamics is concerned with the study of social life. At this point, however, a serious difficulty arises, for here Comte's parallel between physiology or biological dynamics and social dynamics breaks down, since he describes social dynamics as the study of progress.[5] The clue to his position lies, of course, in his adoption of Pascal's analogy between the growth of the individual and the progress of the race, and his rejection of Lamarck's argument to show that species undergo modification in the course of time.

It may be observed, by way of criticism, that the original source of weakness in Comte's attempt to arrive at a science of society lies in the fact that his *Cours de philosophie positive* is not the product of a firsthand investigation of social phenomena. In its essential aspects, it is just a highly elaborated argument to show that a science of society is a desideratum,

[4] *Ibid.*, t. 3, pp. 477, 480.   [5] *Ibid.*, t. 4, pp. 232, 262.

with a demonstration, carried out by the use of deduction and analogy, of the relation in which such a social science might conceivably stand to existing 'natural sciences.' Actually, Comte's achievement consists primarily in his systematization of current ideas on scientific and humanistic subjects, which necessarily were derived in the main from the thought of the eighteenth century.[6]

In considering Comte's reformulation of the specific views of the eighteenth century in regard to the study of man, it is of the highest interest, in the present connection, to observe that he adopted completely the principles of the comparative method, which thus became a central feature of humanistic thought in the nineteenth century.

In sociology, Comte says, it is necessary to consider the principal forms of society in the order of their increasing importance. To determine this order, we must, in the first instance, compare the different states of human society as they exist throughout the world at the present time. Owing to causes which are not well understood, all groups have not yet attained the same level of development, and as a result of this inequality the early stages of civilized groups may all be observed today among primitive peoples distributed in different parts of the

---

[6] "La mérite de Comte est d'avoir arrangé en système une foule de notions éparses dans l'intellectualité de son époque: il a réussi à les fondre en une synthèse parfaitement cohérente. Il est un arrangeur, non un créateur. La cohérence logique est, selon lui, le caractère distinctif d'une science. Mais bien que son œuvre soit cohérente, elle n'est pas scientifique car ses prétendues lois sont rarement la fidèle expression des faits. . . . Il est un homme de transition entre le siècle de déduction et celui de l'observation." Maurice Defourny, *La sociologie positiviste: Auguste Comte* (Louvain, 1902), pp. 353–354.

For discussion of Comte's work, cf. also: Herbert Spencer, *The Classification of the Sciences; to Which Are Added Reasons for Dissenting from the Philosophy of M. Comte* (London, 1864); also in his *Essays, Scientific, Political, and Speculative*, vol. 2 (New York, 1891), pp. 74–144. John Stuart Mill, *Auguste Comte and Positivism* (London, 1865). T. H. Huxley, "The Scientific Aspects of Positivism," in his *Lay Sermons, Addresses, and Reviews* (New York, 1870), pp. 147–173. John Fiske, *Outlines of Cosmic Philosophy* (London, 1874). Franck Alengry, *Essai historique et critique sur la sociologie chez Auguste Comte* (Paris, 1900). Lucien Lévy-Bruhl, *La philosophie d'Auguste Comte* (3e éd., Paris, 1913). Paul Barth, *Die Philosophie der Geschichte als Soziologie*, I. Teil (3–4 Aufl., Leipzig, 1922), pp. 175–221. M. S. Harris, *The Positive Philosophy of Auguste Comte* ([Ithaca, N. Y.], 1923).

globe.[7] The comparative method, therefore, presents to us, at the present moment, all the possible stages of human development as something to be submitted to direct scrutiny. Nevertheless, this mode of inquiry is not free from danger. It displays the various social stages existing side by side, but it gives no clue to the sequence of development or to the filiation of social systems. The comparison of existing societies would, indeed, lead inevitably to a misconception of the order in which the different states have succeeded each other if the order of succession could not be determined by an independent mode of investigation.[8] The second phase of the comparative method, that by which the different successive stages through which humanity has passed is to be determined, is the 'historical method properly so-called.' Since the use of this 'historical method' (the construction of 'ideal series') permits us to determine the order of human development without risk of error, it necessarily becomes the principal mode of sociological inquiry.[9] It is, however, to be remarked that the first phase of the comparative method is not superseded by the study of history. The lowest stages of human development can be investigated in no other way than by the observation of existing primitive groups. Moreover, as there are aspects of social development of which history (*l'histoire de notre civilisation*) retains no traces, the comparative method must be utilized to fill the gaps which it leaves.[10]

The comparative method, as Comte explains, utilizes two series of facts: those provided by observation of existing societies, and those provided by the study of the past. From these two bodies of evidence Comte proposes to reconstruct the course of human development. His justification of this procedure is based upon three assumptions or presuppositions. First, the successive modifications which constitute the 'forward march of humanity' are always slow, gradual, and continuous. Second, these modifications follow invariably an order which is fixed and determined. Third, the differences between

[7] Auguste Comte, as cited, t. 4, p. 317.

[8] *Ibid.*, t. 4, p. 319.   [9] *Ibid.*, t. 4, p. 322.   [10] *Ibid.*, t. 4, p. 318.

groups are due to the inequality in the speed (*vitesse*) with which they pass through the consecutive stages.[11]

These assumptions have important implications. In the first place, each and every group will, in the course of time, pass through the entire series of steps or stages which has marked the development of mankind as a whole. At any given moment, then, every existing group will be in a definite stage, the relative position of which may be determined by reference to the general scheme of development. In the second place, human development being uniform, the development of all the different aspects of human activity will be concurrent and uniform. We may, therefore, facilitate inquiry by subjecting the totality of social phenomena to a process of analytical decomposition (*à une décomposition rationelle permanente*). In other words, we may follow the general movement of human development by restricting attention and observation to any one of the different elementary aspects of human existence—physical, moral, intellectual, political,—abstraction being made of all the others.[12] In the third place, the development of each separate art, institution, custom, and mode of thought will follow the same series of steps in every group. Hence, in the investigation of human progress, we may restrict inquiry to the development of the most advanced nations, the elite or vanguard of humanity, the population of western Europe,[13] and, within this field, we may limit ourselves to the single element of intellectual development.[14]

One other point in Comte's exposition of the comparative method must be mentioned. He accounts for the similarities in the customs, institutions, arts, and ideas of peoples widely separated in time and place on the assumption that the course of human development is uniform in the midst of all diversities of climate and of race.[15] It might have been expected that Comte would have attempted to verify or establish this point of view by examination of the facts. He supports his assump-

---

[11] Auguste Comte, as cited, t. 4, pp. 285, 320.　　[12] *Ibid.*, t. 4, pp. 267, 459.
[13] *Ibid.*, t. 5, p. 7.　　[14] *Ibid.*, t. 4, pp. 268, 328, 458.　　[15] *Ibid.*, t. 4, pp. 318–319.

tion of uniform development, however, not by direct investigation, but by appeal to what he terms the invariability of human nature. In his opinion, human characteristics, physical, moral, and intellectual, are essentially the same at every step of the ladder of progress.[16] The course of development is uniform, because the working of the human mind is always uniform.

As a result of the foregoing observations on Comte's mode of procedure we are in a position to see that his 'social physics' or sociology includes two distinct types of inquiry.

In the first of these, he envisages a science which would stand in the same relation to the social as anatomy and physiology to the physical body. Now, if used merely for the purpose of illustration, this parallel may serve to indicate the aim of one phase of the study of society. Unfortunately, from the time of Hobbes the analogy between the human body and the body politic has proved strangely attractive to humanists, and, following Comte, men such as Spencer, Lilienfeld, Schaeffle, and Worms have in turn devoted themselves to enumerating likenesses and to discovering what appeared to them to be identities between biological organisms and social organizations. As a result, it has become an established convention among sociologists to express their ideas in biological metaphors, and to describe and interpret social relations in terms of a pseudo-biological symbolism. More recently, however, sociologists have in a measure succeeded in liberating themselves from these verbal entanglements, and in recognizing what was originally valuable in the comparison of the organic body and the social group. It is now generally understood that, just as anatomy and physiology investigate the forms and modes of working of the constituent elements of living bodies, sociology may investigate the structure and working of the elements of social organizations. "The central line in the path of methodological progress in sociology is marked by the gradual shifting of effort from analogical representation of social structures to real analysis of social processes."[17] In other words, later inquirers, get-

[16] *Ibid.*, t. 4, p. 343.   [17] A. W. Small, *General Sociology* (Chicago [1905]), p. ix.

ting rid of Comte's misleading analogies by an expenditure of much time and effort, have come to see that one aspect of a science of society will be the investigation of how society is constituted; but whether this inquiry can be successfully conducted by following the procedure of the eighteenth century is a matter which admits of grave doubt.[18]

In the second place, Comte identifies the scientific study of 'social dynamics' with the theory of progress and the construction of 'ideal series.'

In considering this aspect of his work, it is of importance to note Comte's dependence upon older modes of thought. Thus, so little was he influenced by the new scientific ideas of his time that he accepted Bossuet's *Discourse on Universal History* as a model, *un imposant modèle,* for the statement of the final results of his social dynamics.[19] He accepted the form of Bossuet's *Discourse,* but followed Turgot in substituting *l'idée mère* of continuous progress for Bossuet's doctrine of providence.[20] In Comte's view progress is a necessary product of the slow, gradual, continuous accumulation of successive modifications.[21] These modifications, in his opinion, have definite limits,[22] and always follow in a fixed and determined order,[23] which is the same for the race as a whole, for all peoples, however distant and independent, and for the individual.[24] Since these modifications always follow in the same order, the primary object of inquiry will be to trace the fixed and necessary steps in the continuous succession of human development. Comte's dependence upon eighteenth-century thought is revealed in an interesting manner at this point in his exposition. He proceeds to make what he describes as 'an indispensable scientific abstraction.' For clearness, he says, it is of importance to set up, following the 'happy artifice' of Condorcet, the hy-

---

[18] Cf. J. S. Mill, *Logic,* bk. vi, ch. x, § 7.

[19] Auguste Comte, as cited, t. 4, pp. 204–205; t. 5, p. 8.

[20] *Ibid.,* t. 4, p. 262.

[21] *Ibid.,* t. 4, pp. 265, 278.

[22] *Ibid.,* t. 4, p. 285.

[23] *Ibid.,* t. 4, pp. 266–268.

[24] *Ibid.,* t. 4, p. 446.

pothesis or rational fiction of a unique people to which we may refer ideally all the consecutive social modifications which are to be observed among different human groups.[25] One cannot imagine, he says, any nuance or shade of variation in human evolution which is not now to be found somewhere on the earth's surface.[26] The task of social dynamics is to coördinate these variations into one ideal series which will include all the successive steps in human development. In Comte's view, this fiction of a unique social series is analogous, first, to the life cycle of the individual, and second, to the 'fundamental organic series,' the entire series of the forms of life as represented in the biological hierarchy. Any possible doubt of his meaning, it may be said, is removed when, following Pascal,[27] he represents the human species, past, present, and future, as constituting an immense and eternal social unity, of which the different individual and national elements, joined together by an intimate and universal solidarity, contribute, each in its own way, to the development of humanity. With this analogy in mind, Comte proceeds to discuss the general direction, the rate, and the necessary order of human progress. This leads him to the definition of *la grande loi philosophique* of the three successive states—theological, metaphysical, and positive—through which, in his view, knowledge passes in dealing with every type of speculation or inquiry.[28]

It was Comte's main contention that his procedure advanced the study of society to the positive or scientific plane. His adoption of the 'rational fiction' of Pascal and Condorcet would seem to indicate that what he actually accomplished was to establish the 'dynamic' phase of sociology in the 'theological' state, since he himself describes this state as one in which "free play is given to spontaneous fictions admitting of no proof."[29]

Comte's identification of social dynamics with the study of

---

[25] *Ibid.*, t. 4, p. 263.   [27] *Ibid.*, t. 4, p. 293.

[26] *Ibid.*, t. 4, pp. 317–318.   [28] *Ibid.*, t. 4, p. 463.

[29] Auguste Comte, *Système de politique positive* (4ᵉ éd., Paris, 1912), t. 1, p. 33. Cf. W. R. Inge, *Outspoken Essays*, 2d series (London, 1922), p. 171.

progress, and with the construction of 'ideal series,' has had two results. In the first place, his procedure has been accepted without question by sociologists as representing an essential aspect of the study of society, and as being in accordance with the method of 'natural science.' In the second place, his procedure has been unhesitatingly rejected by historians, and has led them to oppose the whole idea of introducing scientific method—that is, Comte's conception of scientific method—in the field of humanistic study.

The reason for the opposition of historians to Comte's procedure is not far to seek. Comte asserts that the employment of the 'historical method' gives to sociology its distinctive philosophical character,[30] but what he means by 'historical method' is entirely distinct from its meaning for historians. In Comte's view, history, in order to be scientific, must be abstract; in order to pass from the concrete to the abstract state it must be cleared of all particular circumstances,[31] and, ideally, even of the names of men and of peoples.[32] For Comte, the 'events' upon which academic history lays stress are to be regarded as 'essentially insignificant,' and as comparable to 'monstrosities' in biology.[33] It follows, therefore, that since history, identified with Comte's 'historical method,' represents the method of 'natural science,' history as the study of events must fall outside the domain of 'natural science.' We have already seen, however, that this is precisely the conclusion of modern logic. What is here to be observed is that both historians and sociologists have been willing to concur in this judgment, and to accept the conclusion that logic has 'justified' this distinction between the two subjects.[34] On the other hand, as has previously been remarked, logic cannot 'justify,' its business being merely to describe, the different modes of procedure followed in the pursuit of knowledge. It follows, therefore, that the judgment

---

[30] Auguste Comte, *Cours de philosophie positive* (4e éd., Paris, 1877), t. 4, p. 323.

[31] *Ibid.*, t. 5, p. 17.   [32] *Ibid.*, t. 5, p. 14.   [33] *Ibid.*, t. 5, p. 12.

[34] Cf. R. E. Park and E. W. Burgess, *Introduction to the Science of Sociology* (Chicago, 1921), pp. 6–12.

of the logicians is simply a late reflection of the situation created by Comte's identification of scientific work in the historical field with the construction of 'ideal series.'

As far, then, as the present argument is concerned, it will be evident that Comte's formulation of the method of 'social dynamics' has had the result of contributing in an important manner to the perpetuation, in the nineteenth century, of the eighteenth-century separation between the study of events and the study of change in the course of time.

Chapter 10

The Influence of Comte on the Study of Anthropology

THE INFLUENCE of Comte's perpetuation of the separation between the study of events and the study of change in time is to be observed, not only in the subject designated 'sociology,' but also in the methodological discussions which, for half a century, have been so conspicuous a feature of the literature of anthropology and ethnology. A consideration of the movement of thought in this field, however, will bring to light the significant fact that, notwithstanding the tenacious adherence of anthropologists, in the nineteenth century, to the use of the comparative method, they have, more recently, been led to recognize the necessity of taking historical events into account in the study of change. While historians have concentrated attention on the study of situations and events, anthropologists have concerned themselves primarily with the study of conditions and of change. In the pursuit of these interests, they have come to realize that the conception, here identified with the thought of the eighteenth century and with the system of Comte, that the study of change may be carried on without reference to the influence of historical events, constitutes an obstacle of the most serious description to the advancement of the study of man. The newer emphasis on the influence of historical events in the study of anthropology will, therefore, be recognized as of particular importance for the present discussion.

It has been suggested by more than one writer of distinction that "the birth of anthropology followed almost immediately the promulgation of the evolution theory by Darwin and Wallace in 1858."[1] The continued repetition of this statement makes it necessary to point out that Darwin's book appeared (in 1859) just too late to have an effect upon the remarkable development of ethnological study in the second half of the nineteenth century. The notable works which initiate this movement in ethnology were published to all intents and purposes contemporaneously with the *Origin of Species*. The distinctive contributions of Waitz, Bastian, and Bachofen, of Maine, McLennan, and Tylor, all appeared between 1859 and 1865. The significance of this fact is made clear when we find Tylor, in 1873, and McLennan, in 1876, disclaiming dependence upon Darwin, and maintaining their allegiance to an earlier tradition of development or evolution.[2] The concept of 'evolution' in ethnology is, in fact, distinct from the type of evolutionary study represented in Darwin's writings. In the pre-Darwinian tradition, the term 'evolution' is synonymous with 'development,' and is intimately associated with the doctrine of the fixity of species. Ethnology has followed Comte in regarding the study of 'evolution' as concerned with tracing the course of development of mankind, and with the construction of 'ideal series.'[3]

Comte's influence upon ethnology appears, then, in the wide acceptance of his idea that the aim of evolutionary study is the construction of generalized or theoretical histories. It appears equally, on the other hand, in the reiterated opposition to his theory of the uniformity of human development; indeed, since his time, this opposition has been one of the most

[1] Sir J. G. Frazer, "The Scope and Method of Mental Anthropology," *Science Progress*, 16 (1922), p. 581. Cf. Franz Boas, *The Mind of Primitive Man* (New York, 1911), p. 175. P. A. Means, *Racial Factors in Democracy* (Boston, 1918), p. 7. R. R. Marett, *Psychology and Folk-lore* (New York, 1920), p. 102. Also identified with the work of Herbert Spencer: A. A. Goldenweiser, *Early Civilization* (New York, 1922), pp. 21–23.

[2] E. B. Tylor, *Primitive Culture*, vol. 1 (3d ed., London, 1891), p. vii. J. F. McLennan, *Studies in Ancient History* (new ed., London, 1886), p. xv. Cf. Frederick Pollock, *Essays in Jurisprudence and Ethics* (London, 1882), pp. 366–367. A. W. Benn, *The History of English Rationalism in the Nineteenth Century*, vol. 2 (London, 1906), p. 460.

[3] Note Tylor's references to Comte: *Primitive Culture*, as cited, vol. 1, pp. 19, 477; vol. 2, pp. 144, 242, 354.

constant characteristics of ethnological literature. In 1859, Waitz argued that any attempt to give an outline of 'the natural history of human society' could lead to nothing but 'the so-called philosophy of history.' His own inquiries proved, he said, that differences in the culture of peoples depend, in the main, upon change in the general conditions of life, and upon the vicissitudes of history. Powerful impulses are, he believed, always required to change existing conditions.[4] In the same year Latham, as a result of his survey of the races of mankind, expressed the view that civilization or advancement was "a result of the contact of more peoples than one."[5] In 1861, Sir Henry Maine published his *Ancient Law*. While an explicit statement of his views on the uniformity of development was not made until 1883, it may be presumed that these views are implicit in his first work. It is of interest, therefore, to find him saying, in opposition to McLennan, that "there has been room . . . for many courses of modification and development, each proceeding within its own area. So far as I am aware," he continues, "there is nothing in the recorded history of society to justify the belief that, during the vast chapter of its growth which is wholly unwritten, the same transformations of social constitution succeeded one another everywhere, uniformly if not simultaneously."[6] In 1863, there appeared Taine's *Histoire de la littérature anglaise*. In giving reasons for his choice of this subject, Taine (who was one of the foremost exponents of 'positivism' in France) presented the consideration that there is a peculiarity in the civilization of England: apart from its spontaneous development, he said, it presents a forced deviation due to the Norman Conquest. In it, therefore, we may observe the two most powerful influences in human transformations—nature (i.e., climate and race) and constraint.[7]

---

[4] Theodor Waitz, *Anthropologie der Naturvölker*, I. Th. (2 Aufl., Leipzig, 1877), p. 473.

[5] R. G. Latham, *Descriptive Ethnology*, vol. 2 (London, 1859), p. 502.

[6] Sir H. S. Maine, *Dissertations on Early Law and Custom* (London, 1883), pp. 218–219.

[7] Henri Taine, *Histoire de la littérature anglaise*, t. 1 (2e éd., Paris, 1866), pp. xlviii–xlix.

With the year 1865 we come to the first of the works of Sir Edward Burnett Tylor, his *Researches into the Early History of Mankind.* At this point it will be well to recall that the comparative method had its origin in the perception of *similarities* in the manners and customs, arts and ideas, of peoples widely separated in place and time. Comte's theory of uniformity is based upon the comparison of similarities, and this orientation of thought has been retained in ethnology down to the present. How this point of view, when accepted without reservation, may affect inquiry appears in the statement of McLennan that he had found such similarity among races usually considered distinct that he regarded the ethnological differences of the several families of mankind as of little or no weight compared with what they had in common.[8] Few writers have followed McLennan in the completeness of his adherence to Comte in this particular, but many have adopted the practice of Lord Avebury, whose *Origin of Civilisation* (1870) is simply a compendium of illustrations of "the remarkable similarities between different races."[9] Now the particular interest of Tylor's first book lies in the fact that in it he made the problem of similarity the subject of a sustained critical inquiry. In his view, similarity "sometimes may be ascribed to the like working of men's minds under like conditions, and sometimes it is a proof of blood relationship or of intercourse, direct or indirect, between the races among whom it is found."[10] The aim of the *Researches* is to arrive at a technique of investigation for determining what similarities may be used as evidence for the reconstruction of the early history of mankind. Of any particular custom which is found in two distant places, Tylor reasoned that if it appears likely that a similar state of things may have produced it more than once, then the similarity discovered cannot be used as historical evidence of connection between

[8] J. F. McLennan, *Studies in Ancient History* (new ed., London, 1886), p. xvii.

[9] Lord Avebury, *The Origin of Civilisation and the Primitive Condition of Man* (6th ed., London, 1902), p. 11.

[10] E. B. Tylor, *Researches into the Early History of Mankind and the Development of Civilization* (2d ed., London, 1870), p. 5; cf. pp. 175, 376–379.

the two groups; if, on the other hand, it appears impossible that such a thing should have grown up independently in the places where it is found, then the similarity becomes evidence for historical connection.[11] The entire book is given over to the analysis of similarities with a view to sorting out those which may be utilized for establishing connections between groups in the past. Tylor's interest lay in discovering similarities which were only to be accounted for by transmission, by diffusion from a common center, by propagation from district to district. In this work we have the first systematic contribution to a subject which has occupied a central position in recent ethnological inquiry.

The ethnologist who is to deal critically with similarities must, Tylor thought, have "a general notion of what man does and does not do";[12] consequently, in his second book, *Primitive Culture* (1871), he turned to "the investigation of the laws of human nature."[13] Now in this, his most widely read work, the influence of Comte is apparent throughout, and in a manner which is not evident in the *Researches*. It should be observed, nevertheless, that here also Tylor keeps before him the importance of the historical aspect of similarity. He points out that, in dealing with the elements of culture, the ethnologist will consider such details "with a view to making out their distribution in geography and history, and the relation which exists among them," and he suggests a 'working analogy' between the diffusion of plants and animals and the diffusion of civilization.[14] The specific problem which, however, he sets himself is that of "determining the relation of the mental condition of savages to that of civilized men."[15]

Tylor's work, as a whole, presents certain points of interest which may be briefly summarized. It inherits from the eighteenth century the point of view which places similarity in the

---

[11] E. B. Tylor, *Researches,* as cited, p. 275.

[12] *Ibid.,* p. 275.

[13] E. B. Tylor, *Primitive Culture,* as cited, vol. 1, p. 3.

[14] *Ibid.,* p. 8; cf. pp. 9, 35, 39, 53, etc.

[15] *Ibid.,* p. 68.

foreground. It inherits from earlier English anthropology a
strong realization of the importance of the contact of peoples
and of the diffusion of culture elements in the advancement
of civilization. It shows the characteristic critical attitude which
later ethnological discussion has taken in opposition to Comte's
assumption of uniformity, and points out, by contrast, that
there are three ways to explain "how any particular piece of
skill or knowledge has come into any particular place where
it is found . . . independent invention, inheritance from ancestors in a distant region, transmission from one race to another."[16] It takes over from Comte, and transmits to English
ethnology, a definite interest in the psychological analysis of
primitive or savage culture with the object of determining the
characteristic traits of primitive modes of thought. We find
thus established in the main current of ethnological literature
two distinct lines of inquiry, which may, for convenience, be
distinguished as the 'psychology' and the 'history' of primitive
man. A brief consideration of the later development of these
inquiries will bring out certain points of interest in the present
discussion.

The argument which has led one group of English ethnologists to lay stress upon the study of primitive psychology appears, in 1884, in Andrew Lang's *Custom and Myth.* In this
book there is no lack of appreciation of the importance of
diffusion, borrowing, contact, and migration in accounting for
similarities. What, however, Lang sets before himself as a definite object of inquiry is "the study of the mental condition of
savages," and the investigation of "the common simple ideas"
of humanity.[17] This point of view has been maintained by a
group of scholars, of which the most widely known members,
in addition to Andrew Lang, are Sir J. G. Frazer and E. S.
Hartland.

The point of departure of these men is the observed fact of
similarity. "No one," Mr. Hartland remarks, "can study the

[16] E. B. Tylor, *Researches,* as cited, p. 376.
[17] Andrew Lang, *Custom and Myth* (2d ed., London, 1885), pp. 9, 20.

habits of mankind, the processes of thought and the institutions
of savage races without being deeply impressed with the unity
which underlies all diversities."[18] With this background, the
specific aim of inquiry is to determine the mental characteristics and modes of thought of the 'simpler' peoples, of the 'backward' elements in the human population of the globe, and, in
the last analysis, to make a comparative study of the mind of
man.[19] Such an examination of how primitive man thinks is
not to be confused with inquiry into historical origins, or into
historical connections between distant peoples in order to account for similarities in particular elements of culture. The
two types of study have different aims, and must necessarily
make different use of common materials. However designated—
Social Psychology, Mental Anthropology, *Völkerpsychologie*—
we have here a fundamental study[20] which has a service to perform which is distinct from the investigation of the 'history' of
early man. We are not here concerned with the question of
whether this plan of inquiry has been successfully prosecuted,
further than to remark that its exponents have left themselves
open to criticism from the tendency, evident in their writings,
to follow Comte in presenting their results under the form of
"a philosophy of primæval history."[21]

The study of the 'history' of primitive man has various
aspects. Comte, as we have seen, regarded the reconstruction
of the stages in a single line of development of humanity as

[18] E. S. Hartland, *Mythology and Folk Tales: Their Relation and Interpretation*
(2d ed., London, 1914), p. 32.

[19] Sir J. G. Frazer, as cited, p. 585.

[20] Cf. Herbert Spencer, "Primitive Ideas," in his *Principles of Sociology*, vol. 1
(London, 1876), chs. 8–16. Andrew Lang, "The Mental Condition of Savages,"
in his *Myth, Ritual, and Religion*, vol. 1 (London, 1887), chs. 3–4. E. S. Hartland,
"Savage Ideas," in his *Science of Fairy Tales* (London, 1891), ch. 2. Franz Boas,
"Some Traits of Primitive Culture," in his *Mind of Primitive Man* (New York,
1911), ch. 8. Wilhelm Wundt, *Elements of Folk Psychology*, tr. by E. L. Schaub
(London, 1916). Lucien Lévy-Bruhl, *La mentalité primitive* (Paris, 1922); *Primi-
tive Mentality*, tr. by L. A. Clare (New York [1923]). A. A. Goldenweiser, "The
Ideas of Early Man," in his *Early Civilization* (New York, 1922), pp. 327–415.
Richard Thurnwald, *Psychologie des primitiven Menschen*, in Gustav Kafka, ed.,
Handbuch der vergleichenden Psychologie, Bd. I, Abt. 2 (München [1922]).

[21] E. B. Tylor, *Primitive Culture*, as cited, vol. 1, p. 25.

the principal aim of scientific inquiry in the field of 'social dynamics.' Since his time, ethnologists and sociologists have exhausted ingenuity in the attempt to arrive at a system of classification which would exhibit the different peoples of the earth, past and present, in a fixed and determined order. This activity has also given rise to a large number of works in which human development is described in terms of religion, art, marriage, property, government, and other single aspects of culture. Pitt-Rivers, for example, devoted himself, in Comte's spirit, to establishing 'series' of objects with a view to tracing the stages in the evolution of the material arts of mankind, and his object was "by this means to provide really reliable materials for a philosophy of progress."[22] In agreement with Comte again, Westermarck maintained that these generalized presentations are to be regarded as 'scientific history.' "Only when treated in this way," he stated, "can history lay claim to the rank and honour of a science in the highest sense of the term, as forming an important branch of sociology."[23]

The more immediate interest of ethnology in this type of inquiry arises from the fact that any conception of history involves the determination of a point of departure or a beginning. In academic history, as we have seen, the beginning is a situation in human affairs identified by reference to a given time and place. In Comte's system, on the other hand, scientific history is history cleared of reference to specific names and dates. Stages of development are not defined in terms of years; they represent a sequence which is conceptual and ideal, not chronological. It follows that the attempt to construct an 'ideal series,' to exhibit the course of development or 'evolution' of any phase of human activity, must begin, not with a point in time and a position in space, but with a *theory of origins.* Comte himself was aware of the danger incident to this mode of procedure. He pointed out, first, that the earliest stages of

---

[22] A. Lane-Fox Pitt-Rivers, *The Evolution of Culture, and Other Essays,* ed. by J. L. Myres (Oxford, 1906), p. 10.

[23] Edward Westermarck, *The History of Human Marriage* (London, 1891), p. 1.

development are to be determined only by the analysis of existing societies, and second, that, where the actual historical data
are not available for purposes of verification, the analysis of
existing societies must lead inevitably to erroneous notions of
the order of succession of social states. It is agreed on all sides
that actual historical knowledge of origins is not to be looked
for, yet speculation as to origins is accepted as one of the essential features of ethnological inquiry.[24] With such speculations
a great part of all works on the 'origin and development' or the
'evolution' of arts, institutions, and ideas is taken up, and one
of the most persistently debated points in current ethnological
discussions is how we are to proceed, through the use of inference and analogy, in the reconstruction of a history for which
no historical evidence is available.

To give an example of the difficulties which have arisen as
a result of the desire to reach back to beginnings, we may
instance the procedure which seeks for 'absolute' or psychological, in default of historical, origins. In the middle of the
nineteenth century there was much discussion of the irrational
and unnatural element in myths and folktales. The prevailing
theory in explanation of this phenomenon, expounded in England by Max Müller and Sir George Cox, was based upon the
etymological analysis of mythical names. The most vigorous
opponent of this philological school was Andrew Lang. The
theory which he urged was that the origin of the irrational
element in myth and tale was to be found in the qualities of
the uncivilized imagination, that this feature was "derived and
inherited from the savage state of man, from the savage conditions of life, and the savage way of regarding the world."[25]
The proof which Lang offered of this theory was his demonstration that there existed an actual and historical state of

---

[24] In criticism of speculation upon origins, cf. W. G. Sumner, *Folkways* (Boston,
1906), pp. 7–8. G. L. Gomme, *Folklore As an Historical Science* (London, 1908),
pp. 225–226. A. R. Brown, *The Andaman Islanders* (Cambridge, 1922), p. 229, n. 1.

[25] Andrew Lang, "Introduction," in *Grimm's Household Tales,* tr. by Margaret
Hunt [1884] (London, 1901), pp. xli, xliii. Cf. J. A. Farrer, *Primitive Manners
and Customs* (London, 1879), pp. 257, 281.

mind, or condition of the human intellect, "in which things seemed natural and rational that now appear unnatural and devoid of reason, and in which, if myths were evolved, they would, if they survived into civilization, be such as civilized men would find strange and perplexing."[26] In its immediate setting, as an explanation of the presence of a particular element in myth, this theory is unambiguous. The theory implied, however, is that a state of mind might be considered as the origin of a particular element in culture,[27] and hence that the study of beginnings might be pursued without reference to historical evidence. As a device for recovering origins in the absence of actual information, this procedure has commended itself to a large number of ethnologists. Thus Henry Balfour is of the opinion that, although the 'true history' of the growth of decorative art is lost and can never be written, we may, nevertheless, discover how patterns and designs have grown up from earlier stages, and trace the evolution of some of them to their 'absolute' origin.[28] Westermarck thinks that "the difficulties in finding the ultimate psychological origins of ceremonies are frequently increased by the obscurity of their historical origins,"[29] but Crawley holds to the view that "all study of the origins of social institutions must be based on what ethnology can teach us of the psychology of the lower races."[30]

It must not be overlooked that many ethnologists interested in the 'history' of culture have maintained that the problem of diffusion is "of prior urgency to that of origins."[31] The study of diffusion represents a characteristic phase of the ethnological investigation of the history of mankind. It constitutes, as we have seen, the subject matter of Tylor's *Researches,* and is one

---

[26] Andrew Lang, *Myth, Ritual, and Religion* [1887], vol. 1 (London, 1913), pp. 32–33.

[27] *Ibid.,* p. 8.

[28] Henry Balfour, *The Evolution of Decorative Art* (London, 1893), p. 17.

[29] Edward Westermarck, *Marriage Ceremonies in Morocco* (London, 1914), p. 9.

[30] Ernest Crawley, *The Mystic Rose: A Study of Primitive Marriage* (London, 1902), p. 1.

[31] Joseph Jacobs, *Folk-lore,* 2 (1891), p. 125.

of the foremost interests of ethnology at the present time. The aim of this type of inquiry is the reconstruction of the actual lines followed in the geographical distribution of single or of multiple elements of culture from area to area in the course of time. Now the fact is that the study of the geographical distribution of culture elements has been one of the most distinctive results, in every branch of humanistic investigation, of the introduction of the comparative method. Thus the history of religion, in one important aspect, is the study of the geographical spread or diffusion of Buddhism, Mithraism, Christianity, and other world faiths. The history of literature is similarly concerned with the influence of Greek and Latin, Hebrew and Arabic, writers upon medieval and modern Europe, and with the relations of the various literatures of Europe to one another during the modern period. The histories of art, philosophy, and science have similar interests. Whether, in short, we consider language or mythology, symbols or designs, alphabets or systems of counting, weapons or modes of transport, the domestication of animals or the cultivation of cereals, clothing or types of dwellings, megalithic monuments or the practice of mummification, there is scarcely an element of culture which has not been made the subject of investigation with special reference to its geographical distribution and its diffusion in time. This type of activity is the direct result of the concentration of attention upon the study of similarities.[32]

There is still another aspect of the 'ethnological study of history' which must be considered. Instead of following Comte in the attempt to support an *a priori* philosophy of history, instead of attempting to reach back to origins through the avenue of speculation, instead of attempting to account for geographical discontinuities in the distribution of specific elements of culture, the ethnologist may undertake an analysis of the *present condition* of culture in a given region in terms of historical

[32] For recent discussions of 'diffusion,' see: A. A. Goldenweiser, *Early Civilization* (New York, 1922), pp. 301–324. R. H. Lowie, *Primitive Society* (New York, 1922), see index under "Diffusion." A. L. Kroeber, *Anthropology* (New York [1923]), ch. 8. Clark Wissler, *Man and Culture* (New York [1923]), chs. 8, 9.

perspective. Now the interest of this mode of approach is that, when analysis is made of the culture of a given area, and the history of the area is taken into consideration, it will be found at once that the present status of the culture submitted to examination cannot possibly be explained on the basis of the assumption that any given condition was the outcome of a slow, gradual, continuous modification through a series of fixed and determined stages. It will be found that the 'ideal' course of development has been interfered with by cultural intrusions from other areas. It will be found that there is no 'ideal' or fixed and determined course of development at all. It will be found, in short, that the eighteenth-century separation between the study of history and the study of change in time, which is crystallized in Comte's system, cannot be maintained.

The application of the historical analysis of culture in criticism of current theories of uniformity of development appears in the work of Sir Arthur Mitchell, whose book *The Past in the Present,* representing lectures delivered in 1876 and 1878, was published in 1880. On the basis of a study of culture in Scotland, Mitchell came to the conclusion that it seemed "highly improbable, if not altogether absurd, that the human mind, at some particular stage of its development, should, here, there, and everywhere—independently, and as the result of reaching that stage—discover that an alloy of copper and tin yields a hard metal, useful in the manufacture of tools and weapons."[33] Our knowledge of what is happening, and of what has happened, he believed, must lead to the inference that "no man in isolation can become civilized,"[34] that progress is not so much a result of independent discoveries or inventions as an outcome of communications made by one society to another.[35] It is of importance to notice that Mitchell maintains that the investigation of human advancement must be based upon the separate examination of the antiquities of each country.[36]

---

[33] Arthur Mitchell, *The Past in the Present* (Edinburgh, 1880), p. 114.

[34] *Ibid.,* p. 186.   [36] *Ibid.,* p. 114.

[35] *Ibid.,* p. 196.

The most devoted advocate of the historical study of ethnology has been Sir George Laurence Gomme. The point of departure of Gomme's work is that "all studies of this kind must begin from the standpoint of a definite culture area."[37] He questioned the manner in which ethnologists occupied themselves chiefly with the study of some one element of culture, such as animism, bride capture, or totemism; he criticized the practice by which investigators subtracted a particular custom of one tribe to compare it with an apparently similar custom subtracted from another without taking into consideration the place this custom occupied in the culture of the respective peoples.[38] He drew attention to the danger, illustrated in Frazer's researches, of seeking to derive a general system of belief and worship from the beliefs and rites of peoples not ethnically, geographically, or politically connected.[39] He insisted that the object of inquiry should be the culture "of whole human groups rather than that of particular sections of each human group, of the whole corpus of social, religious, and economic elements residing in each human group rather than that of separated items."[40] He took exception to the habitual practice of academic historians in ignoring the backward and emphasizing exclusively the advanced parts of nations.[41] Gomme's constructive aim, throughout his writings, was to demonstrate the presence, in English civilization, of different culture layers or strata associated with a succession of intrusions of races (Iberic, Celtic, and Teutonic), and of culture elements (in particular, Christianity). Further, he sought to analyze the ways in which such intrusions had affected the earlier cultures with which they came in contact, and the ways in which the submerged or arrested culture elements of the older inhabitants maintained an existence.[42]

---

[37] G. L. Gomme, *Folklore As an Historical Science* (London, 1908), p. xxi, cf. p. 365.

[38] G. L. Gomme, "Recent Research on Institutions," *Folk-lore*, 2 (1891), p. 486.

[39] G. L. Gomme, *Folklore As an Historical Science*, p. 110.

[40] *Ibid.*, p. 234.   [41] G. L. Gomme, *Ethnology in Folklore* (London, 1892), p. 3.

[42] *Ibid.*, pp. 7, 12, 13, 41, etc.

In Gomme's hands the comparative method underwent a distinct modification. He utilized comparison, not to identify similarities, but to determine what is to be looked for in the study of the culture of a particular area. He saw clearly that the history of English culture, or rather of culture in England, would be unintelligible without a knowledge of the history of culture in other areas. He saw that the study of any one culture must be carried on in the light of the available body of anthropological knowledge. His basic idea is that the study of human evolution must be founded on the comparison of group with group.[43] On the other hand, the final aim of his own endeavors was simply to fill out and extend the knowledge of English history; he defended his own activities with the argument that "every nation has the right to go back as far in its history as it is possible to reach."[44]

The type of analysis which Gomme applied to English culture might, he thought, be extended to that of the Zulus or any other backward people. In 1890, he expressed the opinion that the difficulties of such an undertaking would be enormous, and the profitable result but small.[45] By 1908, however, he had reached the conclusion that it is a mistake to suppose "that survivals can only be studied when they are embedded in a high civilization. It is almost a more fruitful method," he thought, "to study them as they appear in the lower strata," as, for example, among the Australian aborigines.[46] Since that time, indeed, Gomme's general point of view has had wide application in the study of backward groups, and Dr. Rivers has given the designation of 'historical method' to the analysis of an existing culture, basing his investigations on the presupposition that similarities are due, in the main, if not wholly, to the spread of customs and institutions from some one center in which local conditions especially favored their develop-

[43] G. L. Gomme, *Folk-lore*, 2 (1891), p. 487.

[44] G. L. Gomme, *Folklore As an Historical Science*, p. 179; *Primitive Folk-moots* (London, 1880), p. 3.

[45] G. L. Gomme, *Handbook of Folklore* (London, 1890), p. 4.

[46] G. L. Gomme, *Folklore As an Historical Science*, p. 156.

ment.[47] If, as has been said, "some of the theories which Gomme formulated were bound to be open to question, because of the uncertainty as to the exact meaning of the materials on which they were based, and the absence of full proof of the racial intercourse on which he laid stress,"[48] it is obvious that this criticism would apply with added force to the analysis of a culture, such as that of Melanesia, for which no corroborative documentary or archaeological evidence was available.

In the foregoing pages the work of English scholars has been dealt with, not because it is assumed to be of greater impor- tance than that of their contemporaries in other countries, but because it illustrates the points under discussion in a readily accessible body of literature. As manifested in current litera- ture, the differences between ethnologists are most frequently expressed in terms of an antithesis, as in England, between the 'evolutionary theory' attributed to Tylor and theories of 'dif- fusion' as advanced, in recent years, by Rivers and G. E. Smith. In Germany, the same antithesis has given rise to the opinion that a new method in ethnological inquiry had been intro- duced by Friedrich Ratzel.[49] The background of Ratzel's de- parture is represented by the work of Adolf Bastian, who,

[47] W. H. R. Rivers, *History and Ethnology* (London, 1922), p. 5; for additional references, see his Bibliography, pp. 30–32.

In concluding his paper, Rivers remarked: "It is interesting to note how closely the views here put forward concerning the nature of ethnological research agree with those of the late Professor Maitland, especially as expressed in his paper on 'The Body Politic.' In that essay Maitland stated his belief that 'by and by an- thropology will have the choice between being history and being nothing' " (p. 29). Maitland's aphorism, however, is purely sporadic, and does not apply to the type of research advocated by Rivers. He was simply reiterating the old op- position to Comte's theory of ideal series. Cf. his *Domesday Book and Beyond* (Cambridge, 1897), pp. 345–346; *Township and Borough* (Cambridge, 1898), pp. 24–25; "The Body Politic," in his *Collected Papers,* ed. by H. A. L. Fisher, vol. 3 (Cambridge, 1911), pp. 294–297.

Cf. also Edward Sapir, *Time Perspective in Aboriginal American Culture: a Study in Method* (Ottawa, 1916).

[48] Edward Clodd, *Folk-lore,* 27 (1916), p. 112.

[49] For discussion of the modern development of ethnology from the point of view of German scholarship, see F. Graebner, "Geschichte der Ethnologie," in *Die Kultur der Gegenwart,* III. Teil, V. Abt., *Anthropologie* (Leipzig & Berlin, 1923), pp. 438–447.

adopting Comte's system as a basis, devoted himself, from 1860 onwards, to the exposition of the 'psychic unity' of mankind. In opposition to Bastian, Ratzel maintained that similarities in the culture of peoples, however distant, are to be attributed exclusively to the dissemination of culture elements from specific centers of invention. It will be seen, as a result of what has already been said, that the school of Ratzel is particularized, not by the introduction of a new method, but by an exclusive attention to and hence a marked elaboration of the mode of explaining similarities by 'diffusion.' What is involved in each of these contrasts (English and German) is simply the old opposition to Comte's 'uniformity of development.' It has been pointed out earlier that Tylor devoted his first book to the investigation of 'diffusion,' and that he maintained the view that, while some similarities might be attributed to the like working of men's minds under like conditions, other similarities were proof of a historical connection between the groups among which they are found. In recent years marked emphasis has been placed on the second mode of explaining similarities, but no evidence has been brought forward to invalidate Tylor's argument that similarity is sometimes due to 'psychic unity.'

We are now in a position to see that the differences between ethnologists at the present time are fully comprehensible only in the light of certain presuppositions and assumptions accepted in the eighteenth century and transmitted to more recent times through the work of Auguste Comte. Thus it has been pointed out that Comte assumed the aim of scientific inquiry in the field of 'social dynamics' to be the construction of 'ideal series,' representing what he considered the steps or stages in the 'natural order' of human development. In furtherance of this aim, he took over and formulated the procedure to be followed in the 'comparative method.' As employed in the eighteenth century, and as described by Comte, the comparative method rests upon the comparison of similarities. Hence the problem which has presented itself insistently is how we are to account for similarities in the culture of peoples remote from each other in place and time. Reduced to this form, the problem calls for concentration of attention upon the study of the distribution of particular culture elements. This restriction or narrowing of inquiry may be illustrated from Tylor's *Researches*. In his investigation of similarity, Tylor supported his argument in favor of historical connection by instancing the occurrence of specific similarities in different areas. What is here to be observed is an unconscious transference of attention from the groups in which the similarity is exhibited to specific culture elements and their geographical diffusion. The result of this inadvertence has been the introduction of an undesigned opposition between elements which are not on the same footing, namely, the development or evolution of groups and the distribution of specific arts and customs. Now, there is no actual basis for opposition between the historical study of the culture of an area and the geographical study of the spread of particular culture elements in the course of time. The two studies are separate aspects of ethnological inquiry, but, it is important to realize, the two studies are distinct. When carried out, inquiry into the distribution of culture elements may account for the presence of the horse, the composite bow, the cultivation of maize in given areas, but it cannot show how the present condition of backward or advanced groups has come to be as it is. Civilization is not merely an aggregate of culture elements; an assemblage of such elements in a given area may be accounted for without suggesting an explanation of the *modus operandi* of human advancement.

A further source of misunderstanding between ethnologists may also be traced to Comte. As we have seen, his conception of the proper task of historical study was the construction of 'ideal series.' The justification of this procedure, for Comte, was the assumption that such series represent the uniform steps in human 'development.' But Comte used the word 'evolution' as a synonym for 'development'; hence 'evolution' in ethnology, meaning the gradual progress of mankind or of any human society through a fixed and determined series of stages, has a significance distinct from that given to it in modern biology. The substitution, where Comte's influence is concerned, of the word 'development' for 'evolution' would put an end to much disagreement and controversy.

The study of ethnology, under Comte's influence, has been involved in difficulties. It is the merit of Sir G. L. Gomme that he recognized the necessity, if a way out of these difficulties was to be discovered, of turning to the study of the actual facts of the history of culture in a specific area. Now, at first sight, this suggests merely the adoption of the point of view of academic history; in reality, it marks a new departure. What Gomme advocated, as we have already seen, was: (1) a historical study of the conditions of life in a given area, more particularly as these conditions have been affected at different times by intrusions and events; (2) a study which should take into consideration the entire culture of the area, treating the unprogressive aspects of culture as no less significant than the advanced; (3) a study which would utilize comparison for the purpose of determining what was peculiar or unusual in the cultural history of the area. This conception of a mode of procedure in ethnology is an important advance toward what is required for the investigation of 'how man has come to be as he is.' It marks a break with the tradition of the eighteenth century and its plan for determining the 'natural' course of change or of progress without reference to 'events.' On the other hand, as a formulation of procedure for the larger investigation, it is incomplete. To arrive at a fuller understanding of what is required, it will be necessary to consider at some length the experience of investigators, in the eighteenth and nineteenth centuries, in dealing with the problem of biological evolution.

Chapter 11

The Study of Evolution in the Nineteenth Century

IT WAS SUGGESTED above that the second major obstacle to the scientific study of man lay in the manner in which humanists and scientists had approached the study of evolution. It has now been shown that, owing to the acceptance of certain methodological conceptions in the eighteenth century, a definite separation was made by humanists between the study of progressive change and the study of events—with results that are abundantly evident. It has now to be pointed out that the biological study of evolution, during the nineteenth century, has been conducted with the aim of discovering *processes of change* which, it is assumed, have produced differentiation in the forms of life in the course of time. If, however, we assume that change in time is the result of the operation of processes of change which are uniform in time and place, it follows, obviously, that the study of change may be conducted without reference to the influence of historical events. The next step in the argument will be to show that the acceptance of this assumption, in the later nineteenth century, is a result of the joint influence of eighteenth-century conceptions of progressive change and of certain ideas associated with the work of Hutton and Lyell in the field of geology. It will be pointed out, further, that the devotion of biologists to the investigation of processes of change, which involves the effort to account for progressive change or evolution without taking events into consideration, lies at the root of the important differences of opinion which are evident among biologists at the present time.

In the 'natural sciences' we are confronted with a condition of things represented by the present state of stars, strata, and species. Until comparatively recent times, these forms were looked upon as existing in one time plane; it was believed that they had been made originally, as they are now visible to us, by the hand of the Creator.

With the scientific revival of the seventeenth century, men began to concern themselves systematically with the diversities exhibited in the different 'kinds' of natural objects. An immediate result of this interest was the effort to reduce the complexity apparent in things to some sort of order. The typical eighteenth-century example of this activity appears in the *Systema naturæ* (1735) and the *Species plantarum* (1753) of Linnaeus. The great Swedish naturalist, in the spirit of Leibniz, regarded species as fixed, and as constituting a continuous series, and, in his classification, endeavored to depict the actual *scala naturae*.

About the middle of the eighteenth century, the influence of the humanistic theory of progressive change, regarded as an orderly development following a definite and fixed series of steps, began to make itself felt. Thus, in opposition to established doctrines, the new conception envisaged the different classes of stars as showing the successive stages in stellar development. This view was formulated by Immanuel Kant (1755), and by Laplace (1796), and has remained a directive principle in astronomy down to the present. Today the celestial bodies are arranged conceptually in an order from nebulae to blue, yellow, and red stars, and this sequence is accepted as indicative of the phases in the life history or course of development of objects in the physical universe.

Similarly, in the eighteenth century, efforts had been made to sort out and arrange conceptually the classes of rocks visible on the surface of the earth. Linnaeus extended his *Systema naturæ* to include the inorganic kingdom, which he divided into rocks, minerals, and fossils. Under the influence of Werner, the knowledge of rocks was summarized, at the beginning of the nineteenth century, in systems of classification which relied upon mineralogical composition and structure to indicate relationship, to the exclusion of age, origin, and mode of occurrence.[1] It was not until 1815 that William Smith discovered that organic forms supply the key to geological history and provide a means for determining the relative chronology of sedimentary deposits. This great discovery "showed that within the crust lie the chronicles of a long history of plant and animal life upon this planet, it supplied the means of arranging the materials for this history in true chronological sequence, and it thus opened out a magnificent vista through a vast series of ages, each marked by its own distinctive types of organic life, which, in proportion to their antiquity, departed more and more from the aspect of the living world."[2]

It will be observed that, as a result of William Smith's discovery, biology, no less than geology, was placed upon a new footing, and the contributions of palaeontology may be said to have brought the civilized world to a belief in the theory of organic evolution.[3]

The introduction of a time perspective into our view of natural objects operated to replace the traditional theory of 'origins' by the theory that the differences which we encounter in the present are the result of changes which have taken place in the past. The significance, for the movement of thought, of this substitution lies in the fact that, whereas the Creation theory could only be stated and maintained as a belief, the theory of change demanded proof. It became necessary, in short, not merely to state that changes had taken place, but to demonstrate how these changes could possibly have been brought about through the action of natural agencies. Here, then, we come to a distinctive contribution of the eighteenth century. It was recognized that, confronted with a given diversity of forms in the present, the business of science must be the

---

[1] H. E. Gregory, "Geology," in L. L. Woodruff, ed., *The Development of the Sciences* (New Haven, 1923), p. 175.

[2] Sir Archibald Geikie, *Landscape in History, and Other Essays* (London, 1905), p. 169.

[3] H. E. Gregory, as cited, p. 197.

investigation of 'how things work' in the course of time. It was recognized that the aim of science must be the determination and description of the processes through the operation of which things have been and still are being modified.

In the field of astronomy, Descartes, in the seventeenth century, had attempted to explain the existing state of the universe by mechanical processes of development. It was a century later, however, before this idea was effectively worked out by Immanuel Kant. In developing his hypothesis, Kant started with the assumption that the materials now composing the solar system had originally been scattered widely throughout the system as diffused particles or atoms. He proceeded from these theoretical conditions to develop the present state of the universe by means of known mechanical laws (i.e., processes) alone.[4] The procedure of astronomers in the twentieth century differs from that of Kant by reason only of the greater knowledge of physical processes which has been gained since his time. Astronomers are limited to a theoretical history of the past.

In geology, Kant had described the changes brought about on the surface of the earth by the action of natural agencies, such as rain and rivers, wind and frost.[5] It was, notwithstanding, left for James Hutton (1785) to establish the importance of the study of processes for the elucidation of the history of the earth. "With the intuition of genius," Geikie says, "Hutton early perceived that the only solid basis from which to explore what has taken place in bygone time is a knowledge of what is taking place today. He felt assured that Nature must be consistent and uniform in her working, and that only in proportion as her operations at the present time are watched and understood will the ancient history of the earth become intelligible. Thus, in his hands, the investigation of the Present

[4] T. H. Huxley, "Geological Reform" [1869], in his *Collected Essays*, vol. 8 (New York, 1894), pp. 320–322. W. W. Campbell, "The Evolution of the Stars and the Formation of the Earth," *Scientific Monthly*, 1 (1915), pp. 187–189. But cf. Gaston Milhaud, "Kant comme savant," *Revue philosophique*, 39 (1895), pp. 492–493.

[5] T. H. Huxley, as cited, p. 322.

became the key to the interpretation of the Past. The establishment of this great truth was the first step toward the inauguration of a true science of the earth."[6] Hutton started from the
observation that the surface of the globe has not always been as
it is today, and based his inquiries upon the principle that it
has come to be as it is through the continued action of the same
agencies of change that are to be observed in operation at the
present time; "we are," he said, "to examine the construction
of the present earth, in order to understand the natural operations of time past." "But how," he asks, "shall we describe a
process which nobody has seen performed, and of which no
written history gives any account? This is only to be investigated, first, in examining the nature of those solid bodies, the
history of which we want to know; and secondly, in examining
the natural operations of the globe, in order to see if there now
actually exist such operations, as, from the nature of the solid
bodies, appear to have been necessary to their formation."[7]
Through the effective expositions of Playfair and Lyell these
ideas have become the underlying principles of the modern
scientific study of the earth.[8]

In biology, the recognition of the importance of the study
of processes in relation to 'evolution' had been arrived at by
the middle of the eighteenth century. The pioneer seems to
have been Maupertuis (1745, 1751), the French reorganizer of
the Berlin Academy. In the opinion of Maupertuis, "a purely
descriptive and classificatory science which was unable to formulate any laws concerning the processes going on in that
part of nature with which it dealt was, strictly speaking, no
science at all." "The general processes which Maupertuis
thought it especially important that zoölogical science should
investigate are those through which animal individuals and
species have come to have the differences of form and function

---

[6] Sir Archibald Geikie, as cited, p. 171.

[7] James Hutton, "Theory of the Earth," *Transactions of the Royal Society of
Edinburgh*, vol. 1, pt. 2, 1, p. 219.

[8] Sir Archibald Geikie, *The Founders of Geology* (London, 1897), pp. 150–184.

that distinguish them.'"[9] Even after this perception of the problem, the work of a century was required before the description of the process of 'natural selection' was put forward by Charles Darwin.

Natural science in the eighteenth century had thus achieved the notable result of envisaging the differences with which we are confronted in the present world as the product of changes which have taken place in the past. It has now to be shown, however, that the influential ideas which the eighteenth century transmitted to the nineteenth consisted in a series of assumptions which have deeply affected evolutionary study down to the present moment. The assumptions which lie at the foundation of the biological study of 'evolution' will be recognized as intimately connected with those formulated earlier in relation to the idea of 'progress.'

The theory of 'evolution' rests, in the first place, upon the assumption that 'progressive change' is 'natural' and to be taken for granted, and that the aim of this progressive movement is the attainment of perfection. In the judgment of Erasmus Darwin (1794), "it would appear that all nature exists in a state of perpetual improvement by laws impressed on the atoms of matter by the great Cause of Causes; and that the world may still be in its infancy, and continue to improve forever and ever."[10] Lamarck's *Zoölogical Philosophy* (1809) shows, as Osborn points out, that he had arrived at 'the truth' "that there is a progressive and perfecting development."[11]

Again, the theory of evolution assumes that Nature has established a plan or 'natural order,' and that, in accordance with this order, 'natural operations' are always constant, always the same, always regular. A fundamental aspect of this view is that 'Nature never makes leaps,' and hence it was accepted that change, under all conditions, is slow, gradual, and continuous,

---

[9] A. O. Lovejoy, "Some Eighteenth-Century Evolutionists," *Popular Science Monthly*, 65 (1904), pp. 244–245.

[10] Quoted from E. Darwin's *Zoönomia* (1794), in L. L. Woodruff, "Biology," in *The Development of the Sciences* (New Haven, 1923), p. 254.

[11] H. F. Osborn, *From the Greeks to Darwin* (2d ed., New York, 1905), p. 161.

and proceeds always by infinitely slight gradations. This doctrine of 'continuity,' it should be observed, is applied by evolutionists indifferently to the conceptual relationships of the classificatory series, to the sequential relationships of the time series, and to the filiation of successive generations. Thus Buffon and Lamarck thought that, by the direct observation of the present, we can descend by imperceptible degrees from the most perfect creature to the most formless matter—this 'degradation' following from the fixed plan of Nature. They also thought that changes in time are made only slowly and imperceptibly. They held the view, expressed by Erasmus Darwin, that the offspring of a parent "cannot be said to be entirely new at the time of its production," since it is "in truth a branch or elongation of the parent."[12]

In Lamarck's view, the Creator had established an order of things which gave existence successively to all that we see. He assumed, consequently, that animals in nature are arranged in a 'natural order,' and, further, that in the natural order of things there would be a perfectly even development proceeding in a straight line throughout the animal scale, a progress toward the 'perfection' exhibited in the organization of man.[13] We would see that the linear series of animals is a perfectly regular and even progress in complexity of organization from *Monas termo* to man—were it not for the presence of certain anomalies or deviations from the straight line of development. These anomalies are, he says, due to the influence of environment and of acquired habits.[14] Lamarck's conception, it will be observed, gains in intelligibility from comparison with the views of the Physiocrats and of Adam Smith to which reference has already been made.

The assumption that change is invariably slow, gradual, and continuous entails the very important condition that we may

---

[12] For Buffon, cf. Arthur Dendy, *Outlines of Evolutionary Biology* (New York, 1923), p. 377. For Erasmus Darwin, *ibid.*, pp. 381–382. For Lamarck, *Zoölogical Philosophy*, tr. by Hugh Elliot (London, 1914), p. 72.

[13] Lamarck, as cited, pp. xxxvii, 14, 22, 56, 60, etc.

[14] *Ibid.*, pp. xxxiv, 69, 105.

neglect the element of time. "For nature," Lamarck thought, "time is nothing. It is never a difficulty, she always has it at her disposal; and it is for her the means by which she has accomplished the greatest as well as the least of her results."[15] As Huxley remarked, evolutionists have "insisted upon a practically unlimited bank of time, ready to discount any quantity of hypothetical paper."[16] In its original setting, this view may be regarded as a healthy reaction against the current belief that the Creation had taken place in the year 4004 B.C. There is no exception to be taken to the tentative suggestion of Erasmus Darwin (1794) that "since the earth began to exist, perhaps millions of ages before the commencement of the history of mankind, . . . all warm-blooded animals have arisen from one living filament, which the great First Cause endued with animality."[17] When, however, it is assumed that Nature always has unlimited time at her disposal, and that change is invariably slow and gradual, the statement is equivalent to the assertion that, in the study of evolution, the possibility of 'events' may be ruled out of consideration. The dictum that 'Nature never makes leaps' thus comes to be accepted as assurance that there never have been 'events' in the history of the forms of life.

In addition to the assumptions of which we have been speaking, biological evolutionists, at the beginning of the nineteenth century, also adopted from the humanists of the eighteenth century the procedure of the 'comparative method.'

As has been pointed out, the comparative method is based upon a philosophy of history, that is, upon the organization of the data of the history of culture in a unilinear series, in the light of the idea of progress. With the perception of similarities between the present condition of 'savage' races and the earlier condition of peoples now advanced, the conception was arrived at that the present observable differences among human groups

---

[15] Quoted from Lamarck's *Hydrogéologie* (1802), in H. F. Osborn, as cited, p. 165.

[16] T. H. Huxley, as cited, p. 324.

[17] Quoted from E. Darwin's *Zoönomia* (1794), in Arthur Dendy, as cited, p. 383.

represent a continuous series from simplest to most complex, and this series of existent forms was equated with the historical series from earliest to most recent. The aim of scientific inquiry was then conceived to be the utilization of these two series for the construction of an 'ideal series' which should present the 'natural order' of human development.

In biology, the construction of the unilinear classificatory series preceded the acceptance of the interpretation of present differences in the forms of life in terms of historical change. Classification, in the eighteenth century, was based upon the notion of a unilinear and continuous series of forms from the simplest to the most complex. The introduction of a historical perspective led to the concept of a unilinear and continuous series in time, parallel with the classificatory series. Hence was formed the idea of a 'natural order' in the arrangement of forms, applicable at once to the differences observable in the present and to the progressive steps exemplified in the historical series. Through the acceptance of the principle of 'continuity,' which asserted that the units in each series were distributed in infinitely fine gradations, evolutionary study became the investigation of the transitions between the exceedingly slight differences or modifications represented in the 'natural order.'

We may now turn to consider the influence of these eighteenth-century ideas on the work of Charles Darwin.

In the first place, it should be understood that Darwin accepted the idea of 'progressive change.' In his view, "the inhabitants of the world at each successive period in its history have beaten their predecessors in the race for life, and are, in so far, higher in the scale";[18] further, in concluding the *Origin of Species,* he remarked that "as natural selection works solely by and for the good of each being, all corporeal and mental endowments will tend to progress toward perfection."[19]

---

[18] Charles Darwin, *The Origin of Species* ([6th ed.], London, John Murray, 1911), p. 492.

[19] *Ibid.,* p. 669.

The form in which the problem of 'evolution' presented itself to Darwin was how species could have been modified in the course of time, how the modifications, variations, transitions in a continuous series could have been brought about. For the purposes of his inquiry, he adopted, as he says,[20] the example of Sir Charles Lyell, and carried over the presuppositions of 'uniformitarianism' into the field of biology. He thus assumed that Nature was uniform in her ways of working, and that, if the factors in the process of change now going on could be discovered, they might with confidence be taken as applicable throughout the past. He assumed, in short, that all change has been brought about through the slow, continuous operation of processes that are now to be observed. His next step was to make the further assumption that the clue to the processes of change or modification in time was to be found through study of the variation of animals under domestication. From this point he was led to the conception that Nature has exercised selection in 'the preservation of favored races in the struggle for life' analogous to the selection exercised by man in the preservation of favored animals for breeding.

Darwin took over and urged insistently the principle that Nature never makes leaps—*natura non facit saltum.* It is to be noted, however, that he appears to have accepted the principle of continuity only in its genealogical form; he did not adopt the view commonly held by his predecessors that the series of existent life forms was also continuous. He regarded the historical series as alone representing the 'natural order.'[21] Hence, in his conception, Nature, in the course of time, moves only by slow, gradual steps, by slight, successive transitions. He was thus led to maintain that the number of intermediate forms which formerly existed *must* have been 'interminable,' 'enormous,' 'inconceivably great.'

The crucial element in the presuppositions accepted by Dar-

---

[20] *Life and Letters of Charles Darwin,* ed. by Francis Darwin, vol. 1 (London, 1889), pp. 67–68.

[21] Charles Darwin, as cited, pp. 629, 655.

win may be given in his statement that, as Nature can act only by short and slow steps, she can produce no great or sudden modifications.[22] Now the point to be observed, in relation to the present discussion, is that Darwin regarded this dictum as possessing a higher validity, for evolutionary study, than the facts of biological history. Indeed, he devoted a chapter of the *Origin of Species*—"On the Imperfection of the Geological Record "—to the argument that, since the available information in regard to the past is imperfect and incomplete, it may be set aside altogether in favor of the canon *natura non facit saltum*.

If we examine the argument in which Darwin maintains the validity of his theory of continuity as against the data of palaeontology, it will be found that, on his own testimony, the evidence does not uphold his view with respect to the number of intermediate forms. "Geology," he says, "assuredly does not reveal any such finely-graded organic chain" as his theory demands.[23] "We do not find infinitely numerous fine transitional forms closely joining species all together."[24] "Geological research ... does not yield the infinitely many fine gradations between past and present species required on the theory."[25] Even "if we confine our attention to any one formation ... we do not therein find closely graduated varieties between the allied species which lived at its commencement and at its close."[26] Again, on Darwin's own testimony, the evidence does not support the contention that nature can act only by short and slow steps. There is evidence that whole groups of species suddenly appear in certain formations, in an abrupt manner;[27] that species belonging to several of the main divisions of the animal kingdom suddenly appear in the lowest known fossiliferous strata.[28] Further, on Darwin's testimony, there is abundant evidence that the appearance of modifications in the past has been highly irregular. It should first be observed that "many species when

[22] Charles Darwin, as cited, p. 646.   [25] *Ibid.*, p. 637.   [27] *Ibid.*, p. 441.
[23] *Ibid.*, p. 413.   [26] *Ibid.*, p. 430.   [28] *Ibid.*, p. 446.
[24] *Ibid.*, p. 452.

once formed never undergo any further change,"[29] that "some species have retained the same specific form for very long periods of time,"[30] and that "a number of species, keeping in a body might remain for a long period unchanged."[31] Change, therefore, is not a universal characteristic; it is a phenomenon manifested, not continuously, but at intervals of time, and then not in all forms, but in "only a few species at the same time."[32] "The periods during which species have undergone modification," he believed, "have probably been short in comparison with the periods during which they retained the same form."[33] It must be remarked, further, that, on Darwin's testimony, change in the forms of life is intimately associated with disturbances in the environment. Changes in the physical conditions of life, he thought, have produced some direct and definite effect in the production of distinct species.[34] He accepted the view that the world at a very early period was subjected to more rapid and violent changes in its physical conditions than those now occurring, and made the inference that such changes would have tended to induce changes at a corresponding rate in the organisms which then existed.[35] He was of the opinion that, in the later history of the earth, "there has probably been more extinction during the periods of subsidence, and more variation during the periods of elevation [of the earth's crust]."[36] As geology plainly proclaims that each land has undergone great physical changes, corresponding changes in organic beings are to be expected.[37] Finally, we may point to his statement that there are regions in which "the manufactory of species" has been particularly active.[38]

This body of evidence, which he acknowledged would, if admitted, be fatal to his theory, Darwin rejected on the ground of "the imperfection of the geological record." In defense of this course, he argued that, though the known facts disproved

[29] *Ibid.,* p. 638.
[30] *Ibid.,* p. 635.
[31] *Ibid.,* p. 668.
[32] *Ibid.,* p. 455.
[33] *Ibid.,* pp. 489, 638.
[34] *Ibid.,* p. 648.
[35] *Ibid.,* p. 448.
[36] *Ibid.,* p. 488.
[37] *Ibid.,* p. 643.
[38] *Ibid.,* p. 644.

his theory, his assumption of an 'inconceivably great' number of intermediate forms would be substantiated if the geological record were complete. Darwin himself recognized that his views on the incompleteness of the record resulted from the discovery that the available evidence was in opposition to his hypothesis: "I do not pretend, that I should ever have suspected how poor was the record in the best preserved geological sections, had not the absence of innumerable transitional links between the species which lived at the commencement and close of each formation pressed so hardly on my theory."[39]

Now, that life forms have undergone change or modification in the past either is or is not a fact. If a fact, it is a fact of history. Hence it would seem imperative, in a scientific inquiry, to consider the data of palaeontology in advance of setting up a theory to account for the way in which change in the forms of life had actually taken place. "In all cases positive palæontological evidence may be implicitly trusted; negative evidence is worthless."[40] On Darwin's own testimony, palaeontological study would certainly not lead to the conclusion that new species had always appeared "very slowly." It is necessary, therefore, to look for some explanation of his tenacity in holding to the dictum *natura non facit saltum* in opposition to the positive evidence. A clue is suggested at the close of the *Origin of Species*. Almost every naturalist, he says, now admits the great principle of evolution. "There are, however, some," he continues, "who still think that species have suddenly given birth . . . to new and totally different forms. . . . Under a scientific point of view, and as leading to further investigation, but little advantage is gained by believing that new forms are suddenly developed . . . over the old belief in the creation of species from the dust of the earth."[41] Evolution is here identified specifically with slow, gradual, and continuous modification, and the consideration of 'events' in relation to change in the course of time is ruled out as affording advantage to 'the old belief' in Creation.

[39] Charles Darwin, as cited, pp. 440–441.   [40] *Ibid.*, p. 441.   [41] *Ibid.*, p. 662.

Chapter 12

Events in Relation to the Study of Evolution

IT MUST BE understood that this is not an inquiry into the validity of the procedure followed in modern biology. The discussion of Darwin's approach to the study of evolution has been made necessary by the observation that there are two conflicting concepts of the *modus operandi* of change: the 'historical' and the 'evolutionary.' Of these, the former assumes that changes are consequent upon 'events,' the latter that changes are produced by slow, continuous modification in an eventless world. Without presuming to pass judgment upon the procedure of biologists, it may be said that no study of 'how things work' to produce something 'new' in the course of time can dispense with historical inquiry and with historical evidence. Evolutionary study cannot be successfully carried on without recognition of the fact that change, if it occur, must take place under specific conditions and within definite limits of time and of place. All change has a temporal and a geographical setting. Viewed in this light, the difficulties and contentions which have occupied so prominent a place in biological literature since 1859 follow inevitably from Darwin's initial acceptance of the idea of 'progressive change,' and his adoption of Lyell's 'uniformitarianism,' with its negation of historical evidence and its emphasis on 'continuity' and 'present processes.'

It is of some importance to observe that Darwin was more rigid in his adherence to the principle of 'uniformity' than either Hutton or Lyell. As far as method is concerned, the work of James Hutton was the immediate point of departure of nineteenth-century evolutionary study in England. As is well known, Hutton started from the observation that the surface of the earth has not always been as it is today, and based his inquiries upon the principle that it has come to be as it is through the continued action of the same agencies of change that are to be observed in operation at the present time. As a corollary to this proposition, Hutton assumed that "Time, which measures everything in our idea, and is often deficient to our schemes, is to nature endless and as nothing."[1] It was on this foundation that Lyell's 'uniformitarianism' was based. Now it has not been generally recognized that Hutton distinctly points out that the postulate of uniformity or slow, gradual modification in unrestricted time is a methodological assumption set up for convenience at the beginning of a complex and difficult inquiry. "We have," he said, "been representing the system of this earth as proceeding with a certain regularity, which is not perhaps in nature, but which is necessary for our clear conception of the system of nature. The system of nature is certainly in rule, although we may not know every circumstance of its regulation. We are under a necessity, therefore, of making regular suppositions [suppositions of regularity], in order to come at certain conclusions which may be compared with the present state of things." "We are not," he stated emphatically, "to limit nature with the uniformity of an equable progression, although it be necessary in our computations to proceed upon equalities."[2] The assumption of continuous, slow modification was, therefore, regarded by Hutton as a methodological postulate necessary in the earlier stages of a particular scientific inquiry, but as one which was not to be permitted to interpose an obstacle to investigation. So, he remarks, "in the use of means, we are not to prescribe to nature those alone which we think suitable for the purpose, in our narrow view. It is our business to learn of nature (that is by

---

[1] James Hutton, "Theory of the Earth," *Transactions of the Royal Society of Edinburgh*, vol. 1, pt. 2, 1, p. 215.

[2] *Ibid.*, pp. 301–302.

observation) the ways and means, which in her wisdom are adopted; and we are to imagine these only in order to find means for further information, and to increase our knowledge from the examination of things which actually have been."[3]

Again, Lyell explained: "I did not lay it down as an axiom that there cannot have been a succession of paroxysms and crises, on which 'à priori reasoning' I was accused of proceeding, but . . . I complained that in attempting to explain geological phenomena, the bias has always been on the wrong side; there has always been a disposition to reason à priori on the extraordinary violence and suddenness of changes, both in the inorganic crust of the earth, and in organic types, instead of attempting strenuously to frame theories in accordance with the ordinary operations of nature."[4]

Furthermore, it is of importance to recognize that, among Darwin's immediate followers, men such as Huxley took exception to his rigid insistence on the principle of uniformity. As everyone knows, Huxley was the great exponent, the publicist, of Darwinism. He accepted and advocated the theory of 'natural selection.' Nevertheless he objected, from the beginning, to the notion that evolution must of necessity be slow and continuous. In Huxley's judgment, Darwin "loaded himself with an unnecessary difficulty in adopting *natura non facit saltum* so unreservedly."[5] "Darwin's position," he thought, "might have been even stronger than it was if he had not embarrassed himself with the aphorism *natura non facit saltum,* which turns up so often in his pages."[6] In 1859, Huxley expressed the belief, both to Lyell and to Darwin,[7] that nature does make 'jumps' now and then; and, in 1894, he wrote to William Bateson that he had always taken this view, "much

---

[3] *Ibid.,* p. 302.

[4] *Life, Letters, and Journals of Sir Charles Lyell,* vol. 2 (London, 1881), p. 3.

[5] *Life and Letters of Thomas Henry Huxley,* vol. 1 (2d ed., London, 1903), p. 254.

[6] T. H. Huxley, "Darwin on the Origin of Species," *Westminster Review,* n.s., 17 (1860), p. 569.

[7] *Life and Letters,* as cited, vol. 1, pp. 250, 251.

to Mr. Darwin's disgust."[8] From the outset some of Darwin's most devoted disciples objected to what we are now in a position to regard as his neglect of the historical or 'event' element in change.

Evolutionary study, then, has something to learn from history. It has been involved in difficulties for over half a century from adherence to Darwin's refusal to take history and events into consideration in the study of change in the course of time. It has been involved in difficulties as a result of the acceptance of the idea, inherited from the eighteenth century, that the study of processes of change or modification renders the study of events unimportant and negligible.

Many biologists, in addition to Huxley, have objected to the assumption that all changes in the forms of life are due exclusively to the cumulation of slow, continuous modifications. The objection rests upon the same basis as the criticism which geologists have expressed in regard to Lyell's 'uniformitarianism.' With the accumulation of historical evidence, it became impossible for geologists to continue to assume that all changes in the earth's crust have been of the same order and on the same scale as the continuous modifications to be observed at the present day. The intensity of geological action has not been uniform throughout the past; at all times the ordinary processes of erosion and deposition have been in operation. At certain times, however, there have been 'critical periods' in the history of the earth,[9] marked by "episodal disturbances of indescribable and overpowering violence."[10] A feature that runs through all geological history is the intervention of great movements between periods of relative quiescence; epochs of deformation and mountain building have succeeded periods of continental

[8] *Life and Letters,* as cited, vol. 3, p. 320. Cf. E. B. Poulton, "Thomas Henry Huxley and the Theory of Natural Selection," in his *Essays on Evolution* (Oxford, 1908), pp. 193–203.

[9] Charles Schuchert, in L. V. Pirsson & C. Schuchert, *A Text-Book of Geology* (New York, 1915), p. 421.

[10] Eduard Suess, *The Face of the Earth,* tr. by H. B. C. Sollas, vol. 1 (Oxford, 1904), p. 18.

depression and flooding. Concurrently, these changes have been accompanied by alterations of climate from extremes of cold, arid, and zonal conditions to conditions which were warm, moist, tropical, and uniform.[11]

The great disastrophic movements represent historical events which have radically affected the conditions of life upon the earth. Without taking these events directly into consideration, it is impossible to arrive at an understanding of the way in which the forms of life have come to be as they are. Evolutionary study must, of necessity, inquire "under what circumstances those marked divergences of type took place whereby distinct classes, orders, families, and genera successively came into existence";[12] it must "find out specifically what kinds of events" were involved in the appearance of new forms;[13] it must regard variation as a definite historical occurrence.[14]

From the beginning of modern evolutionary study, investigators have recognized that, to some extent at least, changes in life forms have been associated with changes in environment. The more commonly accepted opinion on this subject stands in close relation to the assumption of slow, continuous modification. It is believed, in fact, that the forms of life have been subject to slow modification in response to the slow, continuous modification of the environment. Hence it is said that "every successive modification must have been due to a response on the part of the organism to some environmental change.... The whole process of evolution depends upon changes of environment taking place so gradually that the necessary self-adjustment of the organism at every stage is possible."[15] On the other hand, recognition of the 'event' character

[11] T. C. Chamberlin, "The Evolution of the Earth," *Scientific Monthly*, 2 (1916), p. 554.

[12] W. B. Carpenter, *Nature and Man* (London, 1888), p. 113.

[13] T. H. Morgan, *A Critique of the Theory of Evolution* (Princeton, 1916), p. 6.

[14] William Bateson, "President's Address," *Report of the 84th Meeting of the British Association*, Australia, 1914 (London, 1915), pp. 12, 20.

[15] Arthur Dendy, "Progressive Evolution and the Origin of Species," *ibid.*, pp. 389, 390.

of geological change has brought with it a recognition of the historical character of organic change. It has been pointed out, for example, that "the great floral revolutions of geologic history are connected with the great disastrophic movements."[16] Again, "as the earth's shell has been periodically raised into mountain ranges and the oceans have as often flowed widely over the continents, the environment of plants and animals has undergone repeated and vast alterations."[17] "It is very common," another authority states, "to find a new group arising near the end of some geologic period during which vast climatic changes were taking place. Such an incipient group almost regularly becomes the dominant group of the next period, because it developed under the changed conditions which ushered in the new period and was therefore especially favored by the new environment."[18] "There is probably," Merriam says, "close relation between the continuous change of the progressing living world and the fluctuations in condition of earth climate and earth crust. Movements of the crust producing change of topography and variation of distribution of land and water, taken with changes of climate, must have had important influence in keeping the currents of life moving."[19]

It is evident, then, that the acceptance of the historical point of view in relation to the study of change must lead biologists to the study of the conditions of life as they have been affected at different times by intrusions or events.

History, on the other hand, has something to learn from evolutionary study. Events, until they have been brought into relation with some particular thing, object, or entity undergoing change, remain isolated facts which admit only of categorical statement. The historian must extend his horizon to include

---

[16] David White, in R. D. Salisbury, ed., *Outlines of Geologic History* (Chicago, 1910), p. 139.

[17] Charles Schuchert, as cited, p. 420.

[18] H. H. Newman, *Readings in Evolution, Genetics, and Eugenics* (Chicago, 1921), p. 70.

[19] J. C. Merriam, "Earth Sciences As the Background of History," *Scientific Monthly,* 12 (1921), p. 10.

the concept that the phenomena of the past must be considered as affected by processes operative in time. The historian, however, cannot accept the view of Darwin and the evolutionists that change in time is the result of the continuous operation of processes of change.

This is a matter of such importance that, to make sure of our bearings, it will be necessary to return to the 'present,' from which all inquiry sets out, and to keep before ourselves the question 'how things have come to be as they are.' The present condition of the earth reveals to us an assemblage of differing forms of life. These different forms, as the eighteenth century discovered, are not all of the same age, they have existed for longer or shorter periods of time; some have persisted practically unchanged from the earliest observable geological formations, others are of relatively recent origin. A just view of the facts demands recognition, therefore, of the phenomenon of persistence or stability, as well as of the phenomenon of modification or change, in relation to the forms of life. "We are all accustomed," Huxley remarked, "to speak of the number and the extent of the changes in the living population of the globe during geological time as something enormous; . . . but . . . looking only at the positive data furnished by the fossil world from a broader point of view . . . a surprise of another kind dawns upon the mind; and under this aspect the smallness of the total change becomes as astonishing as was its greatness under the other. . . . Any admissible hypothesis of progressive modification," he continued, "must be compatible with persistence without progression, through indefinite periods."[20] As a more recent authority has stated it, "The great question is, Why do organisms progress at all instead of remaining stationary from generation to generation?"[21] If, however, the phenomena of life display a considerable relative stability, the investigation of 'how things have come to be as they are'

[20] T. H. Huxley, "Geological Contemporaneity" [1862], in his *Collected Essays*, vol. 8 (New York, 1894), pp. 289–290, 304.

[21] Arthur Dendy, as cited, p. 384.

must begin with the attempt to determine the processes which are manifested in the remarkable characteristic which Huxley called 'persistence.'

With the acceptance of this point of view, the conceptual model for the study of change in time will be subjected to a radical alteration. Instead of the picture of slow, gradual progression in unrestricted time, there will be introduced the complementary ideas of 'fixity' and 'advancement.'[22] Now, in point of fact, this alternative model has accompanied every questioning of the validity of the Lyell-Darwinian presupposition of uniform, slow modification. To cite but a few instances, it was implied, as we have seen, in Huxley's writings; it was expressed, in 1866, in definite terms, by Sir William Grove,[23] in his presidential address before the British Association, and was put forward, in the same circumstances, by Sir George Darwin, in 1905;[24] it has been accepted by most, if not all, palaeontologists, and, finally, by a small but increasing group of experimental zoölogists. As stated by Zittel, "there have been periods when the process of transformation and the weeding out of organisms were greatly accelerated, and following upon these reconstructive periods long intervals of repose have ensued, during which intervals species have retained their characteristic forms with but little variation."[25] De Vries "supposed that after periods of relative fixity during which they are subject only to fluctuating variations, living beings may pass through shorter periods when their forms are abruptly modified in different directions by discontinuous changes."[26] More recently, Jennings has

[22] A. S. Woodward, [Presidential Address, Section C], *Report of the 79th Meeting of the British Association*, 1909 (London, 1910), p. 468.

[23] W. R. Grove, "Address [of the President]," *Report of the 36th Meeting of the British Association*, 1866 (London, 1867), p. lxxvi. Cf. Clarence King, "Catastrophism and Evolution," *American Naturalist*, 11 (1877), pp. 449–470, referred to by C. S. Peirce, "The Architecture of Theories" [1891], in his *Chance, Love, and Logic*, ed. by M. R. Cohen (New York, 1923), pp. 164–165.

[24] Sir George Darwin, "President's Address," *Report of the 75th Meeting of the British Association*, 1905 (London, 1906), p. 8.

[25] K. A. von Zittel, *Text-Book of Palæontology*, ed. by C. R. Eastman, vol 1 (London, 1913), p. 16.

[26] A. M. Giard, *Congress of Arts and Science, St. Louis, 1904*, vol. 5 (Boston, 1906), p. 277.

reached the conclusion that "the germinal or genotypic constitution in most organisms is extremely stable," and that "the
facts in uniparental reproduction seem to point more toward
the production of evolutionary change by action of the environment on the germ plasm than by any of the other methods."[27] This alternative model, then, envisages the course of
evolution as consisting in (1) antecedent long periods of relative inactivity, stagnation, and fixity (during which slight, continuous modifications may occur, without, however, leading
to 'new' forms), followed by (2) short critical periods during
which forms undergo abrupt change, in which they make sudden fundamental advances or submit to extinction.

It must be understood that the construction of a conceptual
model of the way in which change has taken place is merely a
preliminary step to the investigation of 'how things work' in
the course of time. It is obvious that investigation will proceed
in one way if it is conducted upon the assumption of slow,
continuous modification, in another if it sets out from observation of the facts of 'fixity' and 'advancement.' In the latter
case, the problem will be to discover the relation between the
two sets of facts. Thus it has been thought that an organism
is subject to a process of drilling into habits, from which, on
occasion, it might be set free by some kind of releasing mechanism.[28] It has been thought that organic forms oppose a certain
resistance to change in their life conditions, that this resistance
maintains their state unaltered or stable until the tension produced by the disturbing influences reaches a certain height,
when a crisis is reached and change ensues.[29] It has been conceived that stability is a result of the operation of processes
which control or inhibit the exercise of powers actually possessed by the organism; that this condition will be maintained

---

[27] H. S. Jennings, "Variation in Uniparental Reproduction," *American Naturalist,* vol. 56 (1922), pp. 14, 15.

[28] Francis Darwin, "President's Address," *Report of the 78th Meeting of the
British Association,* 1908 (London, 1909), pp. 5, 26.

[29] F. A. Lange, *History of Materialism,* tr. by E. C. Thomas, vol. 3 (Boston,
1881), pp. 45–46.

until some disturbance of equilibrium takes place, through the operation of changes in the environment; that when such disturbance come in, it gives opportunity for variation, and organic forms experience temporary release from the operation of processes manifested in stability or fixity.[30] While these conceptions have been put forward by different individuals, it must be remembered that post-Darwinian inquiry has been based, almost exclusively, upon the acceptance of Darwin's assumptions, and, consequently, that relatively nothing has been done to define the processes manifested in 'fixity,' or to bring to light the processes shown in rapid 'advancement.'

It will now be recognized that the difficulties in which both the study of history and the study of evolution are involved have their beginning in the eighteenth-century doctrine that 'events' must be excluded from the investigation of the provisions which nature has made for progressive change. If we are to undertake the study of 'how things have come to be as they are,' it will be necessary to eliminate (1) the assumption that progressive change is 'natural' and to be expected, (2) the assumption that the task of science is to discover the orderly provision which nature has made for progressive change, and (3) the idea that 'events' are not an essential part of the *modus operandi* of change in time.

In this situation, it would seem that the historian, already interested in events and unhampered by the tradition of 'slow, continuous modification,' would have less difficulty than the evolutionist in appreciating the fact that the investigation of 'how things have come to be as they are' must of necessity involve an extended program of inquiry. The explanation of any present status or condition will require a determination (1) of the processes manifested in the persistence of old forms, and in the stability of forms in general, (2) of the processes manifested in slow modification (which, however, do not produce

---

[30] William Bateson, as cited, pp. 18–19. Cf. also the view of Cuvier, quoted in J. T. Merz, *A History of European Thought in the Nineteenth Century*, vol. 1 (Edinburgh, 1896), p. 138.

anything 'new'), (3) of the historical conditions under which changes have actually taken place in the past, and (4) of the processes manifested in such circumstances.

It will be apparent, on reflection, that this scheme of inquiry provides a basis for the correlation of the activities represented by the existing studies of 'history' and of 'evolution.' To this new investigation the older evolutionary study will contribute the concept of processes operative in time, though the assumption that there are processes which directly produce 'change' or 'modification' will be eliminated. To the same investigation the older historical study will contribute the concept of 'events,' though the current acceptance of events as important in and for themselves will give place to the concept of events as the active element in change; events will be conceived, not as the expression of the will-acts of individuals, but as 'intrusions,' of whatever sort, affecting conditions in which the processes manifested in 'fixity' have been operative without disturbance.

The identification of 'events' as 'intrusions' is a matter of some importance. To reach an understanding of 'how things work' in the course of time, we may envisage the facts of experience as arranged conceptually in a series of concentric circles. Outermost, we would have the stellar universe; within this, the physical earth; within this, the world of organic life; within this, again, the world of human activities; within this, the larger group or nation; within this, the local community; and, finally, within this, the individual. In such a series, it is obvious that change in any outer circle will affect all that lies within it. We may, then, define an 'event' as an intrusion, from any wider circle, into any circle or condition which may be the object of present interest. It follows that 'events' are not merely happenings which appear to any particular historian to be unusual or important, but are happenings of a particular kind. The new form of investigation will be concerned, in a special degree, with 'intrusions'; it will also be deeply concerned with the working out of the conditions created by such events.

PART THREE

THE STUDY OF THE PRESENT

Chapter 13

The Method of Science

Iɴ ᴀᴄᴄᴏʀᴅᴀɴᴄᴇ with the initial proposal of this inquiry, it has now been shown that the efforts to bring the phenomena of social life within the purview of the method of science have been foredoomed to failure because of the initial acceptance by humanists of conceptions of method which introduced a complete separation between the study of events and the study of change in time. Pursued in isolation, historical study finds its end in the aesthetic appreciation of unusual happenings, while evolutionary study exhausts itself in the vain quest of processes of change. It will be obvious, therefore, that if we are to arrive at the desideratum of a science of man, it will be necessary to bring into one focus the historical study of events and the scientific study of processes operative in time. In other words, if the aim which humanists have set before themselves is to be attained, it will be necessary to reconsider and revise the methodological conceptions in accordance with which the separation between historical and scientific study was introduced in the seventeenth century. The first step toward the reconstruction of the procedure followed in the social sciences must be a consideration of what is meant by 'the method of science.'

As is well known, there is a marked disposition on the part of humanists to insist that their work is 'scientific,' in opposition to the usage which restricts this designation to the activities of the 'natural' sciences. The basis of this insistence appears to be the argument that, historically, 'science' is synonymous with 'knowledge,' or, more explicitly, 'knowledge acquired by study.' It is, in fact, true that 'science' and 'knowledge' represent simply the Latin and Old English words for the same conception. When, however, synonymous words are incorporated into a language, they become differentiated; each tends to acquire a special shade of meaning. In this instance, the use of the word 'science' has come to be particularized during the last century, so that, at the present moment, 'science' stands for certain branches of inquiry characterized by specific aims and modes of procedure.[1] Whether the humanist is within his rights in using the term 'scientific' is not really the point at issue. It is the later meaning, connoting a particular type of interest and activity, that gives the word its present importance and significance. Nothing, indeed, but confusion can result from the reiteration that the term 'scientific' describes accurately the activities of scholars in the field of history. Clarity of thought is not to be attained by insisting that the same word should be weighted with two irreconcilable meanings in the same context.[2]

While, on the one hand, humanists have been accustomed to urge that their work was 'scientific,' many scholars have maintained, on the other hand, that the character of the facts with which they deal differentiates the investigation of human affairs, in a fundamental manner, from that of external nature. "However widely and carefully," says James Bryce, "the materials may be gathered, their character makes it impossible that politics should ever become a science in the sense in which mechanics or chemistry or botany is a science."[3] Clearly, even the genius of a John Stuart Mill has not been able to eradicate this opinion, which has for its basis, as Mill saw, just the fact that a science of human relations has not yet been brought into being.[4] The strength of knowledge lies, not in what it denies,

---

[1] On the words 'science' and 'Wissenschaft,' cf. J. T. Merz, *A History of European Thought in the Nineteenth Century*, vol. 1 (Edinburgh, 1896), pp. 89–90, 168–172, 202–203.

[2] A. A. Cournot, *Essai sur les fondements de nos connaissances* [1851] (nouvelle éd., Paris, 1912), p. 468. C. F. Keary, *The Pursuit of Reason* (Cambridge, 1910), p. 100.

[3] Viscount Bryce, *Modern Democracies*, vol. 1 (New York, 1921), p. 14.

[4] J. S. Mill, *A System of Logic*, bk. vi, ch. 1.

but in what it affirms. To deny the possibility of an intellectual undertaking does not render it impossible; nor is the fact that men have tried to set up or create a humanistic science, and have failed in the attempt, any proof that success is unattainable. The history of each and every science is essentially a record of failure until such time as the problems have been attacked in the right way. To the scientific worker it is a truism that there are no scientific subjects as such. Any facts are fitted in themselves to be subject matter for science. The field of science is unlimited. The unity of science lies, not in its subject matter, but in its method.[5]

In seeking to determine what is meant by 'the method of science,' the humanist is not infrequently confused by finding various criteria of science set up which would rule out any possibility of establishing a 'science' within the range of humanistic studies. One of the obstacles to the recognition of the unity of method in science consists in the variety of the technical operations required for carrying on investigations in the different fields of scientific work. From this variety has arisen a tendency to confuse the technique of investigation with scientific method, and a disposition on the part of many scientists to insist that the technique of some one science, preferably physics, should be regarded as the criterion of scientific work in general.

As one source of confusion to the humanist, in the endeavor to reach an understanding of scientific method, there may be mentioned the very old conception (maintained, for example, by Roger Bacon, Leonardo da Vinci, Descartes, Kant, and von Humboldt) that science consists in reducing all the phenomena of nature to mathematical laws—the idea that the amount of science in any subject is equal to the amount of mathematics it

---

[5] Marcellin Berthelot, in Ernest Renan, *Dialogues et fragments philosophiques* (Paris, 1876), p. 208. W. K. Clifford, *Lectures and Essays,* ed. by Leslie Stephen and Frederick Pollock, vol. 1 (London, 1879), pp. 125–126. William McDougall, "Psycho-physical Method," in *Lectures on the Method of Science,* ed. by T. B. Strong (Oxford, 1906), p. 113. John Dewey, "Science As Subject-matter and As Method," *Science,* n.s., 31 (1910), pp. 121–127. F. G. Kenyon, *Education, Scientific and Humane* (London, 1917), p. 18.

contains.⁸ It is not necessary to involve the discussion in meta-physical arguments to see that, while mathematics is necessary to the study of physics, it is not a prerequisite to the study of biology. Geometry sets out from a collection of axioms; biology begins with a collection of forms of living beings. Mathematics can never pronounce upon questions of actual existence; but other established sciences have found means for dealing with such questions. Mathematics, therefore, cannot be regarded as the *sine qua non* of scientific work.

Again, science cannot be identified with the domain of 'experimentation,' for experiment cannot be applied to the historical content of subjects such as geology and palaeontology.

A notable source of difficulty to humanists consists in the dictum, frequently repeated, that the test of a science is its power to predict. The success of astronomers in announcing in advance the occurrence of eclipses inspired Auguste Comte to set up 'prediction' as the ultimate criterion of science.⁷ Through the instrumentality of J. S. Mill, this idea has been widely disseminated, so that today, and particularly among humanists, 'prediction' is accepted as the aim and the 'ideal perfection' of every science. To predict means, in ordinary language, to foretell, to prophesy; and unquestionably the popular mind has been greatly attracted by this suggestion of looking into the future under authoritative direction. The scientist is not, however, a substitute for the astrologer, haruspex, or card reader. The happenings which the astronomer states beforehand are not 'historical'; they are simply regularities of nature which belong to a more extended time system than that determined by the revolutions of the earth. No one would speak of 'predicting' the rising of the sun tomorrow morning, and eclipses, though coming at wider intervals of time, are occurrences of

⁸ J. T. Merz, as cited, pp. 30, 281, 383. C. F. Keary, as cited, pp. 105, 107, 108. A. D. Lindsay, *The Philosophy of Bergson* (New York [1911]), pp. 9, 12, 16, 32.

⁷ Auguste Comte, *Cours de philosophie positive* (4ᵉ éd., Paris, 1877), t. 2, pp. 19–20; t. 4, p. 226. The idea was, however, taken over by Saint-Simon and Comte from Condorcet, *Esquisse d'un tableau historique des progrès de l'esprit humain* (Paris, 1795), p. 327.

precisely the same order. 'Prediction,' as a term in science, has a different meaning, and one that has only just begun to make its way into the dictionaries. It means to announce the existence of something before the fact has been tested by direct experience, the declaration being the outcome of previous scientific investigation. The formal statement would be, "If my calculations are correct, then you will find a 'new' planet in such a part of the heavens"; that this hypothetical element is always involved is shown by the fact that the discovery of Neptune is associated more directly with the name of Leverrier than with that of J. C. Adams. Prediction, in science, has no reference to historical events.

Unquestionably the greatest obstacle to a clear understanding of the method of science on the part of humanists is the use of the word 'law' as applied to descriptions of regularities in natural operations. The concept of 'law' in science springs ultimately from the perception of an analogy between the organization of political society and that of nature. As Mill remarked, the term 'law of nature' is employed with a sort of tacit reference to the expression of the will of a superior. Whatever the significance of the word 'law' may be to the physicist, it is this imperative, mandatory sense that stands out in the mind of the humanist, with the result that he feels there is something strained and amiss in the statement that the phenomena of the world around us, including the actions of men and of societies, are 'governed by fixed laws,' that they are obedient to 'eternal decrees.'

It would have been fortunate, from the humanist's point of view, if, instead of the conception of enactment and command implied by the word 'law,' there had been taken over, for scientific purposes, the conception of habitual modes of action implied in the word 'custom.' Enactments are promulgations of some exterior or superior individual or body; customs are the forms assumed by the interrelations within given groups. 'Custom' is, in fact, a close approximation to the scientist's point of view, for a 'natural law' describes just what things of a certain kind habitually do; it is a statement of the regular manner in which things act. Considered more strictly, a scientific 'law' is a formula, expressed in words or in symbols, describing the behavior of a selected group of phenomena; and scientific investigation is the effort to find out 'how things act.' The basic interest of science is in the relations of things. The implication in all scientific inquiry is that things 'work' or 'act' with a regularity sufficient to permit this 'working' to be described. For convenience in discourse we may speak of these regular or customary modes of working as *processes*. Obviously it would tend to clarify thought if we were to employ the word 'process,' a term for the actual operation described, in place of the word 'law,' a term for the verbal description.

We may say, then, that the great object of scientific work is not the 'discovery of laws,' but the investigation and description of the processes of nature. "For science, the world of natural phenomena is a complex of procedure going on in time, and its sole function is to construct systematic schemes forming conceptual descriptions of actually observed processes."[8] The line of development in each field of science has been from the observational study of phenomena to the analysis of the observed phenomena in terms of processes. This step is most clearly marked in geology, but it is no less definite in such widely separated fields as chemistry, physiology, psychology, and philology.[9]

If we are to appreciate fully the point of view of the scientific worker, it will be necessary to observe that what we are given in experience is a vast assemblage of results. Whether we look at a mountain range or a piece of quartz, at a tropical forest or a garden flower, an empire or a scrap of paper, we are regarding results. Nowhere in nature are we presented with things in their 'original' form; nowhere are we provided with

[8] Arthur Schuster & A. E. Shipley, *Britain's Heritage of Science* (London, 1917), p. 275.

[9] Cf. C. R. Van Hise, "The Problems of Geology," *Congress of Arts and Science, St. Louis, 1904*, vol. 4 (Boston, 1906), pp. 525–548. R. S. Woodworth, *Dynamic Psychology* (New York, 1918), pp. 34, 35, 42–43.

a labeled collection of their constituent elements. Furthermore, these results do not remain fixed. From day to day the mountain range is subject to modifications, and our garden, our circumstances, and our ideas change. Everywhere in nature there is activity—even within the atom.

The facts of experience are results of activities. There is, however, no one at hand to explain for us how these results have been produced; and so, from the dawn of thought, men have been driven to try to find out for themselves. The first naïve, uncritical way of explaining 'how things work' has always been to attribute these activities to some person or persons. Even in modern times, this type of thought has not disappeared, and men continue to speak of 'Nature' as a conscious agent. It is only with an effort, apparently, that we can rid our minds of this tendency to regard the operations of the external world as personal activities, a tendency unfortunately conventionalized in the use of the word 'cause.' For the scientist, however, phenomena are wholly impersonal; he sees only things in activity, and any concept of 'will' or 'purpose' is out of place.

The initial step toward a scientific attitude is taken when men reach the point of rejecting the notion that the results given in experience are dictated by personal caprice or extra-natural interference. Science begins, in fact, with the assumption that there is such regularity in the operations of nature that these may be described in stated terms, and that, when formulated, these descriptions will be found to hold good for all occurrences of the same phenomenon. In adopting this mode of procedure, the scientist is simply following the experience of men in general when they give names to objects and actions. Scientific classification names, in a systematic way, the objects around us, many of which have escaped specific designation in ordinary language. So, too, the scientist observes the activities going on in the world and describes these more systematically and with greater precision than is possible in everyday life. Science, then, assumes a regularity in nature that makes 'naming' possible, and one of its great objects is to disengage, from the complexity of phenomena, modes of acting which have hitherto escaped attention.

We do not know 'how things work' to produce the results given in experience, and there is no one to tell us. In making the effort to find out for ourselves, the only means at our disposal is the use of the imagination. Attention is directed to some phenomenon; we wonder how it could have been produced, be it an eclipse, lightning, or an earthquake; and the answer we frame for ourselves, correctly or incorrectly, is a hypothesis. In principle, there is nothing unusual in this procedure; we employ it daily in actual life. It is the method adopted when we say, "I wonder what could have done it"; for what ensues, in the effort to follow up our dilemma, is the imagination and examination of one possibility after another. Scientific work proceeds along these lines, not in the haphazard and semiconscious manner of men in general, but by bringing the procedure into the full light of consciousness. As in daily life our best efforts may be baffled, so, in scientific inquiry, the search is not always rewarded. We may fail in the attempt to reconstruct the processes of nature through the exercise of the imagination, but we do not, on that account, doubt the assumption that the results given in experience are the outcome of natural ways of working, and that these ways may be discovered and described. Defeated in one attempt, the scientist starts anew, believing, not that the ways of nature are past finding out, but that he has not yet hit upon the right approach to the specific problem in hand. "The action of the investigator is periodic. He grapples with a subject of enquiry, wrestles with it, and exhausts, it may be, both himself and it for the time being. He breathes a space, and then renews the struggle...."[10]

Every result in nature is a riddle to be solved, and the initial difficulty in investigation is the discovery of a clue which may be followed up. Here the immediate temptation is to interpret the facts in accordance with analogies drawn from some other

---

[10] John Tyndall, "Scientific Use of the Imagination" [1870], in his *Fragments of Science*, vol. 2 (New York, 1892), pp. 102–103.

phase of experience. Thus, at an early period, as already mentioned, men formed the concept of 'laws of nature' by carrying over the idea of political authority to describe the source of the regularities which they observed in the world about them. We need not go back to beginnings, however, to find examples of hypotheses based upon analogy. When men are confronted with some result in nature, and are trying to frame for themselves a description of the way in which this result may possibly have been produced, they are disposed to make use of any resources of thought which may be available. In the employment of analogy, however, they are enlisting a dangerous ally, for, in thus assimilating the unknown to the known, a specious assurance is given by the familiarity of the latter element. Hence it is of importance to recognize that a scientific hypothesis is simply a working model of something going on in the objective world, and that, as such, it must be constructed out of actual information concerning matters of fact.

Scientific hypotheses are not 'made up out of one's own head'; the scientist must have materials to work on. These materials consist, in the first instance, of inherited knowledge. Every investigator has for his intellectual background the acquisitions made by his predecessors, and every competent worker follows the example of Aristotle in making acknowledgment of the work of earlier contributors. The preliminary training of the scientist includes 'learning' what has been achieved in his subject up to the present; from this vantage point, for which he is indebted to others, he may himself proceed to new discoveries. The process of 'learning' is indispensable, but it has an undesirable aspect, for what is first learned imposes constraint upon the movement of thought. What one has been taught becomes in some sort a standard, and new ideas tend to present themselves as violations of an established order. So the past exerts upon thought an ever-present influence; and it is against this background that every step in advance must be made.

The scientific heritage into which the modern investigator

enters consists of collections of facts and of statements of theories. It is not sufficiently recognized that these two elements
are virtually inseparable. Consciously or unconsciously, all
facts observed and set down have reference to some notion,
hypothesis, or theory. It follows that, while all scientific work
is based on 'facts'—things specified as known to have occurred
or to be true—the accumulation of facts as such does not constitute science. Actual scientific inquiry begins, not with 'learning' what is already known of a particular subject, not with
the collection of materials, but with the perception of some
difficulty in current explanations of phenomena.

What ensues upon the perception of a difficulty is sustained
cogitation. This cogitation is aided by a reëxamination of the
'literature' of the subject, by tentative rearrangements or re-
groupings of the data available, and by the extension of observation as far as the investigator may feel it necessary for the
undertaking in hand. This activity proceeds with the question
"How?" insistently in evidence; and the effort in its entirety is
a persistent struggle for mastery between the constructive and
the critical powers of the investigator. The conditions of the
struggle are arduous; all that we are given is a result—the occurrence of granite, the diversity of the forms of life, the relative
'backwardness' or 'advancement' of human groups—and the
problem is to reconstruct the operations by which this result
has been produced. The imagination of the inquirer is put to
the test in the construction of a working model of a process
or processes; his critical ability is called upon at every step to
check his ideas by the facts. Thus it is that while, in theoretical
writings, great stress is laid on the necessity for 'verifying' hypotheses, in actual work 'verification' is an integral part of the
inquiry. Formally, however, verification means that if we say
things 'work' in a particular way, the description we give must
permit of any competent person's testing its accuracy.

The sole function of science is to construct systematic schemes
forming conceptual descriptions of actually observed processes.
If, now, we compare the work of the different sciences, it will

be found that all processes are not of one general type. Newton's law of gravitation and Darwin's theory of natural selection are alike in being descriptions of 'how things work,' but they do not refer to the same order of phenomena. The difference, indeed, is marked, for in experimenting with the action of falling bodies we consider data apart from any historical setting or circumstance—to use an expression in logic, we 'abstract from' the historical series,—whereas, in the study of evolution, the theory of natural selection is one attempt to show how something new could have emerged in the course of time.

The distinction here made runs through all the different fields of scientific inquiry. The chemist abstracts from the particularity of matter as found on the earth; he leaves the description of actual substances, their characteristics and their distribution, to the mineralogist; he isolates the chemical 'elements,' considers their modes of action in relation to each other, and endeavors to determine the processes of chemical change. On the other hand, the geologist bases his study of the structure of the earth's crust on the historical facts of the stratification of the rocks. But while the description of strata is an essential preliminary to all geological investigation, scientific work in geology dates from Hutton's perception that the historical facts are to be considered in terms of processes which are to be observed in operation. The object of the geologist is to show how the earth as we find it has come to be as it is through the action of processes operative in time. Chemistry, then, may be taken as an example of the type of science which seeks to discover the forms and modes of action of the *constituent elements* of which things are made up, whereas geology is an example of the sciences which are occupied in the endeavor to find out *how things have come to be as they are.* The unifying element in these types of inquiry is the common aim of determining 'how things work.'

It is of importance to observe that the high abstraction from the particularity and individuality of objects as found in experience which logicians have insisted upon as the dominant characteristic of all scientific work is distinctive only of the first of these types of inquiry. As we have seen, the physicist— the investigator of *phusis,* the nature of things—abstracts from the particularity of what is given in the external world, and undertakes to sort out the elements of which the object under consideration is composed. He isolates his materials from the actual environment or setting in which they may have been found, and considers them apart from any actual position in historical time. Obviously such investigations proceed under artificial conditions set up in a laboratory, and not under the conditions characteristic of the actual world. Inquiries of this type—the 'laboratory sciences'—involve, at each step, a progressive isolation or abstraction from the results given in the external world. When, on the other hand, we turn to inquire 'how things have come to be as they are,' a different situation confronts us. Here the laboratory gives place to the world, and analysis under experimental conditions is succeeded by the study of 'kinds,' classes, orders, genera, and species, in their actual distribution in space and their actual relation in time. While the first type of investigation aims at results which are dissociated from any limitation of time and place, the second concerns itself directly with the relationships of specific objects in their temporal and geographical distribution.

The distinction here made between inquiry into 'the nature of things' and inquiry into 'how things have come to be as they are' is by no means new.[11] Yet the failure to recognize it as

---

[11] The distinction here made has been recognized, among others, by: Turgot, in 1750, *Œuvres* [nouvelle éd.], par Gustave Schelle, t. 1 (Paris, 1913), pp. 214–215, 276. Cournot, *Traité de l'enchaînement des idées fondamentales dans les sciences et dans l'histoire* (nouvelle éd., Paris, 1922), pp. 219–222. Joseph Le Conte, *Evolution* [1887] (2d ed., New York, 1892), pp. 4, 7. Bernard Bosanquet, *Logic* [1888], vol. 1 (2d ed., Oxford, 1911), p. 201. J. S. Mackenzie, *An Introduction to Social Philosophy* (Glasgow, 1890), pp. 14–15, 18, 22. J. B. Baillie, "Truth and History," *Mind*, n.s., 7 (1898), p. 506. S. H. Hodgson, "Method in Philosophy," *Proceedings of the Aristotelian Society*, n.s., 4 (1903–4), p. 7. A. L. Kimball, "The Relations of the Science of Physics of Matter to Other Branches of Learning," *Congress of Arts and Science, St. Louis, 1904*, vol. 4 (Boston, 1906), pp. 70–71. A. E. Taylor, *Aristotle* (London [1912]), pp. 37–38. Emile Boutroux, *Natural Law in Science and Philosophy*, tr. by F. Rothwell (New York, 1914), pp. 155–156. H. W. Carr,

determining the character of specific scientific inquiries has led to serious misunderstandings of the problems involved in the study of history and of evolution.

" 'Time' and 'History' in Contemporary Philosophy," *Proceedings of the British Academy*, 1917–1918, p. 341. O. G. S. Crawford, *Man and His Past* (London, 1921), p. 85.

Hermann Paul, *Principien der Sprachgeschichte* [1880] (3. Aufl., Halle a. S., 1898), pp. 9–10, made the distinction between 'Gesetzeswissenschaften' and 'Geschichtswissenschaften'; cf. Hanns Oertel, *Lectures on the Study of Language* (New York, 1902), pp. 5–6, footnote. The distinction made in the text is not to be confused with Windelband's classification of the sciences as 'nomothetic' and 'idiographic.' Cf. also Paul Barth, *Die Philosophie der Geschichte als Soziologie*, I. Teil (3 Aufl., Leipzig, 1922), pp. 32–33.

Chapter 14

The Investigation of Differences in Human Groups

Ａs HAS BEEN indicated in the preceding chapter, a distinction is to be made between the sciences which are concerned with the investigation of 'the nature of things' and the sciences which are concerned with the investigation of 'how things have come to be as they are.' As we have seen, these different types of inquiry have the common aim of determining 'how things work' in the world around us, and the common procedure of constructing "systematic schemes forming conceptual descriptions of actually observed processes." It may now be pointed out that these types of inquiry have a third characteristic in common: they are both devoted to the elucidation of the *present* in which men find themselves situated. Thus the physicist concerns himself with the study of the constituent elements of things as given; the geologist or the palaeontologist concerns himself with the study of things as actually distributed in the world. In the latter case, the scientist discovers the objects of his interest distributed in specific places, and his activity is directed to the elucidation of the present condition of these objects as given in experience.

In the effort to render intelligible the data before him, the natural scientist (as distinguished from the physicist) has found it necessary to envisage the different strata and the different forms of life in terms of a time relationship. Strata and species alike exist in the present, but their distribution and condition are best accounted for by attributing a historical significance to the differences encountered. From the evidence before him, the natural scientist reaches the conclusion that, as we work back conceptually from the present, the aggregate of conditions and distributions displays differences which become more apparent from age to age. Moreover, in his effort to introduce intelligibility into the data, the natural scientist has been forced to question how the results, which he envisages in historical perspective, could possibly have been brought about. It might be thought that this question would have led to a marked emphasis on historical inquiry. Under the influence of eighteenth-century modes of thought, however, the natural scientist proceeded by accepting, as a directive concept, the idea of evolution, by which is meant, not merely that the forms of life have undergone change in time, but that this change has always been slow, gradual, and continuous. As a consequence of this theoretical point of view, he was led to assume that continuous change is the product of some constant agency of change (such as 'natural selection') which has been in operation continuously throughout the past. It would appear, indeed, that the natural scientist, having accepted an *a priori* judgment with respect to the character or form of change, has permitted himself to imagine that the facts of history might be discovered by experiment carried on in the laboratory. The natural scientist, then, sets out from the present, and has for his aim to show 'how things have come to be as they are.' In this endeavor, however, he finds himself involved in difficulties. We are now in a position to see that these difficulties arise from the fact that he has assumed at the beginning just what he is most concerned to find out.

In the humanities, the psychologist holds the position of 'physicist'; he is occupied with the study of how man is constituted. The 'social sciences,' on the other hand, are concerned with the investigation of results—situations, conditions, distributions—given in the present. In this field, the general aim of inquiry is to throw light upon the results with which we are confronted in immediate experience. The undertaking thus described presents, obviously, very considerable difficulties. As I have endeavored to show, however, the real obstacles with which we have to contend at the present time lie in the conceptions with which we approach any particular aspect of this study. The crux of the situation consists in the fact that, if we are to arrive at a knowledge of 'how things have come to be as they are,' we cannot dispense with the investigation of how things have worked in the course of time. It follows, therefore, that the possibility of throwing light upon the *present* turns upon the mode of procedure we adopt in the utilization of historical facts.

It is of significance that, during the last few years, historians have come, quite generally, to express the view that the aim of historical inquiry is to show 'how things have come to be as they are.' What this means is that there has been a reversion from the point of view of nineteenth-century 'academic' history, which accepted 'the document' as the primary interest of the historian, to the view of Herodotus and Polybius that the historian is concerned, in the first place, with the elucidation of some present situation in the affairs of men. In the presence of an immediate interest, such as war, the historian today proposes to show how this situation has arisen, and he proposes to do this by going back to some point of departure, accepted as a 'beginning,' and connecting this 'first' or 'original' situation with the present by a narrative of happenings or events.

The procedure thus adopted by the historian is, as has already been pointed out,[1] the same as the 'genealogical method' of the Greeks; but the modern historian, in his search for explanation, feels a need of something more than a mere genealogy of happenings. The desired explanatory element he discovers in the "conscious motives and purposes that appear to have had a determining influence." At first sight, it might seem as if this effort at explanation, on the part of the modern historian, represented an approach to the procedure of the scientist. In evolutionary biology, for example, the problem might be stated in the form: given a continuous series of changes, to find the uniform antecedent of change. Similarly expressed, the prob-

---

[1] Chs. 2, 3, 7.

lem in history would be: given a sequence of events, to find the psychological antecedent of each particular action. In the former problem, the aim of the biologist would be to discover the constant antecedent; in the latter, however, the historian assumes that he is intuitively possessed of the requisite psychological knowledge. If we examine the procedure of the historian more closely, it will be found that the explanatory element in his work must be identified, not with the particular 'motives and purposes' which he intercalates in his narrative, but with the entire series of happenings which he presents as antecedent to the situation of immediate interest. We have seen previously, however, that the series which the historian offers in his narrative does not include all that has actually happened, but such events only as the particular scholar considers necessary or important for his 'synthesis.' It follows, therefore, that the character of the explanation of any present situation given by the historian is to be sought in the nature of the 'whole' which he envisages by abstraction from the actual data. In short, the explanation provided by the historian is of the type represented in art, not of the type represented in science.

If we are to succeed in throwing light upon the present, it will be necessary to consider conditions as well as situations. It is clear, for example, that in any study of the antecedents of war the economic condition of the countries involved must be taken into consideration, as well as the motives of the leading actors. Now, when we turn to this phase of the subject, it becomes evident that, just as the political historian follows a procedure inherited from the Greeks, the student of culture history follows a procedure inherited from the seventeenth century.

What we are given in any present is an assemblage of different things. The Cartesian conception of science required that the investigator should abstract from these differences in order to gain a knowledge of underlying similarities. Descartes himself reached the important conclusion that "whereas the senses reveal to us a world full of unbridgeable qualitative dif-

ferences, thought reveals the deeper fact, that one single phenomenon, infinitely diversified, motion in space, alone takes
place."[2] Before the end of the seventeenth century, this conception of the importance of motion had found a place in
humanistic thought through its embodiment in the 'idea of
progress.' Since the seventeenth century, procedure in the study
of man has been dominated by the theory that, in reference to
human affairs, change represents a necessary and continuous
movement in a desirable direction. In order to exhibit this
movement, the humanist has endeavored (1) to arrange the different forms of culture, existing in the present, in a unilinear
series from the simplest to the most complex, and (2) to arrange
the different forms of culture, known to have existed in the
past, in a unilinear series of stages. In addition to these conceptual arrangements, which are abstractions from the facts
presented in ethnology and history, the exponents of the comparative method in the eighteenth century took a further step,
and, by the superimposition or consolidation of these series,
undertook to determine the 'natural order' of human development. Subsequently, in the nineteenth century, the ambition
of men such as Comte and Spencer was centered upon the formulation of the 'law' or 'laws' of the progressive movement
of mankind thus exhibited, with conscious reference to the
example of the formulation of the 'laws of motion' in physics.

From what has been said, it will appear that there are two
points which must be taken into consideration in any attempt
to reconstruct the procedure of the 'social sciences.' First, it is
evident that the study of 'how things have come to be as they
are' has always started from the *present,* with the aim of throwing light upon this present. Second, it is equally apparent that
the actual status of humanistic inquiries today is the product
of methodological ideas and practices which have been taken
over, without critical examination, from the past. It follows,
therefore, that while the immediate problem, in the study of
man, is the elimination of these inherited conceptions, the first

[2] N. K. Smith, *Studies in the Cartesian Philosophy* (London, 1902), p. 28.

step toward this end must be a return to the present, from which all scientific investigation must of necessity set out.

What we are given in the present is an assemblage of different things. In the study of man, the point of departure must necessarily be observation of the differences which particularize the condition of humanity in different parts of the world. Any survey, however superficial, of the present conditions in which we find ourselves situated, will reveal the existence of human beings engaged in various forms of activity, such as use of language, maintenance of customs, participation in rites and ceremonies, manufacture and utilization of material objects. When we extend our view beyond our own neighborhood, it is found that these activities take on different forms and aspects in different areas of the globe. The initial step, then, in the approach to the scientific study of man, will be the acquisition of an extensive body of information in regard to the geographical distribution of human activities, spoken of, collectively, as 'human culture.' Geography, therefore, must provide the foundation for humanistic inquiry.

The observation of the cultural differences which distinguish human groups leads at once to a recognition of the major problem of the science of man, namely, "How are these differences to be accounted for?" "How have the differences which we observe in the cultural activities of men come to be as we find them at the present time?"

With the recognition of this question, we are immediately confronted with the necessity of instituting a procedure for investigation. Scientific inquiry, as has already been pointed out, must rest upon comparison. Where there is nothing to compare, that is, where the object under consideration is adjudged 'unique,' the only activity open to us is that of aesthetic appreciation. Even a brief consideration of the experience of humanists will, however, afford convincing proof of the need of caution in determining what elements we are to compare in the investigation of differences.

The attempt to account for the differences in human activi-

ties which we encounter in passing from one geographical area
to another has frequently been made. If we turn to inquire how
the problem has been dealt with in the past, it will be found
that, in the first instance, comparison was restricted to the
single element of geographical conditions, with the result that
cultural differences were correlated strictly with differences in
physical environment, and, more particularly, with differences
in climate.

The literature of the subject may be said to begin with Hippocrates, who devoted a large part (§§ 12–24) of his treatise *On
Airs, Waters, Places*[3] to an analysis of the influence of climate,
or rather of the seasons, in producing differences, both physical
and cultural, among men. In his opinion, changes of climate
affect even the land: where the variations of climate are most
violent and most frequent, the land, too, is very wild and very
uneven; but where the seasons do not alter much, the land
is very even (§ 13). So it is with the inhabitants: "where the
changes of the seasons are most frequent and most sharply contrasted, there you will find the greatest diversity in physique,
in character, and in constitution" (§ 24). Plato entertained
much the same view of the influence of climate upon the characteristics of peoples (*Republic,* 435 E), but the best-known
passage on the subject is undoubtedly that in Aristotle's *Politics.* "Those races," he thought, "who live in a cold climate and
in Europe are full of spirit, but wanting in intelligence and
skill; and therefore they keep their freedom, but have no political organization, and are incapable of ruling over others.
Whereas the natives of Asia are intelligent and inventive, but
they are wanting in spirit, and therefore they are always in a
state of subjection and slavery. But the Hellenic race, which
is situated between them, is likewise intermediate in character,
being high-spirited and also intelligent. Hence it continues
free, and is the best governed of any nation."[4] Polybius held

---

[3] Hippocrates, with an English translation by W. H. S. Jones, vol. 1 (London,
1923).

[4] Aristotle *Politics* vii. 7, tr. by Benjamin Jowett.

that men "have an irresistible tendency to yield to climatic influences: and to this cause, and no other, may be traced the great distinctions which prevail amongst us in character, physical formation, and complexion, as well as most of our habits, varying with nationality or wide local separation."[5] Strabo expressed the opinion that "while in a country that is blessed by nature everything tends to peace, in a disagreeable country everything tends to make men warlike and courageous."[6]

The views of the Greeks were embodied in the first modern discussions of the subject. In his *Republic* (1576), Jean Bodin made a study of the differences of peoples, since, he thought, "the nature of the people is much to be regarded in the framing of a Commonweale." In his opinion, animals vary with 'the diversity of regions,' and, similarly, "there is in a manner as great difference in the nature and disposition of men, as there is of countries." On this assumption, Bodin set forth a long series of correlations between the areas which different peoples inhabit and their physical and moral characteristics. Thus he began by stating that "in the same citie, the diversitie of hills and vallies forceth a diversitie of humors and dispositions, and townes seated uppon uneven places, are more subject to seditions and chaunges, than those that are built uppon an equall and plaine ground"; and he ended with the observation that "the nature of the place doth greatly change the nature and pronounciation of men." In short, the mind, morals, and manners of any given population are affected directly by the climatic and geographical conditions of the area which it inhabits.[7] While, thanks to his place in the history of political theory, Bodin's work is well known to students today, it is probable

---

[5] Polybius iv. 21. 2, tr. by E. S. Shuckburgh.

[6] Strabo ii. 127, tr. by H. L. Jones.
On the theory of climatic influences in classical literature, see also Aristotle, *Politics*, ed. by W. L. Newman, vol. 3 (Oxford, 1902), pp. 363–364.

[7] Jean Bodin, *The Six Bookes of a Commonweale* ... done into English by Richard Knolles (London, 1606), pp. 545, 568. Bodin had previously treated of the same subject in his *Methodus ad facilem historiarum cognitionem*, 1566. Cf. Henri Baudrillart, *J. Bodin et son temps* (Paris, 1853), pp. 413–448; Robert Flint, *Historical Philosophy in France* (New York, 1894), pp. 190–200.

that Pierre Charron's book *De la sagesse* (1601) brought the idea of the influence of climate to a much larger audience in the seventeenth century. In this work the author considered (bk. 1, ch. 41) the problem "Of the difference and inequality of men in general." "There is nothing in this lower world," he said, "wherein there is found so great difference as amongst men, and where the differences are so distant and divers in one and the same subject and kinde." Considering these differences, he held (ch. 42) that "the first most notable and universall distinction of men, which concerneth the soule and body, and whole essence of man, is taken and drawne from the divers site of the world, according to which the aspect and influence of heaven, and the sunne, the aire, the climate, the countrie, are divers. So like wise not only the colour, the complexion, the countenance, the manners, are divers, but also the faculties of the soule."[8]

In discussions of the theory of the influence of climate, it is usual to pass at once from the work of Bodin to that of Montesquieu. This procedure overlooks, however, the important fact that the theory was commonly entertained, and frequently set forth, in the seventeenth and eighteenth centuries, by such persons as Bouhours, Chardin, Fontenelle, Madame Dacier, and more especially by the Abbé Du Bos.[9] The most influential contribution of the period seems to have been Dr. John Arbuthnot's *Essay Concerning the Effects of Air on Human Bodies* (London, 1733), which was the source of Montesquieu's treatment of the subject.[10] In *L'esprit des lois* (1748), Montesquieu discussed "the differences of men in different climates" (bk. xiv). In doing so he started with the observation that *le caractère de l'esprit et les passions du cœur* are very different

[8] Peter Charron, *Of Wisdome, Three Bookes,* written in French, translated [1612] by Samson Lennard (London, n.d.), pp. 169, 171.

[9] Cf. Alfred Lombard, *L'Abbé Du Bos, un initiateur de la pensée moderne, 1670–1742* (Paris, 1913), pp. 243–254. On the idea in contemporary England, cf. J. E. Spingarn, *Critical Essays of the Seventeenth Century,* vol. 1 (Oxford, 1908), pp. ci–cii.

[10] Joseph Dedieu, *Montesquieu et la tradition politique anglaise en France* (Paris, 1909), pp. 192–225.

in different places, and undertook to account for these differences in peoples by the direct physiological effects of different climates. Thus he explained the "immutability of the
religion, manners, customs, and laws in Oriental countries" on
the ground that the climate produces a delicacy (*foiblesse*) of
organs which renders Oriental peoples highly sensitive to impressions; the climate also induces indolence of body and mind,
which renders the people incapable of exertion or effort (*contention*); hence, when once the soul has received impressions,
it cannot change them. This, he believed, is the reason why the
laws, manners, and customs are the same today, in the Orient,
as they were a thousand years ago.

It is evident, then, that the first approach to the study of differences in culture led to the assertion of a direct correlation
between differences in culture and differences in climate and
in physical environment. It should be observed, further, that
the restriction of attention to this single 'cause' forced upon
inquirers the necessity of formulating unverifiable hypotheses
in regard to human physiology.

In the nineteenth century, interest in the correlation of cultural differences with differences in climate was, in large measure, superseded by an interest in the correlation of differences
in culture with differences in race. It will be unnecessary to
give examples of this familiar theory. What is of importance,
in the present connection, is contained in the statement of
Waitz (1859) that the assumption of specific physical or psychical differences cuts short the study of cultural differences
ab initio, and thus leaves the various phenomena of civilization
unexplained.[11] The procedure to be followed in the investigation of differences in human activities must, however, be such
as to bring the phenomena of culture into the foreground.

The question of 'race' suggests a point to which reference is
necessary. The study of 'how man has come to be as we find him
everywhere in the world today' is not directly concerned with

---

[11] Theodor Waitz, *Introduction to Anthropology,* ed. by J. F. Collingwood
(London, 1863), p. 329.

the investigation of 'how man is constituted.' Inquiry into the physical differences between the 'black,' 'yellow,' and 'white' divisions of the human family can be conducted only by biologists; the question whether there are psychological differences in human races can be dealt with only by psychologists. In the present inconclusive state of scientific knowledge on these points, it is obvious that the only course open to humanists is to accept man 'as given,' to assume that human groups everywhere are constituted of much the same human elements. It should not be overlooked, however, that, while the acceptance of man 'as given' is a necessity imposed upon humanistic inquiry owing to the absence of positive results in biology and psychology, the assumption receives direct countenance and support from more than one quarter. Thus it is accepted without qualification in the practice of historians; it is accepted commonly by ethnologists on the basis of firsthand observations of 'backward' peoples; it is accepted by various psychologists as a result of tests made upon representative individuals from different cultural groups.[12] The problem has, however,

---

[12] See, for example, Friedrich Ratzel, *The History of Mankind*, tr. by A. J. Butler, vol. 1 (London, 1906), p. 9. D. G. Brinton, *The Basis of Social Relations*, ed. by Livingston Farrand (New York, 1902), p. 20. E. S. Hartland, *Folklore* (2d ed., London, 1904), p. 44. Henry Balfour, *Report of the 74th Meeting of the British Association*, 1904 (London, 1905), p. 698. R. E. Dennett, *At the Back of the Black Man's Mind* (London, 1906), p. 239. Jean Finot, *Race Prejudice*, tr. by Florence Wade-Evans (London, 1906), pp. 315–316. Sir R. C. Temple, "The Evolution of Currency and Coinage," in *Lectures on the Method of Science*, ed. by T. B. Strong (Oxford, 1906), p. 188. G. L. Gomme, *Folklore As an Historical Science* (London, 1908), p. 192. C. F. Keary, *The Pursuit of Reason* (Cambridge, 1910), p. 49. Franz Boas, *The Mind of Primitive Man* (New York, 1911), pp. 29, 122–123, etc. E. H. Gomes, *Seventeen Years among the Sea Dyaks of Borneo* (London, 1911), pp. 262–263. R. R. Marett, *Anthropology* (New York [1911]), pp. 91, 235. W. J. Sollas, *Ancient Hunters and Their Modern Representatives* [1911] (2d ed., London, 1915), pp. 194, 286. Charles Hose & William McDougall, *The Pagan Tribes of Borneo*, vol. 2 (London, 1912), pp. 221–222. G. C. Wheeler, "The Concept of the Causal Relation in Sociological Science," in *Festskrift tillegnad Edvard Westermarck* (Helsingfors, 1912), p. 189. Vilhjálmur Stefánsson, *My Life with the Eskimo* (New York, 1913), pp. 148–149. S. A. Cook, "The Evolution and Survival of Primitive Thought," in *Essays and Studies Presented to William Ridgeway*, ed. by E. C. Quiggin (Cambridge, 1913), p. 412; *The Foundations of Religion* (London [1914]), p. 15. J. Grasset, "Les sciences morales et sociales et la biologie humaine," *Revue philosophique*, 79 (1915), pp. 109–110. A. M. Hocart, "Psychology and Ethnology," *Folk-lore*, 26 (1915), p. 125. Wilhelm Wundt, *Ele-*

another aspect. The present differences in the activities of human groups throughout the world cannot be accounted for in terms of 'environment' or of 'race' alone. Whatever, then, the conclusions of biologists and psychologists in the future may be, the necessity must still remain for the humanist to carry forward the study of 'how man has come to be as he is' as far as the materials at his command will permit.

---

ments of Folk Psychology, tr. by E. L. Schaub (London [1916]), pp. 112–113. W. I. Thomas and F. Znaniecki, *The Polish Peasant in Europe and America,* vol. 1 (Chicago [1918]), p. 26. Viscount Bryce, *Modern Democracies,* vol. 1 (New York, 1921), p. 14.

Chapter 15

The Method of Hume and Turgot

IN HIS INITIAL survey of the world of human activities, the humanist discovers in the present a great series of cultural differences, associated with definable geographical areas. As a result of this survey, he is forced to ask the question: "How are these differences to be accounted for?" Up to the present, almost all attempts to answer this question have been formulated in terms of some one factor, such as 'climate' or 'race,' and, in consequence, the humanist has been led into the discussion of physiological problems. So far, then, it would seem that humanistic inquiry must either adopt the procedure of the historian and fall back upon philosophy for ultimate guidance, or follow the course of the sociologist and stand committed to some theory of the 'original nature' of man.

The way out of this difficult situation was indicated by David Hume in his two essays "Of the Rise and Progress of the Arts and Sciences" (1742) and "Of National Characters" (1748), the latter published in the same year as Montesquieu's *Spirit of Laws*. In direct opposition to the accepted opinion of his time, Hume contended that differences in national characters were not the result of physical causes, and maintained that men do not "owe any thing of their temper or genius to the air, food, or climate."[1] What is of importance, in this change of view, is to notice the remarkable way in which the study of differences opens out, once the narrow correlation of culture with 'climate' is abandoned.

The point of departure, in Hume's two essays, is the question

[1] David Hume, *Essays, Moral, Political, and Literary*, ed. by T. H. Green & T. H. Grose (new ed., London, 1882), vol. 1, p. 246.

why one nation differs from another in politeness and learning[2] or in national character.[3] He assumes that the natural genius of mankind is the same in all ages and in almost all countries,[4] that "as far as observation reaches, there is no universal difference discernible in the human species,"[5] though, in another connection, he expresses doubt in regard to negroes.[6] From this beginning, his study of present differences leads to distinctive results.

He is concerned, first, not with the question of change, but with that of fixity, sameness, or stability. Men acquire, he says, 'a similitude of manners' by association and imitation; and "whatever it be that forms the manners of one generation, the next must imbibe a deeper tincture of the same dye."[7] "If, then," he says, "we run over the globe, or revolve the annals of history, we shall discover every where signs of a sympathy or contagion of manners, none of the influence of air or climate."[8] The stability or persistence of governments he attributes to the exercise of power and authority. In large governments the people are kept in subjection, knowledge is dwarfed by restraint, liberty of reasoning is abridged.[9] The stability of monarchies arises chiefly, in his opinion, from the superstitious reverence for princes and for priests.[10] In a despotic monarchy "no improvement can ever be expected in the sciences, in the liberal arts, in laws, and scarcely in the manual arts and manufactures. The same barbarism and ignorance, with which the government commences, is propagated to all posterity."[11] In China, the authority of Confucius had such influence that "none had the courage to resist the torrent of public opinion, and posterity was not bold enough to dispute what had been universally received by their ancestors."[12] In other words, association, imitation, and education induce characteristic modes of conduct and

---

[2] *Ibid.*, p. 177.
[3] *Ibid.*, p. 244.
[4] *Ibid.*, p. 195.
[5] *Ibid.*, vol. 1, p. 382; vol. 2, p. 68.
[6] *Ibid.*, vol. 1, p. 252, note.
[7] *Ibid.*, p. 248.
[8] *Ibid.*, p. 249.
[9] *Ibid.*, pp. 178 ff.
[10] *Ibid.*, pp. 181, 187.
[11] *Ibid.*, p. 185.
[12] *Ibid.*, p. 183.

thought, and these are perpetuated through the weight of authority, superstition, and public opinion.

Second, notwithstanding the influences which tend to perpetuate any present condition, the manners of a people undergo modification from one age to another. This modification Hume ascribes to alterations in government, the mixture of new people, or to "that inconstancy, to which all human affairs are subject."[13] Thus modification will ensue upon the establishment of law, since "from law arises security: from security curiosity: and from curiosity knowledge."[14] Modification will follow from the proximity of "a number of neighbouring and independent states, connected together by commerce and policy," since this relationship leads to the 'importation' of arts and sciences.[15] Greece, for example, "was a cluster of little principalities, which . . . being united both by their near neighbourhood, and by the ties of the same language and interest, entered into the closest intercourse of commerce and learning." In each city "a variety of objects was presented to the judgment, while each challenged the preference to the rest; and the sciences, not being dwarfed by the restraint of authority, were enabled to make such considerable shoots, as are, even at this time, the objects of our admiration."[16] Intercourse of different groups, importation of arts, and imitation[17] bring about the modification of the culture of any group in the course of time.

Third, Hume makes the important statement: "I have sometimes been inclined to think, that interruptions in the periods of learning, were they not attended by such a destruction of ancient books, and the records of history, would be rather favourable to the arts and sciences, by breaking the progress of authority, and dethroning the tyrannical usurpers over human reason. In this particular, they have the same influence, as interruptions in political governments and societies."[18] He recognizes, therefore, that, in addition to the modification which may be regarded as continuous, it is necessary to take

---

[13] David Hume, as cited, p. 250. [15] *Ibid.*, pp. 181, 196, 254. [17] *Ibid.*, p. 185.
[14] *Ibid.*, p. 180. [16] *Ibid.*, p. 182. [18] *Ibid.*, p. 184.

into consideration the effect of drastic 'interruptions' of a given established order.

The interest in Hume's departure from the conventional point of view of his time is enhanced when we come to examine the group of writings with which, in 1750, Turgot inaugurated his career.[19] Turgot questioned the climatic correlations of Montesquieu,[20] and was thus led to observations like those of Hume, whose essays he had read and even in part translated.[21]

As has been pointed out earlier, Turgot was the first to draw attention to the difference between the types of science represented, on the one hand, by physics, and, on the other, by the joint study of history and of evolution or progress.[22] In scientific inquiry, he held it necessary to begin with the consideration of things as they are—*il faut partir de la nature telle qu'elle est,*[23]—with the existing condition of peoples, both civilized and savage.[24] He took the position that the capabilities of the human species are the same in all places and in all times:[25] "the same senses, the same organs, the spectacle of the same universe," he thought, "have everywhere given to man the same ideas, just as the same needs and the same propensities have everywhere taught him the same arts."[26] Further, it appeared to him that the actual state of the universe presented at the same moment, upon the earth, every possible nuance of barbarism and of civilization, and revealed the existence of 'inequality varied to infinity.'[27] With this background, Turgot expressed ideas on the subject of fixity or stability, of gradual modification, and of the *modus operandi* of change, which may be indicated briefly.

In the first place, he observes that man in isolation and without commerce is everywhere in very much the same condition

---

[19] Turgot, *Œuvres* [nouvelle éd.], par Gustave Schelle, t. 1 (Paris, 1913), pp. 77–364.

[20] *Ibid.*, pp. 140, 262, 304.

[21] Cf. *ibid.*, p. 338, for translation, in part, of Hume's essay on "National Characters."

[22] *Ibid.*, pp. 214–215, 276.

[23] *Ibid.*, p. 219.

[24] *Ibid.*, pp. 138, 257, 260, 279, 284.

[25] *Ibid.*, pp. 118, 139, 217, 277.

[26] *Ibid.*, p. 216.

[27] *Ibid.*, pp. 217, 303–304.

of barbarism.[28] Among more advanced peoples, the *status quo* tends to be maintained through the influence of education, which is one of the great sources of the stability of governments. It is also maintained through the exercise of political power, for despotism induces in the members of the state a lethargic repose, which is opposed to all change and hence to all progress.[29] Finally, it is maintained by a blind conservatism which would confine the sciences within the limits of existing knowledge and preserve unmodified the earliest opinions, and it is in consequence of this spirit that the regions which were the first to become enlightened are not those which have made the greatest advances.[30]

On the other hand, modification of culture is brought about continually through the influence of commerce and intercourse between different peoples;[31] and so it comes about that every nation represents a transition between its neighbors—*chaque nation est la nuance entre les nations ses voisines.*[32] But, apart from contact with others, the culture of any group is always undergoing modification. Thus curiosity multiplies questions, and by dint of groping, and, as it were, by exhausting errors, men arrive finally at some measure of truth.[33] No art can be cultivated during a long period of time without undergoing improvement at the hands of some inventive genius.[34] Consequently, even in the midst of the ignorance of the medieval period, an insensible progress was preparing the way for the brilliant successes of later centuries.[35] Moreover, each step forward gives greater facility for the next, and so the advance of a nation is accelerated day by day.

In the third place, Turgot expresses the view that the human race would have remained forever in a state of mediocrity, had it not been for the disruptive effect of migrations, wars, and conquests. Reason and justice, if heeded, would, in his opinion,

---

[28] David Hume, as cited, pp. 216, 303.

[29] *Ibid.*, pp. 293–294.

[30] *Ibid.*, p. 221.

[31] *Ibid.*, pp. 221–222, 232, 259, 262–263.

[32] *Ibid.*, p. 282.

[33] *Ibid.*, p. 220.

[34] *Ibid.*, pp. 118–119.

[35] *Ibid.*, pp. 133, 230.

have rendered everything fixed, as it has nearly done in China. Vehement fermentation is necessary for the manufacture of good wines, and it is by subversions and ravages that nations have been extended, and governments, in the long run, improved. Only through such means, he thinks, has reason been freed from the constraint of imperfect laws imposed by despotic power.[36] It is particularly noteworthy that Turgot insisted upon the importance of migrations in promoting advance through the mingling of peoples, languages, and customs.[37] "Everything that frees men from their actual state, that opens their eyes to varied scenes, that expands their ideas, that enlightens them, that rouses them, leads them, in the long run, to the good and the true."[38]

Finally, he points out that, after all the fluctuations induced by upheavals, everything must once more approach a state of equilibrium, and reach, eventually, a condition of fixity and tranquillity.[39] So, through alternations of upheaval and calm, mankind as a whole progresses continually toward perfection.[40]

The type of inquiry thus inaugurated does not appear to have been followed up either in the late eighteenth or the early nineteenth century. The reason for this neglect is to be found in the prestige and attractive quality of the 'idea of progress,' which, as we have seen, carries with it the assumption that 'progress' is slow and continuous, necessary and inevitable. In the middle of the nineteenth century, however, the study of differences, taken up in criticism of the racial correlation, led investigators to precisely the same characteristic form of procedure that we have found in the work of Hume and Turgot.

A particularly interesting case is that of W. H. Riehl, who was himself an exponent of the 'race theory' as allied to German nationalism. Riehl's major interest, however, was in the life of the people, and, in his travels through Germany, he came to observe differences between the life of the people in

---

[36] *Ibid.*, pp. 283–285.

[37] *Ibid.*, pp. 120, 137, 217, 222, 223, 230, 232, 260, 261, 272, 280, 281, 289, 345.

[38] *Ibid.*, pp. 283–284.   [39] *Ibid.*, p. 218.   [40] *Ibid.*, p. 285.

the country districts and that of the dwellers in the cities. The result of his observations was the formulation of the idea, in his *Die Naturgeschichte des Volkes* (1854–1855), that there are two great forces in social life. The first force, that of inertia, persistence, conservatism, is represented (*a*) by the peasantry, and (*b*) by the aristocracy; the second force, that of movement, operates primarily in the towns. On the maintenance of equilibrium between the forces of persistence and of movement depend, he thought, the health and well-being of the state.[41]

A more important contribution of the type to which we refer appeared in the *Anthropologie der Naturvölker* (1859–1872) of Theodor Waitz. Adopting, as his point of departure, the study of differences, Waitz went on to show that "the progressive mental development of some peoples, and the remarkable stability of others, depend upon other causes than on the differences of their original mental endowment."[42] In order to understand the various states of civilization in which man is found today, he thought it necessary to investigate, on the one hand, what delays or prevents man's development, or renders his condition stationary, and, on the other, what induces him to leave his natural state, and leads him from one step of development to another.[43] In this investigation, Waitz argued, it will first be necessary to abandon "the false theory, arising from the exclusive view of our European civilization, that there is anything in the nature of man generally, or of some tribes particularly, impelling them to civilization."[44]

In Waitz's judgment, the so-called lower races exhibit no desire to leave the state of barbarism in which they have been from time immemorial; the savage has no romantic longing to see the world; he remains content where he is, unless driven out by want or by enemies.[45] The stationary condition of backward peoples is due to isolation and an unfavorable geographi-

---

[41] G. P. Gooch, *History and Historians in the Nineteenth Century* (3d impression, London, 1920), pp. 574–577.

[42] Theodor Waitz, *Introduction to Anthropology*, ed. by J. F. Collingwood (London, 1863), p. 328.

[43] *Ibid.*, p. 329.   [44] *Ibid.*, p. 352.   [45] *Ibid.*, pp. 328, 342.

cal environment. Thus the backwardness of the Bretons is to be referred to the disadvantages of the area which they inhabit, and the stagnation of the Chinese and Hindus to the relative isolation of their respective countries.[46] In short, he held that "when we see a people, of whatever degree of civilization, not living in contact and reciprocal action with others, we shall generally find a certain stagnation, a mental inertness, and a want of activity, which render any change of social and political condition next to impossible."[47]

Geographical conditions bring about differences in the culture of peoples inhabiting different areas, but do not, of themselves, bring about advancement.[48] Thus the transition from a primitive state to a higher condition of culture was not easier in Europe because of its geographical advantages.[49] Waitz, therefore, proceeds to examine the positive or active influences or stimuli by which men have been induced to leave their primitive state. The most powerful levers acting on civilization are, in his opinion, migrations of peoples and the wars to which these movements lead.[50] A people may be forced to leave its habitat either by a deficiency in the means of subsistence or by a powerful enemy.[51] Migrations, so occasioned, have very important results, Waitz thought, through the reciprocal influence of the various peoples which are brought in contact. In such circumstances, the relationship of peoples is rarely of a peaceful nature. Movement results in war, and while this, unquestionably, has injurious effects on culture, it would appear to be a necessary agency in the advancement of savage peoples. The reason is that war rouses men from mental indolence and physical lethargy; it calls for sustained effort, and stimulates invention; it induces organization, the recognition of common interests, and common action; it brings about the establishment of social classes, which, apparently, is indispensable to the development of higher cultures.[52] In the end, in-

---

[46] *Ibid.*, pp. 340, 342.　　[49] *Ibid.*, p. 342.　　[51] *Ibid.*, p. 344.

[47] *Ibid.*, 348.　　[50] *Ibid.*, p. 344.　　[52] *Ibid.*, pp. 346–348.

[48] *Ibid.*, pp. 329, 341.

termixture produces a remarkable transformation in the temperament and mental characteristics of the peoples affected.[53]

It is apparent, then, that, through following similar steps,
Waitz was led to formulate a scheme of inquiry which was practically the same as that arrived at by Hume and Turgot a
century earlier. This typical form of investigation, it has now
been shown, was developed in each case through taking differences as the point of departure in investigation. The conclusion which follows is, therefore, that the observation of the
present condition of mankind reveals the existence of differences in the culture of different areas, and that the study of
how these differences have come to be as they are leads to a
typical form of inquiry, which is concerned with the investigation of the processes manifested in the phenomena of persistence, modification, and change. It will be recalled that this
procedure coincides with that suggested by Huxley and other
biologists as an alternative to Darwin's procedure in the study
of 'evolution.'

We have seen that, in order to free humanistic inquiry from
the dominating influence of assumptions which we have inherited from the seventeenth and eighteenth centuries, we
must return to the *present* from which, in actuality, all inquiry
sets out. What the present reveals is a world of *differences,* and
the problem that arises is, "How are these differences to be
accounted for?" We have seen, further, that many attempts
have been made in the past to account for cultural differences,
but that almost invariably these efforts have been directed toward the formulation of an explanation in terms of some one
factor, such as 'climate' or 'race,' with the result that the investigation of differences in the culture of human groups has
been narrowed down to special questions in physiology. It has
been pointed out, however, that certain individuals, more particularly Hume and Turgot, who started from the observation
of present differences, followed a different mode of procedure,
and thereby opened out the investigation of cultural differ-

[53] Theodor Waitz, as cited, p. 347.

ences in such a manner as to require the coöperation of all branches of humanistic inquiry. This last point is a matter of such importance that it seems desirable to illustrate, however briefly, the way in which the investigative procedure of Hume and Turgot brings into relation phases of humanistic study which are now being pursued in isolation, and even with mutual distrust.

The point of departure in the scientific study of man must necessarily be the observation of the present condition of human beings throughout the world. The description of the different peoples and cultures of the earth is, today, one of the most significant activities of ethnology, and is an important interest in the study of geography. The descriptive accounts provided by ethnologists and geographers are to be regarded as contributing to the study of man the body of materials without which the major problem of humanistic research could not be formulated in specific terms.

The examination of different cultures as they exist in the present will not, of itself, suffice to show how the given differences have come to be as they are. Valuable as contemporary descriptions unquestionably are, they require to be supported by an equally extensive series of histories. It is obvious that the differences which we find in culture at the present time are recognized as differences of culture in different areas. It is also obvious that all histories are written with respect to the activities of men situated upon restricted parts of the earth's surface. Historical research, as distinguished from historical writing, leads away from 'general' history to the history of more and more limited areas. In order to carry out the study of 'how the differences which we find around us in the world today have come to be as they are,' it will be necessary to make comparison of the experiences of men under different conditions of life, that is, in different areas of the earth's surface; it will be necessary to compare the vicissitudes which have befallen different human groups in the course of time. The scientific study of man must rest, therefore, upon the comparison of histories. As

Buckle, and many others down to Dr. Rivers, have seen, we cannot hope to arrive at scientific knowledge 'solely by studying the history of a single nation.'[54] The reason why many histories must be taken into consideration, in the scientific study of man, is that the aim of this study will be, not the construction of a historical 'synthesis,' but the discovery of processes. We have seen that the diversity of history is a stumbling block for academic historians, and it must remain a difficulty where the object of the historian's activity is the creation of an aesthetic unity. On the other hand, the extraordinary diversity of human experience, in the past, makes possible a scientific study of 'how things work' in the course of time to produce the differences which we are given in the present. The type of inquiry initiated by Hume and Turgot will, therefore, call for the assemblage of historical data upon an unprecedented scale.

On the basis of the materials made available by ethnological, archaeological, and geographical exploration, and by historical research, the initial step in scientific inquiry will be the investigation of the processes which are manifested in fixity and persistence, stagnation and conventionality.

Parenthetically, it may be well to point out that, in speaking of 'fixity' and 'persistence,' what we mean is that, within a given area, certain activities—that is to say, ways of doing things and modes of thought—have been maintained with recognizable uniformity from age to age. These activities constitute the 'culture' of the area in question. It should be observed that the word 'culture' is frequently used to designate the sum total of the acquisitions of any human group, in language, rites, customs, practices, material objects, and ideas. Strictly speaking,

---

[54] T. H. Buckle, *History of Civilization in England*, vol. 1 (new ed., London, 1873), p. 242. Paul Devaux, *Etudes politiques sur l'histoire ancienne et moderne* (Paris, 1875), p. i. Sir H. S. Maine, *Dissertations on Early Law and Custom* (London, 1883), p. 218. Karl Pearson, *The Grammar of Science* (2d ed., London, 1900), p. 359, n. 2. Jean Réville, *Les phases successives de l'histoire des religions* (Paris, 1909), pp. 235–236. Berthold Laufer, *The Beginnings of Porcelain in China* (Chicago, 1917), p. 148. John Dewey, *Human Nature and Conduct* (New York, 1922), p. 110. W. H. R. Rivers, *Social Organization*, ed. by W. J. Perry (New York, 1924), p. 99.

however, 'culture' signifies the work of cultivation; it means the _activity_ through which the products which we assemble in ethnological museums, and which we describe in books, have been brought into existence. Similarly, the word 'tradition' is used at times to designate the sum total of beliefs, opinions, and usages which is handed down from one generation to the next. Yet the word 'tradition' properly means the act of handing down the customs, observances, doctrines of one generation to another. 'Custom' and 'tradition' are terms, therefore, which refer to activities: the doing and thinking of a group, and the transmission of this doing and thinking from generation to generation. The terms 'fixity' and 'persistence' do not refer to the objects which we find in museums, or to the rites and beliefs which we find described in the writings of ethnologists; these terms have reference to the activities of men.

Now, since the publication of John Stuart Mill's *On Liberty* (1859), W. K. Clifford's address "On Some of the Conditions of Mental Development" (1868), Walter Bagehot's *Physics and Politics* (1872), and particularly since the appearance of Gabriel Tarde's *Les lois de l'imitation* (1890), interest in the processes manifested in fixity and persistence has increased with such rapidity that there is no branch of humanistic study in which attention is not now given to these phenomena. It is apparent, for example, that the investigation of the role of imitation and sympathy, of habit and social pressure, in the existence of communities is rapidly becoming the central feature of works on sociology and of social psychology. It would, however, be an error to assume that interest in these processes is restricted to, or that it is attached in some exclusive manner to, sociology and social psychology. The view which recognizes in the investigation of the processes manifested in conservatism, fixity, persistence, and stagnation the point of departure in humanistic study has been arrived at, to all appearance independently, in practically every department of humanistic inquiry. Students of anthropology, history, jurisprudence, politics, of religion, literature, and technology, have all come to perceive the importance of 'social inertia and conservatism'; while folklore is, in its primary aspect, just the study of 'survivals'—a subject fully discussed in *The Doctrine of Survivals* by Margaret T. Hodgen (1936).

The second step in the procedure under consideration calls for the systematic investigation of processes manifested in slow modification.

The study of processes of modification has been most systematically carried out in the field of the history of language. Since even the most cursory examination of linguistic phenomena will reveal the fact that the sounds, syntax, and meaning of words in all languages undergo continuous, slow modification in the course of time, it is not remarkable that a definitely scientific point of view in the investigation of 'linguistic change' should have been attained at a comparatively early date. While the older literature, more especially William Dwight Whitney's *Life and Growth of Language* (1875), is still of interest, the modern study of the history of language dates from the appearance, in 1880, of Hermann Paul's *Principien der Sprachgeschichte*, and its present state is represented by Otto Jespersen's *Language: Its Nature, Development, and Origin* (1923).

Since Plato drew attention to the influence of strangers in modifying the manners of a given group, much has been written on the influence of traders, missionaries, and other intruding individuals in promoting modifications in culture. In consequence, however, of the predominant interest in similarities, inquiry in ethnology, and in other related subjects, such as comparative mythology, has been concerned almost exclusively with the 'diffusion' of culture elements rather than with the investigation of the influence of the adoption of specific culture elements upon the habits and modes of thought of the groups affected. The study of comparative literature, which is given over to the investigation of interchanges between highly cultivated groups, has more nearly approached the procedure in the study of processes of modification established in the history of language.

It is evident, then, that we may regard the investigation of the processes manifested in fixity and persistence, and of the processes manifested in slow modification, as firmly established in contemporary humanistic study. In recognizing this fact, it must also be observed that this type of inquiry cannot be claimed as distinctive of, or as falling exclusively within the jurisdiction of, any one branch of inquiry. The common interest of all humanists in the investigation of these processes points the way, however, to the possibility of a notable advancement of knowledge through coöperative effort and the mutual interchange of ideas.

The third step in the program of study here being considered is the investigation of the *modus operandi* of change.

It is a truism that the thought of the last half-century has been committed to the Darwinian concept of evolution as a slow, continuous process which admits of no 'breaks.' On the other hand, it has not been generally recognized that a generation which has upheld the universal validity of this view of evolution should, at the same time, have entertained a conception which is in direct opposition to that of Darwin. Put in its simplest form, this opposing view is that the 'new' has emerged only at particular moments of history, and then as the result of some fundamental break with the past.

It is not to be assumed that this mode of procedure has been adopted by men who were ignorant of Darwin's work, or who even were consciously opposed to it. For example, in his *Physics and Politics,* Walter Bagehot undertook an exposition of "the application of the principles of 'Natural Selection' and 'Inheritance' to political society." It was the nature of his materials, and not hostility to Darwin, that led him to observe that the action of institutions is "to create what may be called a cake of custom,"[55] and that "the net of custom caught men in distinct spots, and kept each where he stood."[56] From this point of departure, he proceeded to direct attention to the modification of

---

[55] Walter Bagehot, *Physics and Politics* (New York, 1876), p. 27.

[56] *Ibid.,* p. 29.

culture through the influence of the contacts of commerce,[57] and, finally, to insist that "the great difficulty which history records" is that of "breaking the cake of custom."[58] He thus came to lay stress upon the changes which ensue "when the sudden impact of new thoughts and new examples breaks down the compact despotism of the single consecrated code."[59] Again, Ferdinand Brunetière devoted himself to the task of applying the concept of evolution to the study of literature. In his *L'évolution des genres dans l'histoire de la littérature* (1890), he unconsciously follows in the footsteps of Hume, Turgot, Waitz, and Bagehot in pointing out that this task involves (*a*) the study of *la fixation des genres* or of the conditions of stability, (*b*) the study of *les modificateurs des genres,* and (*c*) the study of *la transformation des genres.*[60] The point of view of the philosopher F. A. Lange, already mentioned, might also be referred to in the present connection. It is not questioned that the vogue of Darwinian ideas has had a notable influence in stimulating the interest of humanists in evolutionary problems. It may, however, be said that when any humanist, since 1859, has undertaken an investigation of the *modus operandi* of change, on the basis of his own materials, he has been forced by the evidence before him to formulate, as a minimum, a contrast between conditions characterized by the dominance of custom, conservatism, and fixity, and conditions in which change ensues from some marked disturbance of the established order. As has already been pointed out, this mode of procedure is not new; the point of interest here is that it should have reëmerged with new vigor among men who were predisposed to follow Darwin.

When humanistic students have undertaken the investigation of differences in human groups, they have been led to the observation that change in ways of doing things and in modes of thought has, in the past, been due to some intrusive influence which, for the moment, has interfered with the operation of the

---

[57] Walter Bagehot, as cited, p. 38.   [58] *Ibid.,* p. 53.   [59] *Ibid.,* p. 39.
[60] Ferdinand Brunetière, *L'évolution des genres* (7e éd., Paris, 1922), pp. 20–22.

processes manifested in fixity and persistence. In other words, change ensues only upon the occurrence, at some given time and in some given place, of an intrusion of such a character as to disrupt the established order.

The form in which this theory of intrusions has most deeply impressed itself upon investigators since the middle of the eighteenth century is that significant changes in culture have been due to the influence of migrations of peoples, with the accompanying collision of different types of civilization. A brief indication of inquiries to which this theory leads will provide additional illustration of the way in which scientific procedure in the investigation of change in time brings into close relation separate aspects of humanistic study.

In the first place, it is obvious that the study of migrations must begin with the fullest annalistic statement of what can be known in regard to 'the wanderings of peoples.' Unfortunately, while interest in these movements has been prominent in literature for two centuries, the phenomena have been accepted by academic historians merely as a series of happenings from which selection is to be made for narrative histories of medieval Europe. Even on the historical or purely factual side, therefore, the investigation of migrations in Europe leaves much to be desired, while the study of migrations in Asia is in a seriously backward condition.

Again, the investigation of migrations raises at once the question of the historical conditions under which such movements have taken place. The two outstanding theories on this point, at the present time, are: (*a*) that migrations have been the result of an excess of population in certain areas; and (*b*) that they have been occasioned by desiccation or change of climate. Each of these theories has met with opposition, but on all sides there has been too great a disposition to rely upon *a priori* considerations, and on the strictly historical side the subject has not received the consideration which its importance demands. It must be urged that such a problem as this can be dealt with successfully only on the basis of the comparison of histories of different regions. As bearing upon the interdependence of humanistic studies, it will be observed that the prosecution of this problem would demand not only historical investigation, but also a searching inquiry into the economic question of the increase of human population, and into the relation of population to the means of subsistence.

The most important aspect of the study of migrations, however, will be the investigation of the changes which these movements have occasioned. In the mode of inquiry under consideration, 'change' is presumed to follow from the shock of an intrusion, and the typical instance of an intrusion is that of a migrating group coming into collision with another differing from it considerably in culture, and remaining upon the invaded territory.

The effect of the collision and conflict ensuing from migratory movements which has been most attentively considered is the change in established institutions and social organization. Medieval European history, on the 'constitutional' side, is concerned primarily with the changes brought about by the barbarian invasions. The value of the study of institutional history cannot be overestimated. Intrusions are 'events,' and the historical facts merit the most exhaustive investigation. Unfortunately, these inquiries, as conducted by academic historians, have usually been restricted to one or another of the countries of western Europe. Since, however, the aim of science is to find out 'how things work,' and particularly to discover the processes set in operation in exceptional circumstances, it must be insisted that the study of institutions necessarily involves the comparison of different histories.

The factual inquiry into the effect of collision and conflict in breaking down an established social order is, in itself, to be regarded merely as a preliminary step. The point that has come to impress itself, in recent years, on the minds of students is that, as a result of the breakdown of customary modes of action and of thought, the individual experiences a 'release' from the restraints and constraints to which he has been subject, and gives evidence of this 'release' in aggressive self-assertion. The overexpression of individuality is one of the marked features of all epochs of change. On the other hand, the study of the psychological effects of collision and contact between different groups reveals the fact that the most important aspect of 'release' lies, not in freeing the soldier, warrior, or berserker from the restraint of conventional modes of action, but in freeing the individual judgment from the inhibitions of conventional modes of thought. It will thus be seen that the study of the *modus operandi* of change in time gives a common focus to the efforts of political historians, of the historians of literature and of ideas, of psychologists, and of students of ethics and the theory of education.

The brief survey which has just been made has not been designed as an introduction to a complex and difficult subject of investigation, but as an indication of the way in which the approach to the study of man initiated by Hume and Turgot actually brings into relation phases of humanistic study which, at the present time, are being pursued without a common focus or united aim. Further, it would seem that this coördination of diverse interests constitutes in itself important evidence of the validity of the type of inquiry which has here been presented.

Chapter 16

Illustrations of Present Difficulties

I F WE ARE to overcome the difficulties which stand in the way of a strictly scientific study of man, it will be necessary to bring to light the sources of these embarrassments. The thesis of this book is that our present difficulties, in the field of the humanities, are the direct result of a continued adherence to certain methodological conceptions which had their beginning in the seventeenth century, and which received their characteristic formulation in the first half of the eighteenth century. It is imperative that we should understand that, in a sincere and devoted effort to reach a strictly scientific basis for the study of man, the humanists of the eighteenth century introduced an explicit separation between the study of events and the study of change. Change to them represented nature's orderly procedure for attaining certain predetermined ends; events to them appeared as accidental interferences with the natural order of change. Hence it was believed that the scientific study of change must proceed by making abstraction from the events recorded by historians. Further, the conception of a natural order of change was identified with the idea of progress. The humanists of the eighteenth century devoted themselves to the task of defining the character or nature of progress, and arrived at the conclusion that it was a natural movement which proceeded, slowly and continuously, in a desirable direction. The influence of these methodological conceptions is evident today in the continued separation between history, on the one hand, and the sciences of economics, sociology, and anthropology, on the other, and in the continued acceptance of the idea of progress as the directive concept in humanistic studies. To appreciate the significance of this inheritance, and to recognize fully the influence of the idea of progress on humanistic inquiry, it will be advisable to examine a number of current contributions to different aspects of the study of man. The writings selected for examination are believed to be representative of conditions existing now in the social sciences.

In the study of history, the activities of scholars give evidence of a widespread dissatisfaction with the conventional procedure of 'academic' historians. This dissatisfaction is the result of a number of converging influences. Thus the remarkable extension of our knowledge of ancient history through the prosecution of archaeological exploration during the last half century, and the equally remarkable extension of our insight into the social customs and religious practices of ancient peoples through the enlargement of anthropological knowledge, have led to a new emphasis upon the study of the conditions of culture and the phenomena of change. Again, in an intellectual world of which the most conspicuous characteristic is the activity of scientific workers, it was inevitable that a number of historical students should come eventually to ask themselves whether important results might not also be reached in the field of history through the utilization of scientific modes of procedure.

In this situation, the dissatisfaction of historical students has found expression in the plea for some new departure in history writing. The term 'new history' appears to have been given a certain currency by James Harvey Robinson; his books *The New History* (1912) and *The Mind in the Making* (1921) may, therefore, be presumed to furnish a clue to some of the underlying conceptions of the group of historians opposed to 'traditional' or 'academic' history.

The background of Professor Robinson's discussion appears to be a strong emotional reaction against what he describes as "the shocking derangement of human affairs which now prevails in most civilized countries, including our own."[1] The

---

[1] J. H. Robinson, *The Mind in the Making* (New York, 1921), p. 4.

'predicaments and confusions' of civilization should, he thinks, have supplied an incitement to study, but actually we have made no such advance in the knowledge of man as has been made during the past few centuries in the study of nature.[2] In fact, "the progress of mankind in the scientific knowledge and regulation of human affairs has remained almost stationary for over two thousand years,"[3] with the result that "it seems as if we had not yet got anywhere near a real science of man."[4] The author agrees with Mr. H. G. Wells that the situation with which civilization is confronted is coming more and more to be "a race between education and catastrophe."[5] In these circumstances, what seems to Professor Robinson necessary is "to bring to bear on human affairs that critical type of thought and calculation for which the remunerative thought about molecules and chromosomes has prepared the way."[6] Hence the essential matter for consideration resolves itself into the question of how scientific modes of thought may be introduced in the study of man. Professor Robinson maintains that this result may be accomplished by means of the 'new' history.

It should be observed that the type of history proposed differs from the old merely in respect to the selection of the factual data to be included in the narrative. The writer of the 'new' history, not being interested in battles and sieges or the conduct of kings, will select some other thread for his narrative than the old political one.[7] The 'new' history is to be envisaged, then, as a narrative of the old form in which the facts presented have been selected with a new purpose in view. This purpose is determined for Professor Robinson by his conception of the intellectual activities required for bringing scientific thought to bear upon the problems of society.

If only, Professor Robinson remarks, men could come to look at things differently from the way they now generally do, no inconsiderable part of the evils which afflict society would van-

[2] J. H. Robinson, as cited, p. 7.   [4] *Ibid.*, p. 11.   [6] *Ibid.*, p. 12.

[3] *Ibid.*, p. 8.   [5] *Ibid.*, p. 228.

[7] J. H. Robinson, *The New History* (New York, 1912), pp. 138–139.

ish away or remedy themselves automatically.[8] He appeals to historical evidence to show that in order to clear the way for the modern discoveries in science "it was necessary to discard practically all the consecrated notions of the world and its workings which had been held by the best and wisest and purest of mankind down to three hundred years ago."[9] He infers, therefore, that what is needed, in order to bring about similar results in the study of society, is that we should proceed to "the thorough reconstruction of our mind," that we should create for ourselves "an unprecedented attitude of mind," that our aim should be to "endeavor manfully to change our minds."[10] This needed change is to be effected by permitting certain historical facts, of his selection, "to play a constant part in our thinking." These facts would tend to free our minds so as to permit honest thought; they would "automatically eliminate a very considerable portion of the gross stupidity and blindness which characterize our present thought and conduct in public affairs"; and, above all, they would "contribute greatly to developing the needed scientific attitude towards human concerns."[11] On the basis of this theory of the influence of historical facts, the purpose of the 'new' history will be to utilize historical materials in such a way as to promote a "beneficent change of mind," "intellectual regeneration," and "change of heart."[12]

If we are to have a science of society, then, we must change our minds in regard to the ideas about society which we have inherited from the past. These ideas, however, are adhered to and supported by the conservative element in our present social organization. It is this element, Professor Robinson insists, which actively opposes the change and regeneration of thought which is needed. History has been systematically utilized to substantiate the claims of the conservatives. 'By right,' however, it is the weapon of the radicals, who should wrest it from the hands of their opponents. The 'new' history, therefore, will

[8] *The Mind in the Making*, pp. 3, 198.

[9] *Ibid.*, p. 25. [11] *Ibid.*, p. 14.

[10] *Ibid.*, pp. 5, 13, 211. [12] *Ibid.*, pp. 4, 16, 49, 172, 217.

devote itself to using this weapon 'on the conservative' with the most decisive effect.[13]

Professor Robinson thus advocates the view that what is required in order to arrive at a science of society is a change of mind from the conservative to the radical attitude, this change to be brought about through the instrumentality of the 'new' history. Unusual as this conception may appear to be, it follows, naturally enough, from his theory of progress. The old history, identified with the conservative interest, is indifferent, he says, to the whole question of human development;[14] the older historian uses such terms as 'progress' and 'decline,' 'human nature,' 'historical continuity,' and 'civilization' without any adequate understanding of their meaning.[15] The 'new' history, on the other hand, is directly concerned with 'progress' and 'betterment,'[16] and regards conservatism as "a hopeless and wicked anachronism."[17] The 'new' history recognizes, in the 'natural order,' "a mysterious unconscious impulse" which has always been unsettling the existing conditions and pushing forward; an impulse which represents "the inherent radicalism of nature herself." This impulse or power, he holds, "must be reckoned with by the most exacting historian and the hardest-headed man of science." It is the "innate force of change," which has been silently operating despite the lethargy and indifference of man himself. It follows, therefore, that the one thing needful is that we should "coöperate with the vital principle of betterment."[18] Coöperation with progress or betterment means overcoming the obstacles placed in its way by the conservative element in society, and represents the activity necessary in order to bring social inquiries within the scope of scientific procedure. If, at this point, the suspicion should suggest itself that Professor Robinson seems to place the recommendations of political and social 'radicals' on a footing with the conclusions of scientific investigators, the doubt will not be allayed when

---

[13] *The New History*, p. 252.

[14] *Ibid.*, p. 89.

[15] *Ibid.*, p. 92.

[16] *Ibid.*, pp. 21, 23, 130, 142.

[17] *Ibid.*, p. 265.

[18] *Ibid.*, pp. 264–265.

we find him saying that "we have learned as yet to respect only one class of fundamental innovators, those dedicated to natural science and its applications—the social innovator is still generally suspect,"[19] or when we read that "the conscious reformer who appeals to the future is the final product of a progressive order of things."[20]

Professor Robinson is undoubtedly in earnest, and the reception which his books have been accorded demonstrates that others besides himself feel that civilization is threatened,[21] and that scientific knowledge would enable man to direct his affairs more intelligently.[22] Some part of Professor Robinson's audience may possibly be gratified by his identification of the 'radical' with the 'scientist'; by his inciting phrase that it is only fear that holds us back;[23] by his call for a great revolution which will substitute purpose for tradition.[24] On the other hand, in the presence of this identification the critic will be forced to ask what the author actually means by 'science' and 'scientific knowledge.' Science, he says, "is but the most accurate information available about the world."[25] Scientific method he identifies with "an appreciation of the overwhelming significance of the small, the common, and the obscure, and an unhesitating rejection of all theological, supernatural, and anthropocentric explanations."[26] This statement will certainly appear inadequate, but, if we compare it with his description of the 'achievements' of historical inquiry during the last sixty or seventy years,[27] the conclusion will be forced upon us that Professor Robinson has derived his conceptions of science and of scientific method solely from academic teachers of history. It must be admitted that Professor Robinson has been too deeply absorbed in his generous enthusiasm for 'betterment' to find out how the student of nature actually goes to work.[28] It must be

---

[19] *The Mind in the Making*, p. 138.
[20] *The New History*, p. 264.
[21] *The Mind in the Making*, p. 206.
[22] *Ibid.*, p. 157.
[23] *Ibid.*, p. 209.

[24] *Ibid.*, p. 212.
[25] *Ibid.*, p. 208.
[26] *The New History*, p. 48.
[27] *Ibid.*, p. 75.
[28] Cf. above, ch. 13.

confessed that his plan for arriving at scientific results in the study of society by the process of changing one's mind is somewhat too simple. If we are to set on foot a scientific study of man or of society, we must get beyond Bacon and Descartes, on whose guidance Professor Robinson confidently relies. If we are to undertake scientific investigation in the field of the humanities, we must be prepared to recognize that the acceptance of 'progress' as 'natural' and continuous involves the acceptance of some 'mysterious impulse' to which this necessary and inevitable movement is due.

The views of Professor Robinson betray the influence of three phases of thought which recur insistently in all contemporary discussions of the applicability of scientific method in the study of history. In the first place, the advocates of a 'new' history, while disapproving established conventions in history writing, aim merely at substituting some other content for the politico-military interest of historical narrative. Historiography remains the goal of their efforts. They do not seem to have considered the possibility that the results of a scientific study of historical facts might be expected to take a form differing widely from historical narration. In the second place, the 'new' historian accepts the idea of progress as the directive concept for his efforts, regardless of the fact that he has taken over this idea, without critical examination, from the philosophers of history of the eighteenth and nineteenth centuries, whose work he unhesitatingly condemns. In the third place, the dissenters from historical tradition greatly oversimplify the procedure necessary for arriving at scientific results.

This last phase may here be illustrated from the significant address on "Law in History" which Edward Potts Cheyney delivered, in 1923, as president of the American Historical Association.[29] History, the great course of human affairs, Professor Cheyney says, has not been the result of chance, it has been controlled by immutable, self-existent law.[30] "Man is sim-

---

[29] *American Historical Review,* 29 (1924), pp. 231–248.

[30] *Ibid.,* p. 235.

ply a part of a law-controlled world."[31] What is necessary, then, is that the student should set about the task of reducing the vast multifariousness of history to simplicity, of finding the law or laws which underlie its apparent lawlessness.[32] These natural laws we must accept whether we want to or not; their workings we cannot obviate, however much we may thwart them to our own failure and disadvantage.[33] The conception of 'laws' here expressed raises difficulties in regard to the "free choice and free action of man"[34] which Professor Cheyney, like John Stuart Mill before him, endeavors to face. His conclusion is that "if the action of man has been conformable to law it has been effective; when he has worked along with the great forces of history he has influenced constructively the course of events; when his action has violated historic law the results have been destructive, momentary, subject to reversal. Men have always been and are free to act; the results of their actions will depend on the conformity or nonconformity of these actions to historic law."[35] If, however, we substitute in this passage 'the will of God' for 'historic law,' the statement would appear to satisfy even the exacting theological requirements of our Calvinistic forefathers.

In the body of his address, Professor Cheyney formulates six 'historic laws.' First, "looking over the field of history there is evident a law of continuity. All events, conditions, institutions, personalities, come from immediately preceding events, conditions, institutions, personalities. . . . The continuity of history is not merely a fact; it is a law."[36] "Second, looking over the field of history, there seems to be a law of impermanence, of mutability. The fall of empires is one of the most familiar of historic phenomena. . . . So persistent and infinitely repeated has been this disappearance of successive organizations of men and types of civilization that it gives every indication of being the result of a law rather than of a mere succession of chances."[37] "Thirdly,

---

[31] *Ibid.*, p. 236.
[32] *Ibid.*, p. 236.
[33] *Ibid.*, p. 245.
[34] *Ibid.*, p. 245.
[35] *Ibid.*, p. 246.
[36] *Ibid.*, p. 237.
[37] *Ibid.*, p. 238.

looking over the field of history there seems to be a law of interdependence—interdependence of individuals, of classes, of
tribes, of nations. The human race seems to be essentially an
organism, a unit. No part of the human race in history has
really progressed by the injury of another."[38] "Fourthly, there
seems to be a law of democracy, a tendency for all government
to come under the control of all the people."[39] "Fifthly, looking
over the field of history I am convinced there is a law of necessity for free consent. Human beings are free agents in their
relations to other human beings; they cannot permanently be
compelled. Not only should all government be by the consent
of the governed but all government has been by the consent of
the governed."[40] "Sixthly, and lastly, so far as this groping search
extends, there seems to be a law of moral progress. Obscurely
and slowly, yet visibly and measurably, moral influences in
human affairs have become stronger and more widely extended
than material influences."[41] If we look over these points, as enumerated, it will, I think, become apparent that what Professor
Cheyney has assembled is sentences contributory to a definition of the idea of progress. His 'laws' are heads of discourse
taken unconsciously from the discussions of progress during
the last two hundred and fifty years. His formulation, then, is
simply an added demonstration of the pervading influence of
the idea of progress in our present-day thought, as well as of the
type of result to which this idea inevitably leads.

Professor Cheyney's address is to be accepted as an important
event in American historical scholarship, for it is tangible evidence of the growing appreciation of the need for scientific
method in historical study. It is of importance, therefore, to
examine the procedure which Professor Cheyney thinks proper
for the discovery of laws. "What," he asks, "are these laws like?"
"There is but one way to find out—to do as others in their various fields have done before, to consider the phenomena, to
make a more or less happy guess at some large principle, then
to test it by a wider comparison with the facts; if so be that a

---

[38] *Op. cit.*, p. 240.   [39] *Ibid.*, p. 241.   [40] *Ibid.*, p. 243.   [41] *Ibid.*, p. 244.

generalization can be found which we can fairly call a law of history."[42] Now this statement describes, with essential accuracy, the methodology of the Cartesian period, from which the 'Newtonians' of the early eighteenth century made earnest efforts to escape. The results at which science aims today are not, however, guesses, derived from a general inspection of any broad field of inquiry, but are accurate descriptions of the way in which things work to bring about the results which we are given in experience. It is not sufficient, in our present situation, to echo Buckle. Professor Cheyney's contribution emphasizes the necessity which confronts the humanist of familiarizing himself with the historical background of methodological conceptions in his own field, of recognizing the influence upon his thought of the ever-present idea of progress, of forming a clear conception of the results at which science aims, and of the steps which are necessary for their determination.

The three phases of thought described above are fully represented in the work of M. Henri Berr, the projector and editor of what may be regarded as the most ambitious effort of historical scholarship in our generation, the series of volumes entitled *L'évolution de l'humanité.*[43]

For a quarter of a century, M. Berr has advocated a 'new' history, designated *la synthèse historique,* which he sets in opposition to *l'histoire traditionnelle.* Despite the author's criticism of *la synthèse érudite* and *les historiens intuitifs,*[44] the difference between the new and the old is not readily apparent. Apart from the introductions provided by the editor, the separate volumes of *L'évolution de l'humanité* would scarcely impress the reader as a new departure in historical inquiry. The series, as described by M. Berr, is to constitute a 'universal history.' In

[42] *Ibid.,* p. 236.

[43] For exposition of his views, see: Henri Berr, *L'avenir de la philosophie, esquisse d'une synthèse des connaissances fondée sur l'histoire* (Paris, 1899); *La synthèse en histoire, essai critique et théorique* (Paris, 1911); "Introduction générale," in Edmond Perrier, *La terre avant l'histoire* (Paris, 1920), pp. v–xxvi; *L'histoire traditionnelle et la synthèse historique* (Paris, 1921).

[44] *La synthèse en histoire,* pp. 5–14, 232–242.

his opinion, the mass of detailed information accumulated by
historical scholars in recent times has now forced upon us the
necessity for some kind of synthesis; while the solidarity of
mankind, the unity which a world politics, a world economics,
a world civilization has introduced, "invites us to reflect upon
the rôle which the world factor has played from the beginning." There is room, M. Berr thinks, for a new synthesis
"which shall include Humanity, from its origins, and the Earth
as a whole." The special feature which is to distinguish this
new synthesis is that it will have 'a real unity': history in its entirety, bound together by unity of plan and unity of directive
ideas.[45] The new synthesis will be marked by a preoccupation
with *l'ensemble,* the whole as such.[46] The point of view here expressed is, obviously, a familiar one. Many efforts of the same
sort have been made since the publication of Bossuet's *Discours
sur l'histoire universelle,* and the composition of a world history has at all times implied the presence of a unifying idea in
the mind of the writer. It cannot be said, therefore, that in its
most general aspects the program of M. Berr marks a super-
session of established procedure.

The aim of M. Berr's theoretical discussion of synthesis in
history is to lay the foundation for a narrative of universal
history, and this aim brings him face to face with the problem
of the selection of materials to be incorporated in his construction. Here, again, the phraseology employed is familiar. Some
facts, he says, are insignificant, others are important. We can
dominate and systematize the past only by making elimina-
tions, as accident has already done for the remote past, and we
must consign to oblivion something even of what has been
preserved. The historian must be prepared to reject "negligible
events" (*les contingences négligeables*).[47] In this process of elimination, the new synthesis will, he thinks, be more effective
than the old in determining what is of importance in history,
and what is to be ignored.[48] It would appear, however, that in

---

[45] *Introduction générale*, p. vi.   [47] *Ibid.*, p. xii.

[46] *Ibid.*, p. xix.   [48] *La synthèse en histoire*, p. 21.

taking this point of view, M. Berr has, to a certain extent, over-looked the fact that selection proceeds, under all circumstances, with reference to the particular interests of the individual historian. What is actually implied in his statement is that the new synthesis will be able to decide *plus efficacement* than the old what facts are of importance or the reverse—for the new synthesis. In short, M. Berr's *Synthèse en histoire* is a special logic (*un traité de logique spéciale*) designed to provide a basis for the selection of facts to be presented in his particular universal history.

It is admitted at once that this is not M. Berr's conception of the significance of his efforts. In his view, the great need of the present is that historical synthesis or construction should be placed upon a scientific basis. Scientific inquiry, in his opinion, is the investigation of causes. The procedure of historians in dealing with causation, he points out, has been a naïve reliance upon intuitive estimates of personal motives and of individual character.[49] In opposition to this procedure, he proposes that historical synthesis should be made scientific in the fullest sense of the word[50] by means of an analysis of causation. His ambition is to determine in an exact manner the method of science in relation to history,[51] and to provide a basis for a scientific synthesis of the history of mankind by making a conceptual analysis of the nature of the causes operative in history.[52] It must be understood, however, that M. Berr's inquiry, in *La synthèse en histoire*, is not an investigation of historical facts for the purpose of arriving inductively at 'causes,' but, rather, is a critical examination and putting together of the views of different theorists in regard to causation in the historical field.[53]

In his effort "to unravel the tangled skein of causality," M. Berr discovers three kinds of causal relations in human evolution: relations of mere succession, where the facts are simply

---

[49] *Ibid.*, pp. 48, 53, 117.

[50] *Ibid.*, p. 23; *Introduction générale*, pp. viii, xvi, xxiv.

[51] *La synthèse en histoire*, p. 258.

[52] *Ibid.*, pp. 42, 53, 260.   [53] *Ibid.*, pp. viii, 38–39, 42, 53–54.

determined by others; relations that are constant, where the facts are linked to others by necessity; and relations of internal linkage, where the facts are rationally connected with others. These causal relations correspond to three orders of facts, or elements of history, which he describes as (1) contingent, accidental, or crude facts, representing the fortuitous element or *hasard* in history; (2) necessary facts, institutions or social necessities, representing the element of immobility or repetition; (3) facts of 'inner logic,' representing the element of *tendance et durée,* the direction and continuance of movement.[54] These kinds of relation and types of fact, it should be observed, correspond to the respective interests of 'traditional' history, sociology, and the philosophy of progress or evolution.[55] M. Berr's theory of synthesis, then, is that the construction of a universal history, if it is to be scientific, must embody the results attained in their separate fields by historians, sociologists, and 'evolutionary' philosophers. Since M. Berr remains a theorist, and does not himself essay the task of historical construction, his undertaking is completed when he has arrived at this conclusion.

In his writings, which are wholly theoretical, M. Berr has enumerated certain classes of data, factual and conceptual, with which the humanist of today must be prepared to reckon. He cannot ignore events, institutions, or the idea of progress. The enumeration of these elements, however, does not of itself bring them into relation with one another; for one reason, because they represent different categories of ideas. History, for example, is a record of facts of a particular order, namely, 'events.' Sociology, as described by M. Berr, is the study of institutions, that is, of entities which have a more or less continuous existence, which are subject to modification and change, and which may be affected by events. The idea of progress or of evolution represents the intellectual effort to grasp the significance of change in relation to some given class of entities, this change being conceived of as independent of the influence of

---

[54] *La synthèse en histoire,* p. 159; *Introduction générale,* pp. viii–ix, xv.
[55] Cf. *La synthèse en histoire,* pp. 55 ff., 114 ff., 140 ff.

events. The idea of progress is a product of reflection, and involves the belief that there is a progressive movement in human
affairs, that this movement is continuous, and that it proceeds
in a desirable direction.

In the presence of this highly complex situation in humanistic study, M. Berr surrenders the possibility of introducing a
clarification of thought and of procedure by giving his un-
qualified adherence to the belief in the idea of progress. "We
are concerned," he says, "with retracing the road which humanity has traveled; with retracing that road (which a blind instinct, obscure forces, and a multiplicity of circumstances have
forced it to take) by understanding why it has been followed.
In the course of the ages, amid the efforts, ambitions, struggles,
and the varied destinies of groups, in spite of stumblings,
detours, and setbacks, humanity advances."[56] The influence of
M. Berr's adherence to this belief is apparent throughout his
work. The aim of inquiry, in his opinion, is to render intelligible and to enable us to follow the progressive movement
which gives meaning to the life of humanity.[57] In M. Berr's
procedure, however, an understanding of this movement is to
be derived, not from historical investigation, but from analysis
of what he describes as the 'inner logic' of evolution or progress. This logical factor, he believes, "is explanatory in the most
profound sense of the word; it is that which gives to evolution
its real continuity, its inner law." The logical factor it is which
alone produces the new in the course of time; it alone is creative.[58] Logic itself, however, proceeds from a principle which is
the motive force of history, namely, *la tendance de l'être à per-
sévérer dans son être, la tendance de l'être à être pleinement,
à être sans limites.*[59] So the phenomena of history come to be
explained in terms such as a 'will to change,' a 'will to growth,'

[56] *Introduction générale*, p. xx.

[57] *Ibid.*, p. xvi.

[58] Cf. *La synthèse en histoire*, p. 155; *Introduction générale*, p. xii; *L'histoire
traditionnelle*, p. 47.

[59] *La synthèse en histoire*, p. 158; *Introduction générale*, p. xii.

and a 'will to culture.'[60] In the last analysis, logic is defined by M. Berr as the scientific equivalent of the doctrine of final cause; the inner movement of history is teleological, and represents *la causalité de l'utile ou du bien*.[61]

A consideration of M. Berr's theory of historical synthesis, then, brings to light one or two points of some interest for the present discussion. In the first place, while he says that "it is when we reject negligible events that the role of 'logic' in the life of societies is best realized," what he actually means is that the 'logical factor' can be made to appear only if we reject such historical evidence as is in conflict with this conception. The facts to be incorporated in universal history are to be selected in the light of their accordance with his theory of an 'inner logic.' In the second place, his theory assumes the validity of the idea of progress; if this be rejected, his system disappears. In the third place, his explanation of universal history in terms of 'inner logic,' like all explanations which are based upon an acceptance of the idea of progress, leads beyond any possible scientific activity by requiring the supposition of a 'mysterious impulse,' an 'inner principle,' an *élan vital*. Briefly, the assumption of progress, as a directive concept in the study of history, leads beyond the facts to some such philosophical system as that of M. Bergson.[62]

In no one of the social sciences has the problem of method evoked a wider interest than in anthropology. As has been pointed out earlier, the movement of thought in this field has been toward recognition of the fact that the cultures of backward or primitive groups must be regarded, equally with those of advanced peoples, as products or results of activities in the past, and hence as calling for historical investigation. While it is true that written documents are not available for the study of the cultural history of backward groups, this does not mean that the possibility of historical inquiry must be abandoned;

---

[60] *Introduction générale*, p. xiii: "une 'volonté de changement,' une 'volonté d'accroissement,' une 'volonté de culture.' "

[61] *La synthèse en histoire*, p. 149.   [62] *Ibid.*, p. 144.

it simply means that the anthropologist or ethnologist will be forced to employ a technique in his inquiries different from that employed in the study of the cultures of Europe. This difference in technique must not be permitted, however, to obscure the fact that the methodological problem in anthropology is the same as that in history.

Notwithstanding the movement of thought to which reference has just been made, it must be admitted that anthropologists in general, when they turn from the labor of describing existing cultures to the work of interpreting the data collected, cling tenaciously to methodological conceptions inherited from the eighteenth century. The result of this adherence is that investigation based upon actual historical evidence is still subordinated to the procedure of elaborating arguments in regard to the origin and development of culture in terms of conceptual abstractions. To observe the consequences of this procedure, it will be necessary only to examine Clark Wissler's *Man and Culture.*

In its most general aspect, Dr. Wissler's book is a discussion of "the fundamental similarities between cultures."[63] "A state of parallelism exists," he remarks, "whatever be the cause."[64] As a consequence of this point of departure, a considerable part of the work (chs. 6–9) is occupied with a presentation of the usual views of how cultures have come to be similar, that is, through independent invention, diffusion, and convergence, in which, as was to be expected, the emphasis falls upon the process of 'diffusion,' natural or organized. This statement of accepted views is to be regarded, however, merely as a background for the author's explanation of similarities. Examination of different human groups leads Wissler to observe that, while actual cultures vary in their contents, they fall into types, so that any given culture may be regarded as a variant of some one of a limited number of types.[65] Further, while these types vary, they will all fit into one general picture or pattern, and

[63] Clark Wissler, *Man and Culture* (New York, 1923), p. 77.
[64] *Ibid.,* p. 194.   [65] *Ibid.,* pp. 25, 32, 55, etc.

this general pattern for culture has prevailed since the earliest stone age.[66] The universal pattern is arrived at by observing that when we have made a purely conceptual 'culture scheme' or classification of culture elements, by abstraction from the actual specific cultures existing in the world, "the same general outline will fit all of them."[67] Thus, as a result of an initial concentration of attention on similarities, the author is led to notice that the content of actual cultures may be classified under a number of headings,[68] and this fact he erects into a conceptual entity, designated 'the universal pattern.' Subsequently, it is this entity which takes precedence, and the author discovers, first, that "the universal pattern, like a new kind of germ-plasm, fastens its inherent form upon each infant culture,"[69] and, second, that similarities "stand as the triumphs of the universal pattern."[70] In other words, he find that similarities are the expression of similarity.

More specifically, Wissler takes the view that one of the principal aims of anthropology is the investigation of origins. Since history is unequal to this task, it must devolve upon the analytic student of culture.[71] He argues, then, that the problem of the origin of culture resolves itself into the problem of the origin of the universal pattern,[72] with which history can have nothing to do.[73] Following this step, he is led to discover that the factors which determine the universal pattern lie in the 'original nature' of man, and consequently it is to this we must look for the 'primary' origin of culture.[74] Since there is no great difference between the individual problem and that of the race, we may, he thinks, regard the universal pattern as being largely determined by the number and kind of the inborn responses which the baby possesses. The universal pattern is the functional pattern for inborn human behavior. The pattern is

[66] Clark Wissler, as cited, p. 226.   [67] *Ibid.*, p. 75.
[68] The culture scheme is given on p. 74; its main divisions are: 1. Speech, 2. Material traits, 3. Art, 4. Mythology and scientific knowledge, 5. Religious practices, 6. Family and social systems, 7. Property, 8. Government, 9. War.
[69] *Ibid.*, p. 223.   [71] *Ibid.*, p. 246.   [73] *Ibid.*, p. 263.
[70] *Ibid.*, p. 232.   [72] *Ibid.*, pp. 260–265.   [74] *Ibid.*, p. 269.

based upon psycho-physical functions, which are inborn, and is to be considered nothing less than a 'set' in the germ-plasm of man.[75] Thus similarities are explained as being due to the 'nature' of man, which is just the assumption with which the methodologists of the eighteenth century started out.

A second important aspect of Dr. Wissler's book is his theory of progress. Here it should be observed that the author concerns himself primarily with Culture as an objective body of data, independent of human beings.[76] In his view, therefore, "tribes may come and tribes may go, but culture goes on forever."[77] Culture is a 'true continuum'; it constitutes a unitary series, from which "nothing really important seems to have been lost to the world."[78] Culture has a career,[79] and this Wissler envisages as a march upward and onward which has proceeded with an ever accelerating pace.[80] Culture is a whole which has grown by accumulation.[81] The evolution or progress of this whole consists in the 'elaboration and enrichment' of its content, but it is to be understood that civilization is a matter of bulk rather than of complexity.[82]

While Culture as a whole grows by accumulation, actual culture systems, identified with tribal or national entities, rise and fall, following out their careers according to discoverable laws.[83] "In reality, what we find in culture is one endless round of cycles."[84] "Tribal cultures have life cycles, like individuals of a species; they spring from parent cultures, grow, mature, beget other cultures, decline and eventually die."[85] Life cycles are thus repeated, though the content of different culture systems is not necessarily identical. "It is not to be expected that two cultures will run through their life cycles with the same absolute sequence of events, but they do tend to travel on the same type curve."[86] All culture systems are identified with areas,

---

[75] *Ibid.*, pp. 256, 264, 267, 272, 279.

[76] *Ibid.*, pp. 49, 99, 108, 181, 252, etc.

[77] *Ibid.*, p. 39.

[78] *Ibid.*, pp. 36, 39, 40, 179.

[79] *Ibid.*, p. 326.

[80] *Ibid.*, pp. 255, 326.

[81] *Ibid.*, pp. 34, 40, 41, etc.

[82] *Ibid.*, p. 97.

[83] *Ibid.*, pp. 40, 179, 195, 198, 223, 239, 247.

[84] *Ibid.*, p. 198.

[85] *Ibid.*, p. 212.

[86] *Ibid.*, p. 195.

and, from time to time, the center, or most typical culture, shifts its geographical position, "not unlike the passing of life's activities from father to son."[87]

It will be observed that in these theories of progress we have two distinct conceptions of what has happened in the past, and the separation between them becomes even clearer when we examine Wissler's attitude toward historical inquiry. First, then, corresponding to the unitary theory of culture as a whole growing by accumulation, we find the results of analytical investigation stated in the form of a generalized unilinear history of culture,[88] or of generalized histories of culture traits, such as 'horse culture' and the 'maize complex.'[89] Second, corresponding to the pluralistic theory that separate culture systems are like individuals, we find the results of historical inquiry stated in the form of a scheme or model of the *modus operandi* of change. That this distinction is made consciously is evident from the author's statement that a knowledge of "the worldwide evolution of culture" is not to be attained by "the circumscribed study of historical cultures."[90] In Wissler's view, the work of history is the study of actual culture systems in their temporal relations, as distinguished from the study of culture as a whole. Historical study is concerned with the varying fortunes of the specific cultures of the world, but it appears to him a serious limitation that historical study can do no more than reveal the identity of the 'fortuitous causes' to which differences in culture systems are due.[91] A tribal culture, he says, is a collection of 'trait complexes,'[92] and it is only by historical inquiry that 'the concrete specific content' of the culture of any given group is to be explained.[93] To account for the association of the elements represented in a culture system it is necessary to have information of the events that brought them into relation. The events that have had the most potent influence on the make-up of culture systems have been associated with military activities. "Everywhere in the world the tendency has

[87] Clark Wissler, as cited, p. 204.
[88] *Ibid.*, chs. 11 and 17.
[89] *Ibid.*, pp. 110–127.
[90] *Ibid.*, p. 246.
[91] *Ibid.*, p. 279.
[92] *Ibid.*, p. 71.
[93] *Ibid.*, p. 263.

been for culture areas to develop dominant centers and then to become the seats of militarism."[94] What we see in history, then, is the continual shifting of culture centers as a result of war. While a single geographical area may for a time hold priority, it does so but for a period, to be outstripped in turn by another; at its fall, some other virile center has always been ready to snatch up the torch of light and dash forward, and "in each historic case the scepter has passed on to the hands of a wilder, less domesticated group of people."[95]

It will be seen, then, that there are represented in Dr. Wissler's book two different lines of approach to the study of man, and two conflicting conceptions of the method to be employed. In the first place, by making abstractions from the concrete data of culture, the author arrives at 'similarities,' and, by abstraction from similarities, reaches his idea of a 'universal pattern.' This pattern he undertakes to explain by reference to the 'original nature' of man. In the second place, he begins by pointing out that what we are given in experience is a relatively large number of different cultures, and recognizes throughout the book that the study of differences can be conducted only by the utilization of actual historical facts. The outcome of this procedure is a generalized model of the way in which change has been brought about in the course of time. The conclusion to which we are brought is that the presence of conflicting and irreconcilable modes of procedure in the work of an anthropologist of note is evidence of the need for revision of existing conceptions of method in humanistic inquiry.

It is evident, then, that in the fields of history and anthropology the discussions of method which have occupied so important a place in the literature of these subjects during the last quarter century have contributed nothing toward overcoming the separation between historical and 'scientific' inquiries in the study of society, or toward bringing to light the difficulties created by the acceptance of the idea of progress as the directive concept in the humanities.

---

[94] *Ibid.,* pp. 164–180, 341.   [95] *Ibid.,* pp. 179, 221, 358.

When we turn to consider the activities of economists and sociologists, we find that, in these fields, no revision of the methodological conceptions inherited from the nineteenth and eighteenth centuries has been made. So evident is this fact that extended analyses are not called for to bring it to light. The vigorous efforts of the 'historical school' of economists in the nineteenth century resulted merely in adding the study of economic history to the older study of economic theory; and while dissatisfaction is openly expressed, at the present time, with the condition of economic theory, the theoretical foundations upon which it is based appear to be accepted simply 'as given.' In sociology the field is still divided, as in Comte's system, between the analytical study of 'society' (with an ever-increasing emphasis on ameliorative interests) and the discussion of theories of 'progress.' So little attention, indeed, has been given to the consideration of the procedure followed in this subject that, in 1924, a prominent sociologist, proposing to give a historical account of the *Origins of Sociology,* could make the statement that nothing had been written before 1800 that could be connected with "the creative course of our specialty."

In the year 1859, three approaches to the investigation of 'how things have come to be as they are' were open to humanists: first, that of Auguste Comte, inspired by the idea of 'progress' and based upon the conception that the aim of scientific inquiry is the formulation of the 'law' of progress, meaning thereby a generalized description of the successive steps in the uniform development of mankind; second, that of Charles Darwin, inspired by the idea of 'evolution,' based upon the conception (suggested by the work of the geologists Hutton and Lyell) that the aim of scientific inquiry is the discovery of the process or processes uniformly manifested in changes in the forms of life, these changes being assumed to be invariably slow, gradual, and continuous; third, that of Hume and Turgot, inspired by the observation of the marked differences in the present condition of mankind, and having for its aim the determination of the processes manifested in persistence and in slow modification, of the determination of the conditions under which rapid change actually takes place, and of the processes manifested in such circumstances.

The first and second of these modes of procedure have their origin, so far as modern thought is concerned, in the Cartesian assumption of motion as the basic phenomenon of the universe. The common element in the thought of Comte and Darwin is an acceptance of the reality of a progressive movement in time. Each alike assumes that this progressive movement is 'natural,' that it is independent of the 'accidental' circumstances of which history and experience are constituted. Each alike assumes that this progressive movement proceeds slowly and continuously toward a determined end in perfection. This form of thought appears both in the eighteenth and the nineteenth centuries as a reaction against the Christian doctrine of the constant participation of Providence in the direction of the affairs of men. The philosophy of Descartes, however, accepted the view that God is continuously modifying things in accordance with a plan, and deviated from the accepted theology simply in maintaining that the direction of the affairs of the universe was not carried on by sporadic arbitrary actions, but in accordance with fixed modes of procedure, the laws of nature, which had been arbitrarily set up. The teleology of Descartes has entered into all theories of progress and of evolution, and hence it is not remarkable that contemporary logicians should have reached the conclusion that these theories involve the postulate of a 'vital principle.'

The difficulties which the humanist must meet at the present time arise from his acceptance of the idea of progress as the directive concept in the study of man. In consequence of the assumption that science is concerned with what is 'natural,' as distinguished from what is 'accidental,' separation was made between historical inquiry and the 'social sciences,' with the result that each of these types of investigation continues to pursue its course in isolation from the other. All social phenomena, however, are in the strictest sense 'historical,' and there can be no scientific study of man until this separation has been overcome.

If, then, we are to arrive at the desideratum of a science of man (or of 'society'), we must face the problem presented by the current acceptance of the idea of progress as an interpretation of human history. The difficulty will, in large measure, be resolved if we recognize the difference between a belief in progress and a belief in the possibility of progress. To believe in progress is to adopt a supine attitude toward existence; is to cultivate an enthusiasm for whatever chance may bring; is to assume that perfection and happiness lie ahead, whatever may be the course of human action in the present. To restrict belief to the possibility of progress implies recognition of the fact that change may result in destruction as readily as in advancement; implies consciousness of the precariousness of human achievement, as witnessed in the fate of 'Nineveh and Tyre.' Belief in progress rests upon the assumption that 'all is for the best,' but wavers between the views (1) that the 'natural' activities of men, if freed from artificial restraints, must necessarily lead to a perfect condition of social existence, and (2) that this desirable condition is to be reached only through the regulation of 'natural' activities by legislation—based upon intuitive judgments. Belief in the possibility of progress forces upon us the question, "How may this possibility be realized?"; it leads us to understand that, if human advancement is to be assured, the activities of men must be directed by knowledge. This knowledge cannot be acquired by any mere expression of good-will; it cannot be achieved even by the most complete coöperation with "the mysterious unconscious impulse" which is "the vital principle of betterment." The knowledge upon which the future depends will require the full utilization of the resources which society has accumulated in institutions of learning. The acquisition of this knowledge is the task to which humanists must set themselves in the interests of their fellow men.

THE PROCESSES OF HISTORY

Introduction

THE QUESTION "Is History a science?" has been debated by successive generations of historians, but no general agreement has yet been reached. It would seem, therefore, that in some particular the problem has been wrongly stated. Hence, following the critique presented in my *Prolegomena to History,* I have approached the whole matter from a new angle by asking what sort of results might be obtained by application of the method of science to the facts of history. The outcome of this procedure, stated in general terms, is an attempt to do for human history what biologists are engaged in doing for the history of the forms of life, and this publication offers in summary form a first analysis of the factors and processes manifested in the history of man.

For the sake of clearness, and in order that the essential considerations might be brought within a brief comprehensive view, the argument has been condensed and made as explicit as circumstances would permit. Since footnotes and citations of authorities have also been eliminated in the interest of brevity and directness, it should be understood that there is no view expressed which, I believe, is not already familiar to students in one or another branch of humanistic inquiry. So far as I am aware, all that is new in the present contribution is the coördination into one consistent statement of results which are well known, but which are widely scattered throughout the literature of history, political science, philology, anthropology, education, geography, and other studies. Further than this, the most significant feature of the book is an insistence that, in dealing with a problem of this magnitude, the prime requisite must be an exacting care in regard to the method employed. Hence it seems to me that the questions for immediate consideration are: first, whether the problems of method have been correctly stated; and, second, whether the factors and processes indicated are correctly described.

More generally, there is no disguising the fact that the present world situation is imperative in forcing men to question searchingly the validity of their own activities. Are, then, those of us who are engaged in the study of History doing all that lies within our power to make our inquiries contributory to the well-being of our fellow men? We must admit that while, during the last fifty years, the students of Nature have most significantly enlarged the knowledge of the world in which we live, the students of Man have made no such striking advance in their field of investigation. It is true that we have been persistent in the collection of facts, and in the refinement of the technique of investigation, but it would seem as if the utilization of all this accumulated knowledge in the spirit of modern science might now be undertaken. What, then, is presented here is a tentative statement, based upon the application of the method of science to the facts of History, made in the earnest belief that inquiry conducted along the lines marked out must ultimately lead to an understanding of the difficulties that beset our civilization, and to a furtherance of the welfare of mankind.

Chapter 1

The Nature and Scope of the Inquiry

SCIENCE IS, in principle, a method of dealing with problems, and the initial step in any scientific undertaking is the determination of the problem to be investigated.

A survey of the present situation, in which men everywhere find themselves involved in conflict, stimulates interest in the wide differences that exist between the many and various groups into which mankind is broken up. Thus, in the foreground, we are vividly conscious of differing characteristics when we speak of French, Germans, and Italians, and impressions associate themselves with the thought of Canadians, Australians, and New Zealanders which are not suggested by mention of English, Scotch, and Irish. But the conflicts of today are not restricted to inheritors of a western European tradition, and the sense of difference becomes more acute when we turn to think of the peoples bordering on the Black Sea—Russians, Rumanians, Bulgarians, and Turks. Even the daily recurrence of these names fails to remove the feeling that attaches to them of remoteness and unfamiliarity. Yet farther off, in Asia, peoples of a wholly un-European aspect are also engaged in warfare.

There are differences enough and to spare, and, at times, when the subject is brought forward, we recollect that in appearance, practices, and beliefs the men who people the earth are of the most heterogeneous description; but, ordinarily, we dismiss the fact, or entertain it momentarily as contributory to our self-esteem. These others, indeed, are 'different,' are 'backward,' are 'colored,' while we (whoever we may be) are 'civilized' and 'progressive.' With such indefinite phrases we escape the sense of a problem, and shield ourselves from the embarrassment of the direct question: "In what respect are these others different from ourselves?" Furthermore, though the knowledge is a commonplace, we tend, in forming judgments of our contemporaries, to forget that, not many generations back, our own progenitors fought with crude weapons, wore skins, and painted their bodies. We tend, for example, to forget that even in the eighteenth century the civilization of China was regarded by European travelers as superior to their own. We ignore the consideration that our religion was derived from a land we now regard as 'backward,' and the fundamentals of our thought from a people whose present representatives we are disposed to patronize.

Nevertheless, the conflicts of the twentieth century have had the result of lessening the exclusiveness and self-confidence of the western European, and have induced in him an awakening appreciation of the manhood and common human quality of outlying peoples. In truth, a new current of feeling has made itself felt, and we have come to regard the differences and contrasts among men, not as a basis for disparagement, but as something to be explained. And here we may discern the nature of the problem with which we are confronted. Every human group, white, black, or yellow, entertains precisely the same attitude of superiority toward all the others, and the vindication of this attitude in ourselves requires that we, for the sake of all, should endeavor to determine, not the reason for our own superiority, but *how man everywhere has come to be as he is*.

2) The problem so stated is not new, and many theories have been advanced to account for the manifest differences in human groups. Of these theories, the most popular and persistent is that which attributes the diversities among peoples to physical differences in race. Thus it is widely believed that difference of race implies a real and deep-rooted distinction in physical, mental, and moral qualities, and that the contrasts in the achievements of the various peoples are due to differences in physical characteristics. Hence it is thought that one race be-

comes a master because of its physique, courage, brain power, and morale, while another sinks in the struggle or lags behind, owing to its inferiority in these qualities. This view naturally implies that the same race preserves its character, not only in every region of the world, but also in every period of history, and so the course of history would appear as a sustained process of selection between the races that are sluggish, cowardly, and retrogressive, and those that are energetic, brave, and progressive—while the latter press forward, the former die out or stagnate in lazy passivity. A slightly different turn is given to the explanation by those who maintain that the present savage races are those which have been left impoverished and stationary as a result of the migration of their more vigorous or stronger elements; the younger and more alert in each generation, it is thought, go out to seek new homes, and leave the older and more conservative to perpetuate the original group.

While the explanation in terms of race has been supported, in recent discussions, by an appeal to biology, there can be little doubt that its principal foundation lies in the inevitable human propensity to classify all those who are in any way unlike ourselves, or who merely lie outside our own group, as 'fiends,' 'aliens,' and 'barbarians.' The Hebrews, though perhaps the best-known example, have not been the only group to regard themselves a 'chosen people'; and while we may point to Dante's opinion that the Romans of his time were ordained to command, and to the modern German equivalent of the same doctrine, it must be admitted that the passionate assertion of nationality in the nineteenth century has been colored at least by this feeling of a special worth or importance in ourselves as contrasted with others, a feeling, we must not forget, which the Negro, Hindu, and Chinaman share with the most progressive of Europeans.

Once entertained, the idea that there have been certain unique races in the past, and that there is one such race in the present, yields itself readily to interested elaboration. So the Hegelian theory has been replaced, on further consideration, by the view which sees all human advancement as the varied expression of the power and genius, not of the Absolute, but of the Aryan race; and while this conception permitted, at first, of a fairly generous interpretation, a more thorough application has restricted the definition of the conquering race to the dolichocephalic (or long-headed) blonds from northern Europe. Wherever this race has penetrated, there, it would appear, the surrounding peoples have been subjugated, and there prosperity and a great civilization have sprung up. So complete is this clue, indeed, that any manifestation of genius, whether in Palestine, Greece, Italy, or Germany, becomes an unequivocal proof of the presence of at least some members of this supreme race. Conversely, wherever the brachycephalic (or short-headed) races have made their appearance, decadence has straightway followed; nor do the advocates of this thorough-going conception shrink from the conclusion that progress in the future must depend upon the increased propagation and the physical dominance of the long-headed variety.

An equally positive, though perhaps less animating, theory places the emphasis, in the endeavor to account for the differences of human groups, not on the physical, but on the mental characteristics of races, and from this root has grown the extensive literature of 'race psychology.' According to this view, the part played in history by any aggregation of men is a direct reflection of its collective character and mentality. The subject and method of this psychology, initiated by Wilhelm von Humboldt, seems first to have been cultivated by Steinthal and Lazarus, but owes its vogue, apparently, to men like Mommsen and Renan. While the interest enlisted by the summary descriptions of the psychology of peoples has been widely extended, the explanation afforded by the procedure is not illuminating, for it consists merely in saying that events and institutions are the outcome of the genius of peoples. Thus, for example, it appears that the Greeks were a people distinctly marked out by nature as freer than other mortals from all that hinders and oppresses the activities of the spirit; or, briefly, that Greek civilization was the creation of the inborn genius of the Greek race. Furthermore, the mode of determining the collective characteristics of groups leaves much room for debate, since, while one authority may regard the Celt as 'a gentle obstinate,' another thinks him 'turbulent and vain,' and a third declares him to be the embodiment of 'an indomitable passion for danger and adventure.'

When pressed, each of these theories, physical and psychological, tends more and more to fall back upon the influence of habitat or climate in determining the character of groups, and we are thus led to consider the type of explanation offered by anthropogeography. It is argued, for instance, that all human varieties are the outcome of their several environments. Groups are what climate, soil, diet, pursuits, and inherited qualities have made them. What is true of man himself is no less true of his works, and so it follows that racial and cultural zones must coincide, while a correspondence must exist between these and the zones of temperature. Hence we arrive at the theory that, in both hemispheres, the isocultural bands follow the isothermal bands in all their deflections. In this view, it is evident, all the specific characteristics of humanity— physique, temperament, institutions, occupations, and ideas— are the more or less immediate reflection of habitat, and it is maintained that each breed of man which has changed its place of domicile has had to adopt the type of culture appropriate to the region into which it has penetrated.

The forms taken by this theory of the dependence of man on habitat are very numerous, but a few illustrations may serve to suggest the wide scope of its applications. Thus it has long been held that the advancement of man in northern Europe was a direct result of the inhospitable conditions which forced him to cultivate unprecedented habits of industry. Again, it has been explained that the extremes of character attributed to the Slav are due to the extremes of climate on the wind- swept steppes. The long and bitter cold, it is said, has enabled the Russian peasants to survive, since it has fostered the spirit of comradeship, and this, in turn, has held them together in their *mir* or village community. The habitat, it also seems, provides the conditions which determine the progress or stagnation of the group, for agricultural tribes, being bound to the soil, are conservative, apathetic, and nonprogressive, while the nomadic or seminomadic life sharpens the wits and calls forth courage, self-reliance, and ingenuity. By others, again, it is argued that the birth and precocious growth of civilization are encouraged by a small, isolated, and protected habitat, though at a later stage this cramps progress, and lends the stamp of arrested development to a people like the Greeks.

The types of theory thus briefly indicated have this in common, that they attempt to describe factors which may be regarded as operative in all human groups, and are thus to be considered as offering an explanation on a scientific basis. To all appearance, however, it has not seemed necessary to the exponents of these views to show how the factors described could have produced the differences which we see around us. Indeed, the mode of procedure adopted has been simply to explain evident differences by alleging the antecedence of other differences, less obvious, but still unexplained. Knowledge is not really advanced by asserting that all human advancement has been due to the presence of some particular race. In point of method, the failure lies in the fact that the theory gives no insight into the processes through which the assumed physical superiority of the Aryan or Teuton has been transmuted into cultural advancement. But, taken on its own terms, and supposing, for the moment, that the beginnings of cultural development in China and India were associated with the intrusion of Aryans, the theory does not suggest how later advances have taken place in these lands, and it ignores the fact that there is ample evidence of notable advancement in Mesopotamia and in Egypt prior to any appearance of the Aryan race. Similarly, it throws no light upon the problem in hand to attribute the special cultural characteristics of a people to correspondingly particularized innate qualities.

In regard to anthropogeography, it may be said more particularly that it represents not so much an explicit theory as
an almost unlimited mass of correlations, some vague and
unimportant, others penetrating and of the highest value. In
some respects, indeed, this subject, at once new and of a remote antiquity, represents, at the present time, one of the most
hopeful aspects of the study of man, for, from its association,
however indeterminate, with geology, it has gained a breadth
and an inclusiveness of vision that has been denied the better-
established humanistic studies. Nevertheless, a too close association with a science already highly elaborated, and a too great
dependence upon the work of pioneers who had not fully entered into the spirit of modern scientific method, have led to
a logical formalism in dealing with its subject matter which
has not been wholly in the interests of scientific progress. Anthropogeography, in short, provides a great body of observations assembled under logically arranged headings, but has
failed to recognize that investigation, to be effective, must be
conducted in the presence of a specific problem.

Furthermore, in the actual consideration of the influence
of habitat upon human affairs, there is almost invariably apparent, on the part of geographers, a certain laxity in regard
to the facts of historical change. Though habitat and climate
have, in general, remained constant throughout the historical
period, civilizations have arisen and decayed, to be followed
by other civilizations under different environmental conditions. If it is the hardy northerner who is 'progressive' at one
time, at another it is the Akkadian and Sumerian in the hot-
house of the Persian Gulf. If the village community is a response to the relentless winter of the Russian steppes, it has also
persisted in torrid India. Egypt, Phoenicia, Crete, and Greece
may possibly be regarded as protected areas, but if the rise of
civilization is dependent upon isolation, how shall we account
for the early development of Lagash and Nippur? How, too,
shall we account for the absence of such developments in a hundred spots more isolated and protected still? If Greek climate

and habitat are to be accepted as prepotent influences in the production of Periclean Athens, and German climate and habitat as determining factors in the development of the military power of today, why have not these relatively constant factors been equally operative in past and present times?

Evidently, then, neither the race theory nor that of habitat offers an adequate basis for an explanation of how man has come to be as he is, and hence we are driven to inquire what other types of theory have been advanced.

3) From a wholly different point of view there has been presented a theory to account for the inequalities among men which has been accorded an acceptance as wide as the theory of race, but by a very different constituency, for while the former may be said to appeal more directly to militarists and certain groups attracted by modern biological ideas, the economic theory of Marx and Engels has found the great body of its adherents among the workers immediately involved in the 'class struggle.'

Constructively, the point of departure of Marx is the idea that the economic factor dominates all the other factors of human existence, and his insistence on this view, notwithstanding the exaggeration it involves, has had the beneficial effect of directing the attention of students to the importance of a series of facts which previously had been very generally ignored. In a measure, Marx may also be said to have employed the method of science, for what he attempted to do was to isolate and describe a particular factor or process manifested in human affairs. But in this undertaking, notwithstanding the profound influence which his writings have had upon modern thought, the limitations of his outlook, and his imperfect appreciation of the complexities of the problem, have stood in the way of a permanent success. It should, however, be remembered that Marx did not set himself to work out a scientific problem, but to carry forward a social propaganda. He was not attempting the special problem of labor under modern conditions, and to analyze the elements of history; his interest was excited by

his dominating aim was to account for this particular phenomenon in its present aspect. Hence he neither considered the
entire field of economic activity in modern life, nor the conditions of labor in any other than the capitalistic form of society.

It must not be supposed, however, that Marx and Engels,
while maintaining that the great moving power in all historical events was the economic development of society, failed to
recognize that they had investigated only that form of economic
organization under which they themselves were actually living.
"We ought," Engels remarked, "to study, at least in their essential features and taken as terms of comparison, the other forms
which have preceded it in time, or exist alongside of it in less
developed countries." And he stated frankly: "Marx and I are
partly responsible for the fact that the younger men have sometimes laid more stress on the economic fact than was necessary"; but this overemphasis, as he explained, arose from the
exigencies of the debate into which their main contention
precipitated them. It is not remarkable, therefore, that the
Marxian interpretation of history should have failed to elucidate the means through which such different results have been
arrived at in Asia and in Europe, in ancient and in modern
times. The fault, if there be any, lies not with these great ini-
tiators who demonstrated the practical utility of an investigation of the elements of history, but with their successors who
have failed to carry forward and to broaden the scope of the
inquiries which they set on foot.

This theory, then, like those previously mentioned, is unacceptable as an explanation of how man has come to be as he
is, for, like the others, it is based upon a limited view of the
facts, and represents a projection of a single factor upon the
complexity of human experience. Practically speaking, the failure in all these attempts has been due to a lack of appreciation
of the necessity for a preliminary study of method. To be acceptable, any such theory must be applicable to 'backward'
as well as to 'advanced' groups; it must apply equally to all
periods of history in all lands; it must apply, furthermore,

to the 'backward' and 'advanced' members of all groups, and hence to the experience of the individual in the world today.

4) The number and variety of the theories which have heretofore been advanced should be convincing proof that in approaching a problem of this magnitude we must first endeavor to arrive at a clear understanding of the method to be followed in conducting the inquiry. It can hardly be questioned that the investigation before us must rest upon an examination of the facts of human history, for we ourselves are aware that any present situation in which we may happen to be involved is the outcome of what has gone before. But the practical problem with which we are confronted appears only when we come to ask how the concrete facts of history are to be utilized in order to explain the status of man as we find him everywhere throughout the world.

During the nineteenth century, and, indeed, up to the present, the student of history has carried on his work in accordance with the assumption that such an explanation would be afforded by a statement, in the form of narrative, of what had happened in the past.

Now, of all possible modes of explanation, the earliest and the most universal is that naïve form which is represented in storytelling. This consists in going back to some selected beginning and carrying forward a narrative of happenings from that point to the situation which the narrator has undertaken to make clear. It matters nothing that, in its earliest manifestations, historical narrative starts with some imaginary beginning, such as the Mosaic account of Creation or Hesiod's Golden Age; the principle is always the same, namely, the acceptance of a situation that comes first, and the emergence from this of a complexity which has its conclusion in a known eventuality.

The initial difficulty for the historian, once his starting point has been decided upon, is that he cannot include all the available facts of past occurrences in the narrative which, as a literary artist, he is bent upon creating. The creation, as in all art, involves the selection of facts for presentation, and while this selection must depend ultimately upon what the narrator or artist himself is, it can be made only in the light of some conception he has formed of the course of events, of some interest or emotion awakened by what he believes has taken place.

The most obvious basis of selection is the interest enlisted by what is simply curious or unusual. This is represented, in earlier writings, by the miscellaneous nature of the records set down by medieval chroniclers and annalists, and, in the work of contemporary scholars, by the recurrent statement: "What really happened was not what you and everyone else has believed, but this that I alone have discovered." On a broader plane, the selection is determined by the interest taken in the outcome of some specific series of events, more particularly when this leads to an impressive denouement, such as the defeat of Xerxes by the relatively insignificant forces of the Greeks. As, however, events but rarely work out to a completely satisfactory ending—witness Thucydides,—historical writers have fallen back upon the method, characteristic in the drama, of depicting personal character revealing itself in the stress of critical circumstances. Following this line of development, historiography has tended to emphasize the part played by the individual in what has happened, relying more and more for its explanations upon the speculative interpretation of individual motives, and justifying this procedure on an assumed similarity of the workings of the human mind in similar situations.

At a later stage, reflection on the seemingly meaningless changes of fortune revealed in events leads to the conscious effort to reach an explanatory basis through the formulation of some concept of the underlying meaning of the course of history. Thus, for example, one recent effort is directed toward showing that the meaning lies in "the existence of a mental conflict as to the means by which happiness is to be attained," while another discovers history to be "the story of man's increasing ability to control energy." Such projections of abstract points of view have been infinite in their variety, ranging from

that of Orosius, who saw in events the hand of God so ordering
at all times the affairs of men that dire calamity should unfail-
ingly overtake neglect of His service, to that of a contemporary
who believes that "modern science is crowned by the conception of an ordered progress in history." But while, at this point,
an extended résumé of theories would be of advantage as
emphasizing the fact that every successive generation attains
new points of view, one must perforce assume familiarity with
such expositions of philosophies of history as have been provided by Flint and Barth, for what is really germane to the
present discussion is the residual fact that today the search for
an underlying principle in history is dominated by the concept
of 'progress.'

It may be well here to point out that the idea of 'progress'
stands in much the same relation to the study of man as that
of 'evolution' to the study of the forms of life. But whereas,
in the hands of Darwin, the study of biological evolution passed
from the merely speculative into the scientific stage, the study
of human progress is still in the pre-Darwinian period. Thus
the sociologist still sets before himself the aim of discovering
'the law of progress,' while the historian, assuming 'progress'
without further question, displays in narrative form the gradual emergence of features which he personally regards as dis-
tinctively modern or as particularly desirable. In neither the
one case nor the other has the investigator concerned himself
with applying to the subject matter in hand the method of
analysis by which Darwin was enabled to support the speculative concept of 'evolution' by the scientific theory of 'natural
selection.'

If we are to appreciate the implications of the idea of 'progress,' it will be necessary to observe that this concept is based
upon the assumption that history—the entire course of events
in time—is unitary, that it constitutes a single sequence of
happenings in which progress is revealed. Now, if we disregard
the use which is being made of this idea in contemporary philosophical discussions, and concern ourselves only with its

place in historical study, it will readily be perceived that the
concept of 'progress' is just the reflection of a convention in
accordance with which we base our presentation of what has
happened on the records handed down to us by certain European peoples with whose languages we are more or less familiar.
Frankly, our concepts are at the mercy of such information as
we have at our command, and so the term 'ancient history' suggests, not diversified series of facts embodying the experiences
of mankind during a certain period of time, but a narrative
restatement of accounts which record the varying fortunes of
some of the political units of Mediterranean lands, more particularly Greece and Rome. We of the twentieth century, with
all our opportunities for acquaintance with the history of Asia,
have not risen above the limitations of our predecessors, and
continue to imagine that we have arrived at a synthesis of human history when we have constructed a narrative by selecting
parts or periods of the history of one European country after
another which seem to us as of special and peculiar significance.
On the other hand, if we look a little farther, it will be to discover that human history is not unitary, but pluralistic; that
what we are given is not one history, but many; and that the
concept of 'progress' is arrived at by the maintenance of a Eu-
ropocentric tradition and the elimination from consideration
of the activities of all peoples whose civilization does not at
once appear to be contributory to our own.

What, then, is essential for us to realize is that the methodological assumption upon which the work of the historian is
based, namely, that we may hope to arrive at an explanation
of how man has come to be as he is through the narrative statement of what has happened in the past, is, critically considered,
inadmissible. Narrative is a form or genre of literature, and in
this lies its forceful appeal, for, so long as men endure, the tale
of what men have done, and how they have striven, will never
lose its interest and attraction. Furthermore, so long as men
continue to question the meaning of life, the attempt to grasp
the ultimate significance of the course taken by events in the

past will be continually renewed. But beyond the romance of human deeds, and quite apart from any effort to penetrate the future, there remains for investigation the vital problem of how man in all his diversity has come to be as we find him now.

There are many histories, and this pluralism reveals our task as historical students, which is not to explain occurrences by the intercalation of hypothetical motives, or to create narratives based upon the selection of events which seem to us of importance in view of some unverified theory of progress, but to compare these several histories with the object of finding out what it is they hold in common. The fact is that an understanding of 'how things have come to be as they are' can be arrived at only through a study of what has happened in the past, but this understanding is not furthered by the conventional construction of narratives. What is requisite is that we should compare the events, the things that have happened, without the intervention of the subjective interests, often unacknowledged because unconsciously held, of historical writers. Precisely what we need to begin with are great bodies of historical data, annals or *fasti,* relating to all human groups without distinction, which have not been subjected to the selective activities of the literary artist and the philosopher.

The inadequacy of the conventionalized method of the historian having thus been pointed out, it now remains to inquire how the concrete facts of history may be utilized in dealing with the problem before us.

5) As it is imperative for us to arrive at an understanding of the method to be employed in dealing with the problem of how man has come to be as he is, and as the narrative method hitherto relied upon by the historian sacrifices the wealth of concrete detail to the personal or speculative interest of individuals, it may be well to observe how men in other fields of history, such as Astronomy, Geology, and Biology, have conducted their investigations.

In the first place, each of these subjects is confronted with the complexity of a present status which is assumed to be the outcome of all the changes that have taken place up to the present time. Second, in each of them the object or aim of the investigation is to arrive at an understanding of how this present status has come to be as it is, and the inquiry takes the form of an examination of the nature of the changes which have taken place.

What disguises the identity of the problem that presents itself to the student of nature and the student of man is that, while the latter is provided with a great body of dated evidence for what has happened in the past, the former is left without any strictly chronological data, and is forced to be content with a merely relative time order in his historical facts. In short, in his efforts to interpret the records of the past, the historian of nature must pursue his quest unaided by the testimony of human witnesses. Nevertheless, while this handicap has immeasurably increased the difficulties in his way, it has not prevented him from contributing in a most notable manner to the sum of human knowledge.

It may fairly be said that the greater success of the student of nature in arriving at a scientific method for dealing with any history has been due to the greater difficulties which he has encountered. Thus, while the historian of man has engaged his efforts in creating narratives based upon details arranged in chronological order, the historian of nature has been forced to prove that the facts upon which he must rely may even be regarded as historical data. Indeed, this proof was the main endeavor of the great group of scientists in the first half of the nineteenth century whose work may be said to have culminated in the publication of Darwin's *Origin of Species* in 1859. The difficulties of the situation in which the advocates of a historical point of view were placed, not the least being the almost universal acceptance of the theory of a single creation, necessitated a careful consideration of the method to be employed, and so forced the recognition of the axiom that any present status is to be regarded as the outcome of the continued operation of natural processes.

Thus the geologist, having arrived at criteria for determining the time order of strata, proceeded to examine the disposition of the rocks in every accessible area of the earth's surface. Now, while the rocks are assumed to have been laid down, as a result of the operation of natural processes, in horizontal layers, they are actually found in an infinite variety of positions. Hence it became necessary to show how these dislocations had been effected, and what one might speak of as the explanatory 'stock in trade' of the geologist consists in the various processes which are manifested in the geological history of the earth. As a result of this way of looking at things, the geologist comes to see around him the evidences of how the earth has come to be as it is, and he comes to regard the landscape before him, not merely as a static disposition of picturesque form, but as an embodiment of constant activities which, in the course of time, have brought this scenery to its present aspect and will continue to modify it throughout all time to come. He can still feel the grandeur of the Alps, and still appreciate the beauty of Fujiyama, but, in addition to the aesthetic pleasure, the sights convey to his mind an added wealth of suggestion regarding the ceaseless workings of Nature.

Again, the biologist has at all times endeavored to account for the infinite variety of the forms of life, but even in the eighteenth century little had been accomplished to provide a substitute for the belief that species were just so many distinct and permanent creations of God. In the nineteenth century, however, a new perspective was gained, and men began to perceive a historical depth in the relations of species. When the systematic classification of plants and animals had been carried to a certain elaboration, it was discerned, through the coöperation of geology, that the arrangement in order from simplest to most complex represented a time order from early to late. As an additional result of the close association of geologists and biologists, the latter also adopted from their co-workers the axiom that things had come to be as they are through the continued operation of natural processes. Darwin's method, in

Darwin

fact, is just that of his geological contemporaries applied to a new subject matter; and his object was the discovery of the process or processes through which new species have successively come into existence. In other words, what he planned to carry out was an analysis of the elements of biological history.

Whether Darwin was successful in his undertaking is for biologists to decide, though up to the present time they have not given sufficient attention to his method and to the nature of the assumptions upon which his theory was based. All that need be observed in the present connection, however, is that, in putting forward his theory of 'natural selection,' Darwin believed that he had described the process through which the forms of life have come to be as they are today. Should it nevertheless appear that 'natural selection' is inadequate to explain the origin of species, this conclusion would not invalidate the fundamental assumption that such processes are actually in operation; it would simply mean that Darwin's particular attempt at analysis was incomplete, perhaps even erroneous throughout. What would then remain to be done would be to make an entirely new analysis with greater regard to precision in method. It must be remembered, whatever the decision, that the theory of 'natural selection' has created an interest in even the lowliest forms of life that did not previously exist, and that it has opened the eyes of men, in a wholly new sense, to the ways by which Nature accomplishes her ever-varying and ever-wonderful results. Nor should it be overlooked that the method of historical inquiry by which the natural scientist has attempted to explain how things have come to be as they are has led to results which have been of the highest practical importance to mankind.

It has been suggested above that astronomers, geologists, and biologists have been compelled to conduct historical inquiries without the aid of specifically dated materials, and there can be little doubt that this deficiency has not only been difficult to overcome, but has, in biology at least, led to far-reaching controversies and misunderstandings, and even to unconscious assumptions which have become stumbling blocks in the path of knowledge. When, therefore, we consider the obstacles which have been encountered by the students of nature, it must be apparent that the student of man is placed in a unique and enviable position, through the possession of dated evidence, for the investigation of the elements of human history. Indeed, the chronological record, such as it is, frees the historian from many of the difficulties which embarrass the naturalist.

On the other hand, it would seem that this unparalleled aid to investigation has, in itself, threatened to become an insurmountable obstacle to the advancement of science, for the interest excited by the effort to perfect this record blinds us, apparently, to the infinite possibilities which it places in our hands. The historian, fortified by an ancient convention, is so completely absorbed in the details before him, and in perfecting his own critical technique, that he leaves to one side the wider problems of historical method. When, however, these problems are actually taken up, it comes to be seen that historical method is the same whatever the history investigated—whether that of the stellar universe, of the earth, of the forms of life upon the earth, or of man. It comes to be seen that in each case the problem is the same, namely, to show how things have come to be as they are; that in each case the investigation presupposes the antecedence of innumerable series of historical events; that in each case the inquiry is based upon the assumption or axiom that things have come to be as they are through the continued operation of natural processes, and that these processes are to be discovered only through examination of what has happened in the past. And here it must be clearly stated, since this is a point upon which much misunderstanding has arisen through Darwin's acceptance of Lyell's method, that the investigation of the processes of change must be based upon the facts of history, and cannot be discovered by examination of the results given in the present. On the other hand, if our inferences from the historical data are correct, they should be verifiable by application to things as they are.

6) It has been urged repeatedly that the endeavor to arrive at an analysis of the elements of history is no longer 'history,' since this, of necessity, has its sole end in narrative. It might be urged in contravention of this argument that the word 'history' originally meant 'inquiry,' and only secondarily came to be applied to the embodiment of the results of inquiry in the particular form of narrative. But, in reality, the situation is too serious to admit of debate in regard to the application of a word having already many recognized meanings. 'History,' in the widest sense, means all that has happened in the past, and, more particularly, all that has happened to the human race. Now, the whole body of historical students is in possession of a vast accumulation of information in regard to the former activities and experiences of mankind, and the problem which is uppermost at the present time is how this accumulated information—which already far exceeds the possibility of statement in any narrative synthesis—may be utilized to throw light upon the difficulties that confront mankind. In the world as it is today, is the historical scholar to look forward to contributing the results of his specialized researches to some later *Cambridge Modern History,* or is he to entertain the hope that his investigations may stand beside those of the biologist, for example, as contributing, through an added knowledge of the operations of nature, to the welfare of humanity?

Yet, while there are many who insist upon the conventional aim of reducing all historical facts to narrative, there are unmistakable evidences that other historical students are seeking a new outlet for their activities, and a new utilization for their knowledge. It is only necessary to observe the interest accorded to Lord Acton's project for a History of Freedom, it is only necessary to take cognizance of the studies which multiply daily on the religious, economic, geographical, and other phases of modern history, to see that men are reaching out in directions unknown to the older historiography, directions which are manifestly tentative approximations to a scientific standpoint. For the undercurrent of all this awakened interest is analytical;

and whether we set ourselves to isolate the strand of 'freedom' or that of 'class struggle,' the influence of 'sea power' or that of 'religious revivals,' we are contributing, in the long run, to an analysis of the elements of history.

Only an optimist, however, would suggest that this new movement in historical study had found itself, and was thoroughly conscious of its methodological foundations. The fact is that, while we are gradually escaping from the dominance of narrative, we have not as yet acquired the width of outlook necessary for the pursuit of analysis on a truly humanistic basis. Our vision is still focused upon Europe and the doings of Europeans, and while we look with a kindly interest at "the map of the world as known to Herodotus," we seem unable to appreciate the fact that relatively the scope of our own historical inquiries is less extensive than his. By one or another eminent contemporary authority, the study of history has been regarded as limited to the investigation of written documents; as limited to the Christian era; as limited to southern and western Europe; as limited to political events. Nevertheless, there has long been a tendency toward a wider outlook, but, as a matter of fact, the development of this broader interest has been forced to wait upon an extension of knowledge which has only been achieved within the last few decades through the progress of archaeological discoveries and of Oriental studies. With this difficulty removed, we may face the situation that the analytical study of history must be founded upon a comparison of the particular histories of all human groups, and must be actuated by the conscious effort to take cognizance of all the available facts. If this seems too much, let us remember that in a generation we have moved back from Greece to Egypt, from Egypt to Babylonia, and that now other remote vistas have been opened up by the excavations at Mohenjo-dāro. The minimal unit of history is not a series of empires, following each other in time, from the plain of Shinar to the British Isles, but the continental mass of the Older World taken as a whole, and throughout the time occupied by the generations of men. Only

with such an outlook may we hope, through the application
of analysis, to discover the factors and processes of history, and
thus arrive at a scientific knowledge of the way in which man
has come to be as he is.

Observation of the groups into which mankind is broken
up leads us to question how the differences between them have
come to be what they are, and hence to examine such explanations of the problem as have hitherto been advanced. A consideration of certain typical solutions that have been offered
brings us to the conclusion that in every case these have been
based upon a restricted view of the facts, and thus forces upon
us the necessity of taking up the entire problem anew.

Since, however, this problem is one of great magnitude and
difficulty, it would seem to be a proper precaution, in advance
of embarking upon the undertaking, to examine the methodological equipment on which we shall be forced to rely. As a
result of such an examination, the fact emerges that the traditional method still adhered to by the historian, the statement
of what has taken place in the form of narrative, does not lead
to any explanatory conclusion; and so, if the whole attempt
is not to be abandoned as vain and chimerical, it next becomes
necessary to find out how investigators have proceeded in other
fields of history. This inquiry leads in turn to the discovery
that geologists and biologists utilize the historical information
at their command, not for the purpose of constructing narratives of happenings, but to determine what have been the processes through which things have come to be as they are.

The point of view thus gained at once clarifies the situation,
for it reveals the significance of the chronological data which
the human historian of today has inherited from his predecessors; it throws light upon the nature of the activities of a large
and increasing number of historical students; and it displays
the importance and utility of the great residuary body of
historical facts which historiographers have been unable to incorporate in their narratives. Furthermore, it shows that the
objections which have been urged regarding the applicability of

scientific method within the province of the historical student are negligible, for a knowledge of the factors and processes of history can be arrived at only through the study of history, and this type of inquiry provides an opportunity by which the extraordinary wealth of dated material that is characteristic of human history may be made to subserve the highest interests of mankind.

Chapter 2

The Geographical Factor in History

A FORMULATION of the problem to be investigated and a general conception of the method to be followed having been arrived at, it next becomes necessary to consider the character of the evidence to be employed. Freeman was far from being alone in the belief that, while the recovery of the ancient records of Eastern peoples was to be regarded with pleasure, the historian could not accept these as materials for the study which was his own. This is an artificial distinction and an improper limitation to research, and, indeed, the greatest obstacle to the scientific study of history has been the conventional attitude, of which Freeman's remark is an example, by which the attention of historians has been restricted to Europe and the activities of Europeans, for such limitation would interpose an effective barrier to the use of the comparative method. If, however, the many histories with which we are confronted, histories of India, China, and Europe, are to be compared, the assumption must be made that the essential content of history is everywhere the same, that human history is made up of the same materials throughout, and woven upon the same loom. Simple as this declaration may appear to be, it involves conclusions of such far-reaching importance that it forces us to examine the bases for an acceptance of the homogeneity of history.

Europe and Asia are indissoluble, and are separated in name only. When we stop to consider the map of the Eastern Hemisphere, it is at once apparent that Europe is just a westward extension or peninsula of the great land mass of Eurasia. The convention by which we regard the two continents as divided is not an outgrowth of modern geographical knowledge, but represents simply a traditional nomenclature which we have inherited from immemorial antiquity. Physically, Europe and Asia are continuous: the great northern plain of Asia penetrates into the heart of Europe; the mountain barrier which, alternately expanding to enclose great basins like those of Hungary, Persia, and Tibet, and focusing in knots like the Alps, Ararat, and the Pamirs, stretches from Atlantic to Pacific, is crossed only by occasional passes; the line of depressions, conspicuous in the Mediterranean, runs through the Black, the Caspian, and the Aral seas, through lakes like Balkash, Issik, Zaisan, and Baikal, from west to farthest east; the desert belt lies stretched, a veritable cincture, Sahara, Arabia, Iran, Turkestan, and Taklamakan, across the body of the Older World.

Again, if we consider the distribution of peoples, there is no point at which we may draw a line of separation between Asia and Europe. There are representatives of European stocks to be found throughout the eastern continent, while, conversely, in the West there is no nation without its quantum of Asiatic blood: there are Finns in the North, Mongols in Central Europe, Arabs in Spain, Turks on the Aegean, and Semites everywhere.

Furthermore, in their history, the two parts of Eurasia are inextricably bound together. Mackinder has shown how much light may be thrown upon European history by regarding it as subordinate to Asiatic; and while we may question Ujfalvy's saying that Rome fell because the Chinese built a wall, we cannot deny that the ancient history of Europe is as incomprehensible without a knowledge of the Nearer East as medieval history without reference to the migrations of Asiatic peoples from the northern steppes. The oldest of historians held the idea that the epochs of European history were marked by alternating movements across the imaginary line that separates East and West; to us these movements are distinguishable in remotely prehistoric times, they have left their legible traces on the languages we speak, they are evident in periods of Greek history unknown to Herodotus, and are already modern with the expeditions of Darius and Alexander, with the appearance of Huns and Moslems in the West and of Frankish kingdoms in the East. The tide has turned, we may say, since Russia conquered Siberia and Britain became paramount in Hindustan, but the East has not been vanquished, and, possibly, the returning tide may not long be delayed.

Something more than this intimacy of relation, however, is necessary in order to demonstrate that the history of man in Europe and Asia is homogeneous. The fundamental basis of argument for holding that the history of man everywhere is of the same fabric does not rest upon the interconnections of events, but may be stated in the form that the varying experiences of human groups have been similarly conditioned by the varying aspects of the conformation of the globe. Man cannot escape the physical world in which he lives, nor its infinite diversification; this is obvious, but it will require some illustration to make clear the fact that the even-handed dominance of nature leads inevitably to widely different results in the lives of men.

2) Europe is visibly a projection from the block of Eurasia, but if we examine the configuration of the larger area, it will be found that there are other projections to the south and east. India, indeed, is easily recognizable as a peninsula, but China lies quite as completely outside the quadrilateral of the central mass. From a comparison of these three, which, incidentally, contain together by far the greater part of all the inhabitants of the globe, it will be discovered that China and India, though seemingly more closely united to the central block, are, so far as human accessibility is concerned, much more completely set apart than Europe. For while the latter lies exposed and open to the center, through the level plains of Russia and the convenient approach of the Aegean and the eastern Mediterranean, the former lie behind the protecting bulk of the highest and most difficult mountain system in the world. Hence India may be reached only by utilizing one or other of a few tortuous

routes through the towering mountains on its northwestern frontier, while China, similarly, enjoys the protection of the inaccessible mountains of Tibet on its western flank, and of the wide-extending deserts to the northwest. The routes by which the borders of either country may be reached are few and strictly defined, and are impracticable in face of an organized defense; and it will also be observed that both in China and in India the entire country stretches away from the gateway by which alone access may be gained, and the defense of this protects the land from molestation. For Europe, all this is changed, as there is no single or restricted strategic point at which the whole area may be defended, and, as a consequence, its penetration to the farthest recesses has been repeated and complete. Here, then, in its very simplest form is an example of homogeneity, inasmuch as the fortunes, expressed in history, of the inhabitants of these areas have turned primarily upon the relative accessibility of the land.

The principal reason, apart from the concentration of attention upon the affairs of Europe, why this close dependence of history upon the irregularities of the surface of the earth has not been fully recognized, seems to be the unavoidable tendency to regard as interchangeable or synonymous the geographical name of a land and the title of its dominant political power. Thus we speak of 'the history of China,' thinking at once of political happenings and of a certain area of the earth's surface which we Europeans have agreed to call by this name. But the subject of the historian's discourse is not an actual physical land; he considers this only as the seat of a particular political organization; and hence a more careful usage would distinguish between the title of the political unit and the name of the country over which its jurisdiction extends. It would, indeed, obviate misunderstanding if we were to speak habitually of the governmental unit, coincident with the geographical area which we call 'China,' as the 'Middle Kingdom,' or any of the titles used by the Chinese themselves, for then we should recognize more easily that the political organization has not always been, and strictly speaking is not now, equated with the geographical area.

This consideration leads to the recognition of another aspect of homogeneity, which is that the political organizations dealt with in history have all come into being at definite and restricted spots, from which, subsequently, they have expanded. Indeed, no intimate knowledge of history is necessary to reveal how limited were the original geographical areas from which grew the political units known as the Roman, Chinese, Russian, and British empires. A uniformity of this sort is clearly of interest in and for itself; it becomes of great significance, however, when we turn to examine the elements common to all such cases, and to see in these small beginnings the universal influence of geographical factors.

Various attempts, already alluded to, have been made to discover common elements in the beginnings of early civilizations. The difficulty in all these attempts has been that the investigator has limited his observation to the lands of the Nearer East, and has failed to extend the comparison to all known instances of the emergence of political units. So, while at first sight it may appear that these beginnings have some relation to the irrigable valleys of rivers like the Nile and the Euphrates, further consideration will show, on the one hand, that there were valleys of this character in which civilizations did not arise, and, on the other, that civilizations have made their appearance in quite different situations. Some part of the difficulty that has been experienced in the attempt to isolate the common factors in the different instances of the emergence of advanced groups is unquestionably due to the use of such vague and all-inclusive terms as 'civilization.' If, however, we restrict the inquiry, for the moment, to the beginnings of political organization, a working basis for comparison will be obtained which will be found to lead to definite and verifiable results.

When, therefore, we come to compare the different situations in which political units can be seen to emerge, it is first to be observed that these units are restricted to small areas, and, when the common character of these areas is examined, it is demonstrable that they are termini of routes of travel, and hence points of pressure which have been strictly determined by the physical conformation of the earth's surface.

It may be well, as far as possible, to envisage the situation. South of the great Eurasian plain, the mountain barrier and the desert belt offer very real obstacles to human movement; the actual ways, restricted to practicable passes and sufficiently watered routes, provide but limited possibilities in lines of travel. Hence, supposing that any considerable body of men should, for any reason whatever, be driven from an established habitat to seek a new place of abode, the world would be 'open' to it only in the most general sense. Indeed, any one choice would severely restrict all the movements that were to follow, and with each step in any given direction the options for the future would become ever fewer. If now we turn to observe the habitable extremities to which the routes lead, it is manifest that a theoretical first migrating group will settle down where conditions are endurable, but a second will find itself confronted by the first as occupants in possession. In whatever manner this situation may be met, and there is evidence that some of the earlier groups have moved on, the time comes when the question of occupancy must be fought out at the gateway. In other words, while a little effort will serve to move a single railroad car on the track, a long line of cars lying ahead cannot be set in motion by any amount of mere human pressure exerted at one end.

Where these conditions have been fulfilled, political organizations have arisen, sooner or later, throughout the Eurasian continent. Thus in China and in India, which, as has already been pointed out, are pockets on a gigantic scale, the earliest appearance of political units is just within the entrance or opening. Something of the same general character is to be seen in England, where the earliest political units came into existence along the line of greatest exposure to the Continent, whereas, just as in China and India, the population of the more remote and inaccessible areas of the kingdom has scarcely been politicized up to the present day.

All the termini of routes are not, however, of this Indo-Chinese pattern, and Mesopotamia affords an example of a different kind. Here, indeed, is a land which is accessible from every quarter, so that it may be regarded as the focus of routes leading in from different directions. Nevertheless, the phenomena exhibited are of exactly the same character; political organizations come into existence at the point of pressure, and the only difference between this case and the former is a difference in the degree of exposure, which turns, not upon the activity of men, but upon the physical disposition of mountains, rivers, and deserts. Furthermore, if we think of the Euphrates and Tigris, we may see that, as water would rise in a river in the presence of some obstacle, political units make their appearance higher and higher upstream as successive entrants make their way along the different avenues of approach.

Stated thus, even in the most general terms, it becomes evident that everywhere the beginnings of political organization have been determined by the physical disposition of the land. It will have been observed, however, that this determinant influence of routes has been dependent upon the presence of human beings, that it comes into play only in the event of the movement of peoples. Hence the origin of these movements becomes a matter of primary importance, more particularly as the homogeneity of history is further exhibited in the dependence of these movements on man's physical surroundings.

3) With practical uniformity, the view taken of the origin of migrations is that these movements have been the necessary outcome or manifestation of the 'natural increase' or 'automatic excess' of population. Nothing, indeed, could well appear simpler to the modern mind than this transference to earlier times of the typically nineteenth-century picture of ever-flowing streams of emigration finding their way to distant colonies. Yet, convincing as it may seem, the explanation conceals a problem of some magnitude and complexity.

To reach the core of the difficulty, it may be pointed out that the great rise in European population during the last century and a half is an altogether exceptional phenomenon. At its very beginning, this increase deeply impressed the minds of thoughtful contemporaries, and, among others, Malthus took up the problem, setting himself "to investigate the causes that have hitherto impeded the progress of mankind." The object of the present inquiry might almost be stated in the same terms, but Malthus, possibly with greater discretion, limited his field of research to an investigation of the effects, in man, of the constant tendency in all life to increase beyond the available means of subsistence. Of this tendency there can be little doubt, and, later on, Darwin took it for granted that organic beings may be regarded as striving to the utmost to increase in numbers. He pointed out that the progeny of a single pair of any species, if unhindered, would soon cover the earth, and Malthus estimated that, under favorable conditions, the human race might double itself four times in every hundred years. Manifestly, however, no such 'natural increase' takes place, either among animals or men, and the crucial point in the investigations both of Malthus and of Darwin was the nature and effect of the 'checks' by which population is limited.

It was argued by Darwin that each organic being lives by a struggle at some period of its life, and, adopting the view expressed by Malthus that those who labor under any original weakness or infirmity would be the first to succumb, he arrived, by inverting the idea, at the conclusion that the survival of the fittest led eventually, not merely to a maintenance of the standard, but to the development of new species. As there has been a marked disposition on the part of humanistic students to apply Darwin's hypothesis to the special case of man, it may be urged that Darwin's adaptation of Malthus' ideas should not be permitted to supersede Malthus' contribution in its own field, and this particularly since, notwithstanding the common tendency of animal and human population to increase, the difference in the nature of the 'checks' applied is so marked as to make separate consideration imperative. Among animals, as Darwin saw, the struggle is a direct physical effort, and results in the elimination of individuals unable to bear their part; among human beings, as Malthus pointed out, actual want of food is, practically speaking, never the immediate check. Indeed, what we have to consider in the latter is the means adopted for the prevention of increase, for in no human group has population been left to grow with perfect freedom or without interference. The inquiry concerning man must concern itself, then, with the results of means adopted, consciously or unconsciously, for the restriction of population; and hence at the outset we are confronted with a substitution of ideas in place of the physical processes represented in 'natural selection.'

In beginning his examination of the influences which have retarded human advancement, Malthus set forth certain "propositions" which he regarded as axiomatic. First, he considered that "population is necessarily limited by the means of subsistence," and, second, that "population always increases where the means of subsistence increase." To the first of these an addendum might be offered, which, though by no means self-evident, is regarded by Bateson as axiomatic from the standpoint of the biologist. This may be stated in the form that, as population is necessarily limited by the means of subsistence, in normal stable conditions it remains stationary. Now it will readily appear that if this addendum is a true statement, mere 'natural increase' cannot be assigned as a reason for migration, and hence some other explanation must be sought to account for this phenomenon. It follows, therefore, that the nature of the arguments which may be advanced in support of the added proposition must be briefly indicated.

The point to be brought out is that, owing to the restrictive measures employed, primitive groups do not multiply to such a degree that an overflow of population takes place. Among animals, the individual arrives on the scene of life to accept the chances of a struggle in which the more vigorous and fortunate have an advantage; among primitive peoples, on the other hand, a continuance of the life of the individual turns, in the first instance, upon the decision of older members of the group into which he is born, and the chances of survival are arbitrarily limited by the forethought, for their own well-being, of those upon whom the new arrival is dependent. Writing in the eighteenth century, Raynal drew attention to "that multitude of singular institutions which retard the progress of population." To convey a clear impression of the extent to which the 'natural increase' of early or lower groups was restricted, it would be necessary to consider each of these various practices; for the present purpose, however, it will be sufficient to take as an example the influence of infanticide.

First, it should be observed that, in order to render population stationary, it would only be necessary that the restricting practices should affect a limited and variable surplus which would remain after allowance had been made for the normal or average infant mortality of a given place and condition of life, and for the number actually necessary to maintain the full complement of the group. This being so, it is of importance to notice that infanticide, the killing of newborn infants, has been practiced universally throughout the world (until superseded in modern times by more remote methods for accomplishing the same ends).

It is not to be assumed that, in its earliest application, the practice of infanticide was inspired by any farsighted concern for the food supply of later years. In its simplest form, the practice seems to have arisen from the readily appreciable difficulty that a mother finds in caring for more than one infant at a time under primitive conditions of life. At a very early period, however, it seems to have been appreciated that if all the children born were allowed to live there would not be food enough to support everybody. This truth, as has frequently been pointed out, would soon force itself upon the attention of islanders; and modern observers have reported that in certain islands from a half to two-thirds of all infants were killed at birth. When forethought had once come to play a part, the practice of infanticide seems to have assumed some fairly definite form, and to have come, in a measure, under public surveillance. So, while in one group the first or even the first two or three infants would be killed, in another all after the first three or four would be done away with. Twins, weakly children, those born on unlucky days or for whom the omens were inauspicious, children whose upper teeth came first, appear, in general, to have met with an untimely end. Before long the selection evidently came into close association with some conception of the needs of the group: Australian women are said, out of an average of six children, to rear as a rule two boys and a girl, and practically everywhere the ratio of boys and girls is a matter of special concern.

As a consequence of the interest excited by McLennan's theory of the origin of exogamy, the question of the prevalence of female infanticide has to a great extent overshadowed the more general problem. Here it may be observed that male infanticide seems to stand in the same relation to mother-rite groups that female infanticide does to patriarchal groups. In the former, since descent passes through the female side, girls are preferred, and boys are less desirable; in the latter, the conditions are reversed. So, too, where daughters could be sold for a good price to husbands, they would be valued, but where a dower had to be given, they would be looked upon as a source of loss. Conversely, with the introduction of the custom of tracing descent through males, boys were preferred, more especially because the dead were dependent upon heirs male for the sacrifices associated with ancestor worship.

If the influence of infanticide in restricting numbers is to be fully appreciated, it must be understood that the practice was not a mere matter of individual caprice, but was commonly regarded as a public concern of moment to the group as a whole. The decision was not by any means universally left to the parents, and in some places the carrying out of the sentence was entrusted to professional practitioners. The most impor-

tant aspect of the matter, however, is that the infant had no
standing in the group into which it was born—was veritably 'a
little stranger'—until it had been formally accepted into the
kin. As van Gennep has pointed out, the attitude of the group
toward the infant was one of self-defense, and it was necessary
that the newcomer should undergo purification, and remain
for a period in a state of probation, before the rite of admission
was celebrated. Very generally, it would appear, the child was
submitted to more or less public inspection, and the rite of
acceptance was performed by the headman of the village or
the head of the family group. At Athens the decision seems,
primitively, to have been arrived at by a family council; later,
the father announced before the altar of Hestia whether the
child was to be accepted or abandoned; finally, it would seem,
the official ceremony was confined to acceptance—failure to
celebrate the birth was tantamount to rejection.

Clearly, then, the practice of infanticide alone must have
gone far toward limiting the numbers of earlier groups and
rendering population stationary, and it must not be overlooked
that this is but one of a number of such practices. That these
methods of keeping population within bounds were effective
may, furthermore, be inferred from the stability of the boundaries between different primitive groups, and from the widespread evidences of a persistent attitude of hostility toward
strangers. The boundaries of tribal territory, as Grierson has
shown, are, in general, clearly defined, not merely by the natural landmarks of rivers, lakes, forests, and mountains, but even
by artificial monuments. The borders are jealously defended,
and, being on either side placed under the protection of supernatural powers who are believed to take upon themselves the
punishment of venturesome intruders, are not violated without
trepidation. Indeed, beyond the group boundary, the world
was necessarily full of menace, for among all lower peoples the
stranger was feared and treated as an enemy, and the relation
between stranger groups was one of persistent hostility. So,
while Holsti has shown conclusively that primitive warfare

consisted more of shouting and terrifying than of fighting with intent to kill, it is not to be assumed that the hostility was factitious; and the fact that peaceful intercourse between neighboring groups was limited in the extreme is shown by the custom of the 'silent trade.' Singular as it may appear, in this mode of bartering, traces of which are still to be found in every quarter of the globe, the traffickers not only do not address but do not even see one another. The silent trade is simply a means by which enemies may mutually exchange goods and at the same time remain in safety; "they, indeed, keep faith with one another, but in so doing they are actuated, not by any feeling of amity, but wholly by the wish to serve their own interests."

It cannot be asserted that the addendum offered to the first proposition of Malthus has the same axiomatic character as the statement that "population is necessarily limited by the means of subsistence"; nor can it be demonstrated from statistics that "in normal stable conditions population remains stationary"; nevertheless, it may now be urged that there are weighty considerations which tend to substantiate such a conclusion. So, as the longevity of the savage is less than that of civilized man, and as the conditions of savage life undoubtedly have an appreciable influence upon fecundity, the prevalence of such customs as infanticide, not to speak of the influence of various forms of marriage, must have made anything like rapid increase of population impossible. Furthermore, all we know of the habits of lower groups, more particularly their dread of strange places and strange people, tends to confirm the view that such groups have long remained practically stationary in numbers. Finally, Keane points out that various aboriginal peoples seem to have remained in their original habitats ever since what may be called the first settlement of the earth by man; and, after an exhaustive inquiry, Willcox arrives at the conclusion that, where the influence of Europe has not been deeply felt, notably in China, and in Japan before its opening to Western influence, population has been nearly or quite stationary or has actually decreased.

4) Presuming, then, that population in normal stable conditions remains stationary, that among primitive peoples there is no 'natural increase' which would lead inevitably to migrations, it becomes pertinent to inquire how movements of peoples have been brought about.

This suggests the second proposition of Malthus, that "population always increases where the means of subsistence increase." If this be true, then, obviously, its converse must be true, and population will decrease when the means of subsistence diminish. The initial point for consideration, it will thus be seen, is not so much the rise and fall of numbers as the increase and decrease of the food supply. Unfortunately, Malthus took up the diminution of numbers, not in relation to contraction of food supply, but merely as illustrating the recuperative power of population after such visitations as plague, pestilence, and famine. The direction of his interest led him to concern himself primarily with the mode by which subsistence is increased, and so he points out that population multiplies rapidly when, in new colonies, the knowledge and industry of an old state are applied to the unappropriated land of a new country. The most notable rise in population of which we have historical knowledge has followed upon modern improvements in agricultural methods, whether in old countries or in new. We may say, in short, that increase of population, in modern times, follows upon increased production of food.

It must now be observed that, while increase of the food supply will permit more people to live upon the same area, there is no reason to suppose that this increase will lead to migration. And, accepting the fact that we know of no period at which the earth was not filled up to the limit of existing conditions—Keane dates the complete occupation of the globe by man in the early Pleistocene epoch—and assuming, from what has been said, that any local advance would simply mean that a greater number would be supported on a given territory, we are still left without a clue to the explanation of the movements of peoples. If, however, we turn to consider, not the

effect of an increase of the means of subsistence, but the effect
of a decrease, the difficulty will, I think, be seen to disappear.
If, briefly, it can be shown that populations have actually been
driven forth in consequence of a shrinkage of food supply due
to a lessening of the productivity of the land, a satisfactory
explanation will be provided for the movements of peoples.

While the productivity of the land is increased by human
activity, it may also be affected injuriously by the same means.
Population shifts, for example, when the methods employed
have led to the working out of the soil, leaving as a memorial
'the abandoned farm.' So, too, population has declined in more
than one area when an invasion has been followed by a lapse
to inferior methods of cultivation, as in the Euphrates-Tigris
valley; or when, as in the Turkish dominions, forms of taxation
have been introduced which bear with undue severity upon the
agricultural class. It is obvious, however, that these occurrences
are incidental to a relatively advanced civilization and cannot
be utilized to throw light upon earlier situations.

What would appear to be a simple illustration of food shrinkage, with its accompanying results, is provided by Livy when
he states that in Gaul, in the time of Ambigatus—whoever
he may have been,—a succession of abundant harvests led to
a rapid increase in numbers, and that subsequently, to relieve
the country from the burden of overpopulation, a rather large
number were sent out to seek a new home. Paulus Diaconus
relates that the same experiment was resorted to by the Lango-
bardi, who, he says, divided their whole group into three parts
and determined by lot which part should go forth. Machiavelli,
improving upon this, regards the increase as constant, and the
method of division and emigration as an established custom.
He seems, like many later writers, to have been impressed by
Paul's explanation that the North, being colder than the South,
is more healthy, and better fitted for the propagation of nations. He thought, indeed, that the whole country was called
'Germania' because such great multitudes sprang up there, a
theory which evidently takes its rise in the etymology of Isi-

dore, who imagined that the word 'Germany' was derived from
germinare; the same idea is represented in Jordanes, who
traces the Goths to this "hive of races or womb of nations."
While Malthus was inclined to follow Paul and Machiavelli,
Gibbon doubted the regularity of these outpourings, and we
can now see that the entire series of explanations, from Livy
down, is simply an effort to account for the one known fact that
migrations occur. Modern scholars, like Chadwick, prefer to
attribute the movements in question to pressure from behind
rather than to the effects of sporadic cases of overpopulation.

Climate is everywhere variable, and wet spells succeed dry
spells in a halting rhythm. Good seasons may possibly stimulate
population, but, after all, sporadic influences of this sort are
not likely to have changed the face of the world by inaugurating the great migrations known to history as 'the wandering
of the peoples.' A more significant effect may be attributed to
a succession of bad seasons, particularly when these take the
form of long-continued droughts. To observe the full effect
of such occurrences it is necessary to turn from Europe to Asia.
Thus in the northwestern provinces of India, the meeting
point of the two great rain currents, scarcity of moisture is frequent, and from time to time the autumn rains fail completely.
Then famine ensues, and the stricken people, to escape destruction, move blindly "in the direction of Mâlwa, that Cathay or
land of plenty, where, in the imagination of the North Indian
rustic, the fields always smile with golden grain and poverty is
unknown." So, too, in southern India the inhabitants, similarly
impelled, have been known to travel in thousands toward the
distant hills. Here, then, is a force strong enough to overcome
the most deeply ingrained immobility, and to break down even
the strongest barriers of caste. Nevertheless, it is difficult to
discover in an exodus of disorganized and starving beings more
than a semblance of those movements which have played so
conspicuous a part in the history of man. If, however, we consider the conditions existing in Central Asia, other important
factors will be found to present themselves.

Since the end of the eighteenth century the idea has been widely entertained by linguistic scholars that the distribution of languages in Europe is best to be explained on the hypothesis of a series of migrations of peoples from Central Asia. While the literature of this discussion is extraordinarily extensive, there does not appear to have been any concerted effort on the part of philologists to inquire into the origin of migrations, though as early as 1820 passages from the *Zend-Avesta* had been cited to show that a sudden lowering of temperature in northern Asia (attributed later to the coming of the Ice Age in Siberia) had compelled the population to seek a warmer habitat. On this basis, seemingly, the phrase 'climatic change' has retained its place without substantiation from direct investigation. A new view of the matter was introduced in 1892 when James Bryce, discussing the origin of migrations, pointed out that "a succession of dry seasons, which may merely diminish the harvest of those who inhabit tolerably humid regions, will produce such a famine in the inner parts of a continent like Asia as to force the people to seek some better dwelling-place." It was not, however, until the narratives of recent explorers like Sven Hedin and Aurel Stein, at the opening of the twentieth century, had directed attention anew to the presence of sand-buried ruins in Central Asia that the underlying problem was vigorously attacked, and this time by geographers.

The active discussion of the origin of the migrations from Central Asia may be said to have been inaugurated in 1904 by two memorable papers in the *Geographical Journal*. In the earlier of these, Mackinder laid emphasis, first, upon the aridity of the heart of the Eurasian land mass, its system of internal drainage, and the fact that it is not a continuous desert like the Sahara, but a steppeland with alternations of desert areas and river-fed oases. Second, he pointed to the mobility of its horse-riding inhabitants—a factor which has also been dwelt upon by Demolins and Vidal de la Blache. In the discussion which followed, Holdich raised the question of the reason for the overflow of peoples from Central Asia, and was emphatic in his opinion that one of the great compelling reasons for all these migrations had been a distinct alteration in the physical conditions of the country. It is of some interest to notice, as showing the views recently held, that Mackinder, in reply, considered that when you had the evidence of this constant succession of descents, it was quite unnecessary to ask for any explanation of it.

In the later paper, Prince Kropotkin developed the theory, on a broad geological foundation, that Central Asia is in a state of rapid desiccation, and, adverting to the existing evidences of a greater population in times past, stated the belief that "it must have been the rapid desiccation of this region which compelled its inhabitants to rush down to the Jungarian Gate, down to the lowlands of the Balkash and the Obi, and thence pushing before them the original inhabitants of the lowlands, to produce those great migrations and invasions of Europe which took place during the first centuries of our era." Here again the discussion brought out important considerations. Mackinder, while accepting Kropotkin's general contention, thought that there was a tendency to exaggerate the rapidity of the desiccation during the historical period; he was inclined to doubt that the invasions of Europe had originated in desiccation, but accepted Hedin's conclusion that the shifting of sand by the wind had frequently brought catastrophe to human settlements. Freshfield, citing various climatologists, was convinced that it was oscillation in climate, and not desiccation, to which all the records pointed. Mill drew attention to the constancy of the total rainfall during historical time, and expressed the opinion that there was a drying up of the plateau regions of all the continents, compensated for by an increase of precipitation elsewhere. Evans insisted that the general question of the desiccation of the globe should be kept distinct from that of the drying up of Central Asia, and pointed to recent changes in the physical geography of the latter region which rendered inevitable the desiccation of the country. The whole problem was thus opened up, with an evident consensus that some change, continuous or fluctuating, had taken place in the climate of Central Asia. At the end of a decade, during which the question of desiccation was warmly debated, Gregory presented an exhaustive review of the opinions embodied in the literature. From this it would appear that the coöperation of geologists and geographers had been able to reach no more definite result than that, as an increased rainfall had been demonstrated for many parts of the world, there was a predisposition in favor of a compensating decrease in Central Asia, though the conflict of opinion on this point might be explained on the hypothesis that the desert is widening in some places and contracting in others.

Now it must be evident that if the discussion of the relation of change of climate to migration is not to remain permanently (like its philological counterpart) on the basis of the advocacy of personal views, actual investigation of the archaeological evidence must be carried out upon the ground, for in this way only may direct proof be obtained. It is to the high credit of Raphael Pumpelly that he envisaged the problem in this way; and it is fortunate that grants from the Carnegie Institution made possible two expeditions to Turkestan, in 1903 and 1904, under his direction. It should be understood that these expeditions were organized, and the grants made, for the specific purpose of investigating the theory that the great civilizations of the East and West had their origins in Central Asia, and of examining the evidence for the supposed occurrence of changes of climate in the same region. The results arrived at in regard to these questions, therefore, were not by-products of some other undertaking, and are further guaranteed by the fact that the work was carried on by a selected group of specialists. (It may be noted that Ellsworth Huntington, whose *Pulse of Asia* has enjoyed a wide popularity, was an assistant on the two expeditions.) In the present connection it is unnecessary to enter into detail in regard to Pumpelly's successes; what is of importance here is the fact that evidence was accumulated to show that, in Turkestan, organized town life, with agriculture and the breeding of animals, goes back possibly thousands of years before the Christian era, and that after these investigations no doubt remains that the inhabitants of the sites explored had been repeatedly driven forth by destructive changes of climate.

Population, then, is limited, in any given habitat, by the means of subsistence; it remains stationary in normal stable conditions, but may increase without disturbing the equilibrium if the food supply be increased through improvements in the methods of production. On the other hand, the inhabitants of a given area will be forced out when, through the operation of natural agencies, such as a diminution of rainfall, the means of subsistence decrease, and from this compulsory movement ensue migrations. Clearly, therefore, it is unnecessary to assume that among certain groups population has been permitted to grow without restraint, or to imagine some 'mighty hive' from which nations have emerged in 'swarms,' or to suppose the existence of specifically 'restless' peoples. It is of some interest to recollect, at this point, that any disturbance of conditions will manifest itself in an increase of population, and it can scarcely be doubted that migratory movements lead to the multiplication of population, instead of being the product of overpopulation in an established community. Finally, migrations are not to be attributed to a spirit of enterprise; peoples do not wander forth seeking for they know not what. We cannot assume in groups long fixed in habitat and ideas the sudden desire for booty, or freedom, or glory, or for 'something unattainable.' Nor may we accept the hypothesis that man is primarily a migratory, restless being, and that his fossilization ensues only when he is temporarily debarred from pursuing his natural impulses and is brought to a standstill. Man is prone to remain where he is, prone to fixity in ideas and in ways of doing things, and only through nature's insistent driving has he been shaken out of his immobility and set wayfaring upon the open road.

5) So far, then, it has been shown that political units have arisen at certain definitely circumscribed places. These places

have not been consciously selected or decided upon by men, but have been determined by the conformation of the earth's surface, that is, by the localization of habitable areas and the possibilities of travel. The common element to be observed is that the places where political organizations have come into being have been points of pressure; they have not merely been lands upon which one group after another might have set covetous eyes, but have been the termini of routes which, of necessity, have been followed by successive migrant groups. The dependence of man upon his physical surroundings, thus exhibited, is made even clearer when it is observed that the human movements which lead eventually to the beginning of political organization have had their origin, not in man's foresight or planning, or as a result of the 'automatic increase' of population, but in changes of climate within a definite area.

If, now, we accept this statement of the dependence of man upon his physical surroundings, it obviously becomes necessary to inquire how migrations have operated to bring political organizations into existence. This inquiry will have the additional advantage of showing the uniform dependence of history upon a second set of natural factors, namely, the fundamental characteristics of man himself.

Chapter 3

The Human Factor in History

POLITICAL ORGANIZATION is a comparatively recent phenomenon which has made its appearance among men in certain restricted places at definite moments in time, and has spread but slowly from different points of origin. This fact has hitherto had little significance for the historian, for, owing to his preoccupation with the study of documents, he has been more interested in questioning the credibility of ancient narratives than in examining the antecedent conditions from which political units have sprung. When, however, the matter is explicitly brought up, it is evident that political organization is an exceptional thing, characteristic only of certain groups, and that all peoples whatsoever have once been or still are organized on a different basis. Furthermore, it is also evident that political organization has been but imperfectly extended over the population of the areas where it is dominant, and, consequently, that 'survivals' of the earlier regime are to be found even in the most highly developed countries. It will, therefore, be seen that the examination of the problem presented by the emergence of political organization is essential to an understanding of how man has come to be as he is, and that the uniformity of origin exhibited in this emergence is a further justification for maintaining the fundamental homogeneity of history.

If we compare 'primitive' and 'civilized' groups of men as we find them in the world today, almost the first point of difference that will strike the observer is that, among the former, the individual identifies himself by particularizing his blood relationships, whereas, in the latter, the individual defines his status in terms of relation to a given territory. For example, "the Saxons brought with them across the Narrow Seas an organization according to families, hundreds, and tribes, dependent, that is to say, on blood-relationship. But the settlement of these units in the conquered land gave rise to the later parishes, hundreds, and counties. Gradually the idea of domicile replaced that of clan as the principle of social order, and whereas the family, or the hundred of families were formerly responsible for the malefactor, the modern police have power of arrest within clearly defined county or municipal areas. Thus, while in later history the physical features of the country are in some ways less coercive, administrative divisions have grown more precise, and have become more constant elements in the machinery of government."

This striking difference seems first to have been emphasized, in 1861, by Sir Henry Maine, and was dealt with, later, from the point of view of the anthropologist, by Lewis Henry Morgan.

Archaic law, Maine remarks, "is full, in all its provinces, of the clearest indications that society in primitive times was not what it is assumed to be at present, a collection of individuals. In fact, and in the view of the men who composed it, it was an aggregation of families." If, then, kinship in blood is the original basis of organization, there is no revolution known to us, he continues, "so startling and so complete as the change which is accomplished when some other principle—such as that, for instance, of local contiguity—established itself for the first time as the basis of common political action." "The idea that a number of persons should exercise political rights in common simply because they happened to live within the same topographical limits was utterly strange and monstrous to primitive antiquity." "The most recent researches into the primitive history of society," he says in a later book, "point to the conclusion that the earliest tie which knitted men together in communities was consanguinity or kinship." "We have next to consider the epoch, reached at some time by all the portions of mankind destined to civilization, at which . . . the land begins to be the basis of society in place of kinship. The change is extremely gradual, and in some particulars it has not even now been fully accomplished, but it has been going on through the whole course of history. The constitution of the family through actual blood-relationship is of course an observable fact, but, for all groups of men larger than the family, the land on which they live tends to become the bond of union between them, at the expense of kinship, ever more and more vaguely conceived."

Morgan, after describing the earlier form of organization, goes on to say that the later form is "founded upon territory and upon property, and may be distinguished as a state (*civitas*). The township or ward, circumscribed by metes and bounds, with the property it contains, is the basis or unit of the latter, and political society is the result. Political society is organized upon territorial areas, and deals with property as well as with persons through territorial relations. . . . In ancient society this territorial plan was unknown. When it came it fixed the boundary line between ancient and modern society."

Now, while the forms and problems presented by the facts of kindred organization are represented in anthropology by an extensive literature, and while the forms and problems of political organization have been described and discussed by all the generations of historians and political theorists from Herodotus and Aristotle to the present day, I am unaware of any sustained effort that has been made to investigate the transition from the one to the other by comparison of all the available data. The question of the relations of the different types of kindred organization forms one of the major interests of anthropology; on the other hand, it is with the experience of men under the conditions of the new organization that history, in the accepted meaning of the term, deals, and it must be apparent now that the only satisfactory approach to the study of history will lie through the investigation of the phenomena of transition wherever this may have taken place. But, while the transition has not yet been made the subject of extended research, there is one fact at least which stands out with such distinctness that it may be utilized at once to exhibit the homogeneity of history and to reveal the source of the most notable characteristics of modern life.

2) To observe this fact in its proper setting, it is necessary to see that, while the distinction between kindred and political units may readily be defined, the description of the difference does not explain how the later condition sprang from the earlier. In other words, there is some step or process involved in the transition which has not been brought to light.

To comprehend the situation fully, we may begin by saying that kindred organization, in whatever form it may assume, reflects the natural facts of human generation. What follows immediately from this is a commonplace of the study of primitive man which must be constantly borne in mind, for kindred organization implies the unquestioned and unremitting dominance of the group over the individual, and this leads to the tenacious and uncompromising maintenance of customary ways and ideas. It will thus be seen that the despotism of custom negatives the idea that kindred organization could have been given up voluntarily, or exchanged, after deliberation, for something invented or considered better. The change, as I have pointed out, has been forced upon men at certain geographical points, determined by the physical distribution of land and water, and by a series of exigencies which go back to specific datable occurrences within a definite area of the earth's surface. Furthermore, the immediate occasion of the breakup of kindred groups has been the collision and conflict, at the termini of routes, which have ensued from the migrations of men; and apparently it has required repeated, long-sustained, and bitter conflict—such, indeed, as Gilbert Murray has depicted in *The Rise of the Greek Epic*—to overcome, even in a limited degree, the adherence of such groups to old customs, old ways of doing things, and old ideas. Wherever political organizations have come into existence these conflicts have taken place, so that there is a direct historical relation between war and this particular step in human advancement.

Now, there is a strong temptation to turn aside here, under the guidance, let us say, of Chadwick's *Heroic Age,* and dwell upon the story of these struggles, dimly conveyed to us through the alluring haze of epic poetry, but it is essential, in the present connection, to keep clearly before us what it is that war has destroyed. The cardinal point is that the conflict, in breaking up the older organization, liberated the individual man, if but for a moment, from the dominance of the group, its observances, its formulas, and its ideas. Briefly, a situation was created in which the old rites and ceremonies could not be performed, one in which the old rules of action were manifestly inadequate, and hence one in which the individual became, in some measure, a law unto himself. This, at bottom, is the fact upon which all history turns.

It is difficult for the modern man to realize that, in the earlier period, individuality did not exist; that the unit was not the single life, but the group; and that this was the embodiment of a relatively fixed system, from which escape was normally impossible. So completely was the individual subordinated to the community that art was just the repetition of tribal designs, literature the repetition of tribal songs, and religion the repetition of tribal rites. Conversely, the breakup which resulted from the ultimate conflict of alien groups had, as its most essential feature, the release of personal initiative, the creation of personal responsibility, and the recognition of personal worth and individuality. These appear in actual life under the form of individual self-assertion, which, in all later developments, remains a significant phenomenon. And here, parenthetically, it may be pointed out that we accept readily enough as characteristic of the transition epoch the spirit of boasting which pervades the literature of such periods, and we set down as the all-pervading motive of action the hunger to win personal glory, but when we come to the discussion of our own times we show no disposition to analyze the conventions that now define the avenues through which the same spirit may find outlet, nor do we seek to discover the means by which this spirit is kept in check under modern conditions, nor the relation that its expression bears to opportunity. Needless to say, the question of the delimitation of the channels through which self-assertion might properly realize itself in desirable activities has never been taken up.

We are now in a position to see that the release of individual self-assertion through the temporary overthrow of the domination of customary restraints has been the necessary prelude to the emergence of territorial organization and the institution of personal ownership. However far apart these two elements may appear to be in modern life, in the beginning they are identical, for the fundamental characteristic of political organization is the attitude of personal ownership assumed by the ruler toward the land and the population over which he has gained control—an attitude expressed to this day in the phrases 'my army' and 'my people.' What we have uniformly at the beginning of the historical period in different lands is the assumption of sovereign ownership by an individual leader or king who relies upon the aid of a military group, caste, or aristocracy to hold in subjection a subordinate population of which little is heard; and later history is, primarily, the record of the unceasing efforts of kings to extend what they regard as their personal possessions. Even today, the most advanced political theory (of German origin, naturally) accepts the view that the state is an institution imposed by a victorious group upon those whom it has conquered, with the single object of regulating the authority of the victor over the vanquished, and guarding against internal rebellion and external assault. Rulership, in this view, has no further purpose than the economic exploitation of the conquered by the conquerors.

The crucial point to be observed here is that kingship and territorial organization represent simply the institutionalization of a situation which arose out of the opportunity for personal self-assertion created by the breakup of primitive organizations. And it should be understood that just as the relative stability of the older units follows from the fact that every human being is born into a given group and becomes assimilated to this in speech, manners, and ideas, so, in the new organization, the *status quo* operates to perpetuate itself, and the mere fact of its existence becomes an argument for regarding it as ordained by some supermundane power. Thus, throughout the past, we are presented with the anomaly of men fighting to maintain the institutionalized vestiges of the self-assertion of aggressive individuals on occasions of long-past upheavals. On the other hand, it must also be observed that—under conditions which it is of paramount importance for the historian to make clear—the spirit of self-assertion has arisen from time to time in the subordinate elements of composite groups. Indeed, what we ordinarily designate 'constitutional history' is largely occupied with the efforts put forth by one or another element, class, or order included within a political group to contest the dominance of a ruling minority and the theory of sovereign ownership. From this internal contest has arisen the theory of individual 'rights' (of which perhaps the most fundamental is that of preventing other people from interfering with a man's use of his own property), and the theory that political authorities may be tested and reformed in accordance with current ideas. But, while these matters constitute the marrow of history, we must leave them here to concern ourselves more particularly with other, less generally recognized, results of the initial self-assertion.

3) The object we have in view is to discover, if possible, how man everywhere has come to be as he is. From what has been said it will appear that this involves a consideration of the facts of 'transition' and 'release,' and a vivid realization that these phenomena have made their appearance only at certain geographical points and at certain moments of time. It has been shown already that political organizations have arisen at points definitely localized and determined by the physical features of the earth's surface, and it follows explicitly that the release of the individual from the dominance of the group, and the stimulus and opportunity necessary for the emergence of in-

dividual initiative and self-assertion, have been similarly restricted. Hence we arrive at an aspect of the matter which is manifestly indispensable for an understanding of the present condition of mankind, namely, that individualization and the politicization of groups have never been other than irregular and incomplete.

The origin of this irregularity is, simply, that pressure and conflict, coming at specific points, have never been evenly distributed geographically; and the breakup of kindred organization, never having been designed, has never been fully and deliberately carried out. Of necessity, some lands and some people, being nearer the immediate seat of conflict, have been more deeply involved in the struggle, and hence more completely exposed to the disturbing influences. Of necessity, too, release, being ultimately personal, has opened different paths of opportunity to different members of the community.

The manifestations of the irregularity have been of the most varied character. Within the groups primarily affected, for example, the breakdown of the old organization has not been accompanied by the revelation of any 'best possible' substitute, and so, in the stress of emergency, the old forms are made over to do service as best they may, new forms are called by old names, and new ideas masquerade in faded habiliments. Furthermore, when the turmoil begins to subside, the lately disturbed groups, as readily as their forefathers, turn to impose their newly acquired modes of thought and action upon the rising generations, and hence the arrangements of a given moment are perpetuated indefinitely.

Outside the original political group, again, the influences of the upheaval spread, as from a center, in ever widening and diminishing waves. To observe the results of this extension, it is necessary to make a distinction which, I think, has not hitherto been observed. If, avoiding the complexity of the situation presented in the countries ordinarily included in 'ancient' history, we turn our attention to China and India, it will be seen that a political organization comes into being in the midst of nonpolitical communities. Typically, the new political unit may be regarded as maintaining contact with tribal or kindred organizations on two frontages, and the distinction to be made arises from differences in the activities which follow from the conditions in the two directions. It has already been pointed out that, in China and India, political units make their appearance just within the exposed frontier; the result of this is that the new organization has behind it, rearward, an extensive country with a quiescent population grouped on the old lines, and, in front, outward, similar groups, subject, however, to perennial uneasiness and disturbance. From this situation there arise two different types of activity on the part of the middle group—and it is not without significance that in other countries besides China there has been a recognized 'middle kingdom.'

If, then, we consider the relations of the political unit toward the 'native' population in its rear (avoiding the error of identifying an assertion of territorial dominion with the politicization of a population), it will readily become apparent that almost never has this population been wholly incorporated into the political organization, or the kindred organization been completely broken down. This condition is manifest in China and India, but the statement holds true equally of Great Britain, and is conspicuous in the New World. The occasion of this unequal politicization of geographically protected peoples may be traced to the aggression or self-assertion of small bodies of men, representing individuals who have not submitted themselves to the process of restabilization in the political organization. It has been usual to classify these men, somewhat invidiously, as 'adventurers,' but in reality they are individuals for whose awakened initiative and desire for purposive action the new arrangement provides no adequate opportunity. It is the case, everywhere and in all times, of "the man who would be king": "we will go away to some other place where a man isn't crowded and can come to his own." So, in India, the Aryan settlement of the Punjab was followed by the rise of small Aryan kingdoms in the neighboring Ganges Valley, and the footsteps of the adventurers may even be traced, still farther south, in the Deccan. Precisely the same course of action is to be seen in China, and is exemplified frequently, in later times, in the colonial expansion of European peoples.

If we turn next to the policy of the 'middle' kingdom in regard to the outward or frontier groups, a wholly different situation comes into view, for here the aggression or pressure is directed against the central political organization, and not exerted by it. What is to be considered primarily is the means of defense adopted by the political unit against migrant invaders. In ancient times, it would seem that one of the earliest expedients for protecting the exposed frontier was the wall, and the barrier erected by the Chinese is but one instance of a practice which has been followed throughout Asia and Europe. On the other hand, it was discovered at a remote period— for example, by the Chinese under the Han dynasty—that a more effective defense of the land might be provided by a military occupation and control of the frontier territory lying beyond the actual boundary of the organized political unit; and the Chinese government followed intermittently the policy of maintaining its hold upon the provinces of Mongolia and Sinkiang. In this procedure we have an example of a strategic policy which has played a most significant part in the history of the world, and is even now a subject of debate in every foreign office on the globe. It is of interest to observe that the Romans should have relied, in general, upon the earlier expedient of the wall, with its accompaniment of a march or no man's land in front. But after the long series of barbarian invasions which brought about the disruption of the Western Empire, the newer political organizations which arose upon its foundations adopted the later Chinese policy and erected for defensive purposes, across Central Europe, that series of *Marken*—frontier provinces under military control—from which have sprung the German and Austrian governments of the present day.

Clearly, then, the extent of the influence exerted by the

'middle' kingdom and its central political organization will differ radically in the two directions; and we may see, in brief, that the present condition of the great contrasting groups of East and West, of China and India on the one hand and Europe on the other, springs from the manner in which the results of localized transitions from kindred to political organization have affected neighboring populations. Upon the interiorly situated groups, the more obvious institutions of the new regime are extended, through the forceful activity of individuals, without great disturbance to the earlier organization of the groups brought under subjection or the extension of any awakening influence to the individual members of these groups. Thus the institution of kingship, with its accompanying theory of sovereign ownership, is imposed in new areas without an attendant breakup of kindred organization, and without a resultant stimulus to personal initiative. Upon exteriorly situated peoples, the influence exerted is, on the other hand, altogether indirect. Beyond the wall, there is no extension of politicization. The frontier is a declaration of personal ownership, and with the internal condition of the exterior barbarians the king has no concern. But the barrier or pale, whether of masonry or of armed men, obviously exerts a pressure of its own; it acts effectively as a dam against which weight accumulates, and so creates a point of pressure for those outside. In the end, the barrier breaks, and with the inundation a new situation is created in which new tribal units are broken up, new individuals awake to self-assertion, and a new redistribution of ownership takes place.

I have remarked earlier that 'transition' has not been made the subject of extended comparative research, and all that has been done here is to suggest the indubitable importance of the study. Nevertheless, even a superficial inquiry brings to light certain points of great interest, and we see that transition is always a result of pressure and conflict at geographical points which are absolutely determined by the configuration of the earth's surface, and that this localization of transition, in place and time, leads everywhere to irregularity and unevenness in the distribution of political institutions. Most significant of all, the central feature of transition is not merely the substitution of territory for blood relationship as the basis of unity in human groups, but the emergence of individuality and of personal self-assertion, and hence it follows that human advance rests ultimately upon the foundation of individual initiative and activity.

4) At an earlier point in this discussion it was found necessary, in order to escape from the vagueness of such terms as 'civilization,' to restrict the inquiry, for the moment, to the beginnings of political organization. If, however, we are ever to understand how man has come to be as he is, the investigation cannot be limited in this manner; for while human life is, unquestionably, conditioned by the organization under which it is conducted, the actual content of life cannot be summed up or expressed in terms of organization. The differences which are to be observed between groups at the present moment, between earlier and later generations of the same group, between individuals, and between earlier and later periods in the life of the same individual, cannot be epitomized in any description of the forms of human association.

Here, for the sake of clearness, it may be pointed out that the practice of any art involves the acceptance of specific limitations and the recognition of conventional forms within which the artist's expression is confined. No student of sculpture or poetry, for example, will confuse the technique of a statue or a sonnet with the thought and emotion which it attempts to convey. In short, the work of art is something more than the technical rules by which it is conditioned. Now the conduct of life is an art, and is limited by specific rules and conventions, but there appears to be a preponderant disposition on the part of students of man to regard the exterior rules and conventions, laws and social usages, as the essential matter for consideration. This is made clear when we observe that legislators, publicists, and 'social workers' hold tenaciously to the opinion that the

advancement of man is to be effected by the simple expedient
of modifying the existing regulations. Whether this be true or
not, there can be no question that in the investigation of the
elements of human history we must set ourselves to inquire,
not merely how the forms and conventions of human aggre-
gates have reached their present status, but how the content of
life has come to possess the infinite variety which it exhibits
today.

In pursuit of this broader inquiry, we may begin by saying
that what differentiates man from animal cannot be what he
shares in common with his closest nonhuman relations, and
hence that, in seeking to account for human advancement, the
common possessions of animal and man must be eliminated
from consideration. Fortunately, there is practical agreement
among all classes of investigators—psychologists, logicians, and
anthropologists—that the differentia of man consists in his possession of articulate speech or spoken language. Speech is a
difference easily determinable, and has in itself proved to be
a subject of profound interest to scholars, but the success that
has attended the study of words and languages during the last
century has somewhat obscured the important fact that speech
does not exist in and for itself. The interest that has been taken
in the changes of form, sound, and meaning of words has hin-
dered, until quite recently, a just appreciation of the fact that
the study of words cannot be separated from the study of what
they designate. Speech comes into existence in response to the
desire on the part of a human being to make himself understood by someone else, and is an instrument for the communi-
cation of ideas. Language is a conveying medium, and the aim
of speech is the conveyance of ideas, not the mere interchange
of words. Hence the humanist, or student of man, will interest
himself not merely in the form of expression, but in what is
expressed; he will pass from the individual words of a language
to examine the ideas conveyed. Linguistic scholars have rendered invaluable service in the composition of grammars and
vocabularies, but they have, not infrequently, lost sight of the

circumstance that any given language is the medium through which a particular system of ideas finds expression. While, then, we may accept speech as the distinguishing mark of humanity, we cannot but recognize that the fundamental object of inquiry will be the system of ideas represented in a given language at a given time.

If, then, we come to compare, not man and brute, but the differing groups that go to make up the human population of the globe, the distinguishing feature of any group will be, not its language, implements, or institutions, but its particular idea system, of which these other manifestations of activity are varying expressions. Without exception, the products of human activity are expressions or aspects of the entire mental content of the group or individual. This mental content, moreover, is not to be conceived of as a mere assemblage of disparate units placed in juxtaposition, but as cohering in an idea system. Ideas are not simply accumulated or heaped up; on the contrary, every 'new' idea added not only modifies, but is in turn modified by, the existing system into which it is incorporated. Thus it appears that no idea system, any more than an actual spoken language, is a deliberate construction. Languages are made up of words, but these are not consciously and systematically elaborated; like the names in a scientific classification, they come into existence only as occasion demands, and are elicited by objects, actions, and events. Before 'plowing,' 'sowing,' and 'reaping' could have been named, these actions must have been performed and recognized. Similarly, the idea system of a group is not to be attributed to foresight or planning, but to the pressure of circumstance. It will appear, then, that if we are to consider the content of life in addition to the exterior forms of human association, the study before us must concern itself with the factors and processes through which the idea systems of different groups have come to be as we find them today.

In justification of thus postulating idea systems as a basis for the comparative study of man, it may be pointed out that what we find in 'civilization' is not the product of primary emotions, which man shares with animals, but of some activity which he has developed in a characteristic manner. This activity may be described as the formation and expression of ideas. The physical and psychological constitution of man being 'given'—a point to which reference will subsequently be made,—what varies from group to group is not this foundation, but the results of mental activity; and we want to know how these results have come to exhibit the differences we find in the world today. Thus human 'evolution' is, fundamentally, intellectual 'evolution,' and the diversity of status in human groups at the present time is to be traced to differences in mental activity. This basis of study will be found to meet all the requirements of the comparative method as exhibited in biological evolution, which is founded upon a comparison of the phylogenetic or historical series, the ontogenetic or biographical series, and the facts of present geographical distribution; and the investigation of how man has come to be as he is must be placed upon such a basis as will make the utilization of these categories possible. Furthermore, this basis has already been found necessary in different lines of humanistic inquiry. Human 'advancement' is not measurable in terms of any one of the classes or categories under which human activities have been grouped for purposes of study. When we consider any one subject like religion, art, language, or political organization by itself, we simply impose a voluntary limitation upon our personal attention; in actual life, on the other hand, the mental activity of man has never been divided into separate compartments. Hence, in dealing with these separate studies, we require some more general basis of comparison. So Hobhouse, tracing the evolution of morals, takes as a foundation "the collective stock of knowledge, the equipment of method and governing conceptions which constitute the working intellectual capital of any community." Similarly, S. A. Cook points out that "for the study of religion it is necessary to observe the tendency of man to blend into one whole his tested and untested knowledge, his own experience and that of others." "A 'body' or system of beliefs, practices, and the like, depends upon people; it is part of their larger total 'body' of thought, and undergoes development." "The development of a man's life and that of his total world of thought are interconnected; and since his profoundest and most valued beliefs are not unchangeable, the most vital part of his physical being and that of his world of thought are both capable of development. Each depends upon the other, and the whole evolves."

All the more, therefore, when we come to take up the broad problem of how man has come to be as he is will it be necessary to adopt the canon that judgment in regard to the mental activity of a given group can be based only upon the totality of the various mental phases of culture—language, custom, myth, and art. And this position is fortified by McDougall's opinion that "man, since he became man, has progressed in the main by means of the increase in volume and improvement in quality of the sum of knowledge, belief, and custom, which constitutes the tradition of any society. It is to the superiority of the moral and intellectual tradition of his society that the superiority of civilized man over existing savages and over his savage forefathers is chiefly, if not wholly, due."

As a result of these considerations, we arrive at the view that the study of how existing idea systems have come to be what they are provides a feasible basis for an investigation of the advancement of man. The alternative bases of study which ordinarily are adopted concern themselves, on the one hand, with the physical constitution of human beings, and, on the other, with the exterior forms of human association. The first of these leads at once to the theory that there have been and are innately superior races, innately superior classes, and innately superior individuals, and that human advancement has followed from the spontaneous activity of these higher elements. As, however, no effort has been made to account for the sporadic emergence of these exceptions to the general rule of backwardness and stagnation, in the long run the argument is just an assertion of the physical superiority of those who have become conspicuous. The second basis of study fixes attention upon the forms of group organization, and provides no opening to a broader consideration of the content of human life; whereas the basis here proposed brings under one view the entire range of activities represented in religion, art, literature, philosophy, and science, and coördinates these activities with the facts of history and of group organization.

5) If we turn to examine the relation of idea systems to group organization, a remarkable parallelism in development becomes apparent. It has already been pointed out that under primitive conditions organization is relatively stable, and that the individual is bound by the authority of the group. The idea systems of primitive groups are highly restricted in content, but, in addition to this limitation, the traditional ideas entertained have, in general, been transmuted into customary actions and ways of doing things. Thus, religious ideas are concentrated in rites and observances, and explanations of natural phenomena are embodied in symbolic ceremonies. In short, the whole body of custom and tradition represents ideas fixed in action. Since these modes of action, which are associated with all the essential activities of life, must be prosecuted with rigid adherence to precedent, it is evident that any reconsideration of the validity of the ideas upon which they rest is practically out of the question. Primitive man does not 'think,' he performs definitely prescribed actions under the eye of the community, which, in turn, is vitally concerned in the exactness with which the repetition of formula or ceremony is carried out. It will thus be observed, as Professor Shotwell suggests, that a study of the relation of custom and observance to idea systems, and of the conditions under which they become 'survivals' when the latter have changed, must ultimately constitute an essential feature of this inquiry; but as yet such study has not been undertaken.

It has been indicated that the breakdown of kindred organization, following upon migration and collision, tended to release the individual from the domination of the group, and to create a situation in which personal initiative and self-assertion became possible. It has now to be pointed out that, while this release may be regarded as affecting primarily the submission of the individual to the mandatory authority of the group, essentially it opens for the individual the possibility of thinking for himself without reference to group precedent. The emergence of individuality, with its accompanying manifestations of personal initiative and self-assertion, is intimately associated with the beginnings of independent mental activity, of thinking which may lead the individual to question the validity of inherited group ideas.

This striking result, it must be understood, is not achieved by the individual of his own volition or accord; it is thrust upon him by the force of circumstances. To make the point clear, we may say, speculatively, that had there ever been but one system of ideas common to all men, advancement would have been impossible, for progress in ideas springs from comparison, and a sense of difference could not arise from contemplation of different instances of the same thing. Conversely, the critical spirit is easily enough aroused by the juxtaposition of different means for attaining the same end; so that different observances for effecting the same result, different mythological explanations of the same phenomena, when brought into contact, may be expected to lead to questionings and comparisons.

That some such path has actually been followed in the past seems clear. Ernst Curtius pointed out, long ago, that the influence of sea navigation upon the development of the Greeks had been very marked, as it suddenly brought face to face men who had been living under widely different conditions, and hence induced an endless comparing, learning, and teaching. A more drastic form of the same process is exhibited, however, when successive migrating groups invade the land, be it ancient Greece or medieval Italy, and a time ensues of "constant warpaths and uprootings of peoples." In such circumstances, the whole traditional body of customs, rites, and observances tends to be overthrown, for the turmoil no longer permits of opportunity to propitiate the slain, or to maintain the sacrifices for the dead; the lines of kindred are broken, and new groups, composed of men whom chance has thrown together, are formed under the leadership of some individual whose self-assertion, backed by strength or craft, seems to offer protection. This is the essence of all 'Dark Ages,' in which, through swiftly moving change, contrasts are made vividly apparent, men awake to the perception of differences in ideas, and criticism is born.

At the present time the view is very widely entertained that human advancement is the outcome of the commingling of ideas through the contact of different groups. Thus Henry Balfour says, typically, "this process of grafting one idea upon another, or, as we may call it, the hybridization of ideas and experience, is a factor in the advancement of culture whose influence cannot be overestimated. It is, in fact, the main secret of progress." So, too, F. W. Maitland holds that "the rapidly progressive groups have been just those which have not worked out their own salvation, but have appropriated alien ideas." While, in the main, these statements may be accepted, it must, nevertheless, be insisted that the great advances of mankind have been due, not to the mere aggregation, assemblage, or acquisition of disparate ideas, but to the emergence of a certain type of mental activity which is set up by the opposition of different idea systems. This is illustrated in Jastrow's remark that civilization is everywhere the result of the stimulus evoked by the friction of one group upon another. The stimulus is mental, and the friction springs from the contact of differing customs and explanations. The simple commingling of ideas undoubtedly takes place, but the important point is that different ideas in regard to the same subject, when maintained in opposition by members of the same group, necessarily evoke comparison and critical discussion. The outcome of this is not always, nor even generally, a choice between two alternatives, for the debate will leave neither of the original positions wholly unchanged, and hence a new idea system will arise which is not a

selection of materials drawn from various sources, but a resultant of the juxtaposition of different bodies of thought.

We may see, then, that, under primitive conditions, the type
of organization operates to maintain a fixity of relations, customs, and ideas; under transitional conditions, however, the
dominant factor is the release of the individual, manifesting
itself in the self-assertion which gives to the new organization
its characteristic form, and in the personal criticism through
which the older idea systems are modified and changed.

6) If, as would thus appear, differences in idea systems have
been of crucial importance in the history of mankind, the question of how these differences have arisen will naturally force
itself upon our consideration.

Differences in idea systems are, substantially, man's response to differences in his surroundings. This fact has been
obscured, in general estimation, by the somewhat exaggerated
use which has been made of it by men like Buckle and Spencer,
who, for example, have attributed the growth of superstition
to the terror inspired by the threatening aspects of nature
in tropical countries. If, however, we keep to a less speculative level, it will readily be admitted that the surroundings
in which their respective lives are passed will present very
different objects for consideration to the Eskimo and to the
Arab; and so, while the language of the one has many different words for 'seal,' that of the other displays a similar elaboration of terms for the 'camel.' This form of dependence of
the group upon its habitat is so far recognized as unequivocal
and precise that it has been made the basis of extended philological research with the object of determining the earliest seat
of various peoples, notably the 'Aryans'; for where the names
of natural objects, such as trees and animals, have been bor-
rowed from other languages it is assumed that these could not
have been known to the particular group in its original home.
It is true that objections have been urged to this course of reasoning, but the fact remains that, where the conditions of life
lead men to pursue the occupation of fishing, the foreground

of their interest will be dominated by terms and ideas which would be entirely different if the same individuals were engaged in cattle raising or farming. In short, the surroundings in which a group is placed determine its primary interests, and these, as Boas has pointed out, affect the entire character of its vocabulary and the make-up of its system of ideas.

This fact is illustrated, for example, in Jastrow's study of Sumerian and Babylonian ideas of beginnings, "which may be summed up," he says, "in the statement that in the early Sumerian view the chief factor in the Creation myth is the bringing about of vegetation and fertility, whereas in the later Babylonian or Akkadian tale the main stress is laid upon the substitution of law and order for primitive chaos and lawlessness." Again, it is difficult to refrain from calling attention, in however condensed a form, to the examination of "The Background of Greek Science" by J. L. Myres, in which he endeavors "to recover some of the limiting conditions under which any scheme of scientific knowledge and scientific method necessarily came into being in Greek lands."

Considered as a theater, a place for observing nature, he says, Greek lands offer in some respects unequaled facilities. They are a region of abrupt contrasts and frank revelations of what nature is, in its infinitely various detail. Its clear air decimates distances—witness Lucretius' remark that far-off lights do not grow smaller; but its strong contrasts of hot and cold, owing to intensity of sunlight and rapidity of radiation, continually present the atmosphere as a perceptible fluid, with shimmering ripples over each roasted rock, and with an upper surface, emphatic as a sea level, on which the wool-pack clouds sit like snowflakes on a window pane. In such a climate, too, 'wet' and 'dry' are as clearly defined in their antagonism as 'hot' and 'cold'; for wet and dry are not only natural opposites, but are here engaged in perpetual struggle, in alternating seasons of rain and rainlessness. With the other great antitheses of the physical philosophy, light and darkness, hard and soft, sweet and bitter, it is the same; but most striking of all, perhaps, is the extraordinary rapidity both of decomposition and of organic growth. All these, Myres continues, "challenge curiosity about the origin and the nature of life, with peculiar insistence, and apparent facility of experiment. Who, then, or what, maintains the world? This, for men, as for Olympians, if Olympians thought about such things, was the supreme question to be asked of nature. It was a question of minor interest, and merely historical value, 'Who made the world?' and 'What shall it be in the end thereof?' This indifference to cosmogony and eschatology is characteristic of Greek physical speculation, and greatly lightened its task. It stands in the strongest contrast to the Oriental, and particularly the Babylonian, insistence on origins, and interest in creation myths; and enhances the Greek insistence on questions about the structure, the maintenance, and the current behavior of the world; questions which Oriental, and particularly Babylonian thought, neglects, or glozes over."

Inferentially, then, differences in idea systems are determined by differences in man's physical surroundings, and these differences are maintained through the discipline exercised by the group over the individual. When, however, we come to examine the factors in human advancement, it appears that radical changes in idea systems follow upon the collision of groups from dissimilar habitats. So it was not, as has been thought, because he rode a horse that the nomad from Central Asia influenced greatly the lives of the dwellers in the outer circle of Eurasian lands, but because the conditions of his life developed a system of ideas which was wholly different from theirs. And here it is of the highest importance to observe, with Hogarth, that the relatively small and well-marked area of the Ancient East, in which the earliest marked advancement of mankind appears to have taken place, contains within itself no less than six divisions characterized by large differences of a geographical nature. These are Asia Minor, Armenia, Syria, Arabia, Mesopotamia, and western Iran, and I am unable, at the moment, to recall any area similarly restricted in which so many distinct types of habitat are placed in close association. Neither lapse of time nor uniformity of government has been able to overcome the striking differences which the variations in habitat have promoted in the idea systems of the peoples of these regions. As has already been indicated, the lower valley of the Euphrates and Tigris represents the natural focal point of human movement in these lands, the terminus of many routes of travel, and we may now see that while this central position implies a maximum exposure to attack, it implies also a maximum exposure to different systems of ideas.

Finally, in confirmation of the hypothesis that the changes which have contributed to human advancement have ensued from the collision of groups from widely different habitats, and hence of different idea systems, we may point to the initial stages of those great outbursts of intellectual activity which have distinguished every people which has risen above the level of primitive man. Thus, the historian of China is forced to repeat, from chapter to chapter, the formula: "first the successful invasion, the destruction of the old power, and then the formation of new nations, governments, and types of men"; and the summary of results is typified in the statement that "not the least of the Mongols' gifts to China was the stimulus and fertilization of the native intellect in the domain of the imagination." Similarly, Vincent Smith, the historian of India, remarks that "the rule of the able and long-lived monarchs of the Gupta dynasty coincided with an extraordinary outburst of intellectual activity of all kinds. The personal patronage of the kings no doubt had some effect, but deeper causes must have been at work to produce such results. Experience proves that the contact or collision of diverse modes of civilization is the most potent stimulus to intellectual and artistic progress, and, in my opinion, the eminent achievements of the Gupta period are mainly due to such contact with foreign civilizations, both on the east and on the west." Again, the entire history of Babylonia and Assyria is an epitome of such situations, and this leads a recent historian to observe: "It may be put down as an axiom that nowhere does a high form of culture arise without the commingling of diverse ethnic elements." "The Euphrates valley from the time that it looms up on the historical horizon," he continues, "is the seat of a mixed population. Egyptian culture is the outcome of the mixture of Semitic with Hamitic elements. Civilization begins in Greece with the movements of Asiatic peoples, partly at least non-Aryan, across the Aegean sea. In Rome we find the old Aryan stock mixed with a strange element, known as Etruscan. In modern times, France, Germany, and England furnish illustrations of the process of the commingling of diverse ethnic elements leading to advanced forms of civilization." Ultimately, attention may be directed to Petrie's conclusion in his memorable study of *The Revolutions of Civilisation* that "every civilization of a settled population tends to incessant decay from its maximum condition; and this decay continues until it is too weak to initiate anything, when a fresh race comes in, and utilizes the old stock to graft on, both in blood and culture. As soon as the mixture is well started, it rapidly grows on the old soil, and produces a new wave of civilization. There is no new generation without a mixture of blood, parthenogenesis is unknown in the birth of nations."

7) At this point, it is necessary to revert for a moment to a theory which has gained wide acceptance in modern times, namely, that human advancement has been the direct result of war. Thus Brinton, himself a veteran of the Civil War, urges that "in spite of the countless miseries which follow in its train, war has probably been the highest stimulus to racial progress. It is the most potent excitant known of all the faculties. The intense instinct of self-preservation will prompt to an intellectual energy which nothing else can awake. The grandest works of imagination, the immortal outbursts of the poets, from Homer to Whitman, have been under the stimulus of the war-cry ringing in their ears." It will not be necessary to epitomize the views to which this idea has given rise, or to indicate the variety of the arguments which have been adduced in its

support. From all that has here been said, it is obvious that war has played a most significant part in the advancement of mankind, but the benefits it has conferred have been confined to the breakup of crystallized systems of organization and of thought. Since man has not become sufficiently self-conscious of the natural processes which dominate his life, he continues to submit to the fixative influences of group discipline, and throws all his weight in favor of maintaining the *status quo*. It follows that, in the past, the gateway of human advance has been the violent conflict of the representatives of old and new ways of thought and action, whether the old and new be embodied, for the occasion, in states, in groups within a given state, or in single individuals. It must, therefore, be regarded as a shortsighted view which imagines the conflict thus precipitated as in itself a desirable thing, though, heretofore, man's ignorance of himself has made such conflicts inevitable. On the other hand, this opinion emphasizes, as perhaps nothing else could at the present moment, the supreme importance of an understanding of the elements of history. To reach this desideratum it has been necessary, first of all, to show that the history of man is homogeneous throughout, and to point out the factors which exercise a determinant influence upon the course of events; but to gain a knowledge which may be of direct service in the consideration of human affairs we must now turn our attention, more specifically, to the processes through the operation of which man everywhere has come to be as he is.

Chapter 4

Method and Results

THE TASK of science in the presence of a history, be it the history of the physical universe, of the earth, of the forms of life upon the earth, or of man, is the discovery of the processes through which things—stars, strata, and species—have come to be as they are, and each of the major sciences, such as Astronomy, Geology, and Biology, has entered upon the modern phase of its activities with the recognition of this fundamental problem. Commonly, this new departure is associated in men's minds with the acceptance of the idea of 'evolution,' which, in its most general form, implies simply that things have come to be as they are through a sequence of changes undergone in the past. As a consequence, it has been affirmed that 'evolution' is just the projection of the idea of human history upon the world of nature; but the restricted sense in which this notion is true is that men have come to observe the phenomena of nature in a time relation or perspective. If, on this account, the student of organic nature may be said to have applied the idea of human history to his own subject matter, he has in no sense adopted the historian's method. He does not attempt to write a narrative of what has happened in the past. In fact, it is not open to him to present his results in chronological form, since the biological record is entirely lacking in specific dates for happenings. From this deficiency most important consequences have ensued, for, on the one hand, the evolutionist has been forced to devote himself to the investigation of the processes of history, while, on the other, in the presence of an undated record he has assumed an eventless world.

The outcome of this situation is apparent in the series of

assumptions upon which Darwin based his work. In a thoroughly scientific spirit he set himself to discover the process or processes manifested in the emergence of new species. Nevertheless, accepting the authority of Sir Charles Lyell, he began by assuming that "Time is to Nature endless and as nothing," and from this proceeded to his second assumption that new species have arisen only through the slow cumulation of infinitely slight modifications. Furthermore, he took over from Lyell the methodological theory that we must interpret the past history of the earth and its inhabitants by the present, that we must seek for an explanation of what has happened by the study of what is happening, on the assumption that the processes manifested have never been different in kind or degree from what they are now. Lastly, he believed that there had been but one process involved in the origin of all species, that of 'natural selection.'

What Darwin attempted was to describe, as simply and directly as possible, the mode by which, in one particular field of nature, interactions result in something new. The character of his theory is immediately traceable to the absence of specific dates in the historical materials upon which he was forced to rely; had dated evidence been available, his conception of unmarked time, of time as an unbroken flow, could not have arisen. It follows that, having dated events to work from, the historian of man, when he comes to investigate processes, will adopt a procedure widely different from that followed by Darwin and his contemporaries. Instead of confining his attention to the present, utilizing the facts of the past for purposes of verification only, he will begin by examining the evidence for the actual changes that have taken place. Hence the procedure which is bound up with the conception that the present is the key to the past will, so to speak, be reversed, and 'history' will remain the study of the past with a view to the elucidation of the processes manifested in the present.

2) The scientific student of human history cannot accept Darwin's assumptions and procedure as a model upon which

to pattern his inquiry, but he is not therefore left without guidance. An alternative method for approaching the investigation of how things have come to be as they are was suggested by Huxley. The great exponent of Darwinism pointed out that any hypothesis of progressive modification must take into consideration the fact of persistence without progression through indefinite periods, and, furthermore, he urged upon Darwin's attention the possibility of occasional 'rapid leaps' or changes in nature. In short, Huxley recognized three different sets of processes as contributory to the emergence of the present status: first, those represented in fixity, stability, or persistence; second, those manifested in slow continuous modifications; and, third, those revealed in explicit changes or events.

In later discussion the elements unrecognized by Darwin have more and more forced themselves into the foreground of debate, and have colored the views held by all investigators. Thus De Vries supposed that after periods of relative fixity, during which they are subject only to fluctuating variations, living beings may pass through shorter periods when their forms are abruptly modified in different directions by discontinuous changes. So, too, George Darwin expressed the opinion that the study of stability and instability furnishes the problems which the physicist and biologist alike attempt to solve, and he envisaged the course of 'evolution,' not as uniform and slow, but as divided between a sequence of slight continuous modifications accumulating through a long period and somewhat sudden transformations which would appear as historical events. Again, his brother, Francis Darwin, regarded 'evolution,' not as a process of modification, but as a process of drilling organisms into habits, and thought of an organism as a machine in which energy can be set free by some kind of releasing mechanism. This latter idea, as will appear later, was carried further by William Bateson, who also believed that variation occurs as a definite event, and that we can see no changes in progress around us in the contemporary world which can be imagined likely to culminate in the evolution of forms distinct in the larger sense. Finally, not to multiply instances unnecessarily, the essential feature of what I have called the alternative mode of approach is brought out by Hans Gadow in asking why it is that mammalian material can produce what is denied to the lower classes. Why have they not all by this time reached the same grade of perfection? "Because," he says, "every new group is less hampered by tradition, much of which must be discarded by the new departure, and some of its energy is set free to follow up this new course, straight, with ever-growing results, until in its turn this becomes an old rut out of which a new jolt leads once more into fresh fields."

In the study of man, the contemporaries of Darwin maintained a tradition of evolutionary inquiry which investigators like Tylor and McLennan regarded as completely independent of biology. This, indeed, is evident when we find that Tylor considered the essential points for inquiry to be "permanence, modification, and survival." Maine had before this insisted that the stable part of our mental, moral, and physical constitution is the largest part of it and offers a resistance to change that is rarely overcome. Clifford, while imbued with the newer biological conceptions of his time, instituted a contrast between positive and negative conditions of development: "a race," he says, "in proportion as it is plastic and capable of change, may be regarded as young and vigorous, while a race which is fixed, persistent in form, unable to change, is as surely effete, worn out, in peril of extinction." Bagehot, again, who wrote his *Physics and Politics* to illustrate the application of the principles of 'natural selection' and 'inheritance' to political society, recurs throughout his book to the influences which have made nations 'stationary.' He sees in revolutions the outbreak of passions long repressed by fixed custom, but starting into life as soon as that repression had been catastrophically removed. Furthermore, he sets a question which must be regarded as fundamental: "If fixity is an invariable ingredient in early civilizations, how then did any civilization become unfixed?"

It is, however, in the study of the history of language that this alternative method has been most clearly defined. So Whitney, whose *Life and Growth of Language* may be regarded as the classic presentation of this subject in English, utilizes explicitly the three types of processes mentioned above. Thus, while, as is usual in the writings of philologists, he devotes the greater part of his book to a description of the processes through which language has been slowly and continuously modified in transmission from generation to generation, he directs attention to the operation of processes which tend to maintain every spoken dialect the same from age to age, and points, as in a third category, to the fact that occasionally whole communities have been led to adopt the speech of another people as a result of some great revolution. Indeed, it may be said that, so far as method is concerned, the historical study of language is one of the few subjects in the whole range of evolutionary inquiry that has been placed upon a satisfactory basis.

Here it may be observed, by way of addendum, how frequently the idea has been expressed, as by Bagehot and L. H. Morgan, that portions of the human race have been halted at certain stages of progress. Henry Balfour, for example, is of opinion that the heterogeneity of groups may readily be explained by assuming that, while the progress of some races has received relatively little check, the culture development of others has been retarded to a greater or less degree. Hocart, again, attributes 'stagnation' to the failure of some factor or factors (described by him as "constant in their operation") which make for continuous progression. This point of view, however, embodies the assumption that 'progress' is to be anticipated, an opinion which Maine was at pains to controvert, and which is in no way justified by the evidence. 'Progress' is exceptional; hence our first concern must be with the processes, which are universal in their operation, that make for fixity and stagnation. Having determined what these processes are, it will then be possible to observe the influences of other processes through which modification and change are brought about.

3) Before proceeding further, there is, however, a point of some importance which must be dealt with parenthetically. Expressed in the simplest terms, this may be stated in the question: "What are the limits of humanistic inquiry?" The query must be faced, for humanists in all branches of the study of man seem to feel it necessary to base their discussions upon what they conceive to be the conclusions of modern biology. In this way the unavoidable difficulties of the study of man have been needlessly complicated, and the student has involved himself in debates over highly technical matters with which he is not competent to deal. Every science involves, as a qualifying condition of its pursuit, the conscious restriction of attention to a particular set of facts, and the success of any scientific undertaking turns upon the consistency and definiteness with which this initial restriction is observed. For scientific purposes, every investigation must be confined within definite limits; no science pretends to deal with the whole complex of natural phenomena, and in the study of man there are obvious reasons why the field of inquiry should be limited wherever possible.

The problem before us is to find out how man has come to be as he is throughout the world today. The unavoidable restriction upon the limits of the inquiry is that the humanist will accept man 'as given,' and leave all questions relating to his origin and physical differences to the biologist.

While, at first sight, this may appear a radical departure, there is ample justification for the step, over and above the fact that neither the biologist nor the humanist is in a position to deal successfully with the entire field. There is, in short, an important body of evidence which indicates the 'psychic unity of mankind.' A typical example may be found in the remarks of Stefánsson on the Eskimo: "Commonly," he says, "primitive people are supposed to have certain mental qualities, designated as instinctive, through which they vastly excel us along certain lines; and to make up for this excellence they are supposed to be far our inferiors in certain other mental characteristics. My own observations incline me to believe that there are no points in which they, as a race, are any more inferior to us than might be expected from the environment under which they have grown up from childhood; and neither have they any points of superiority over the white man, except those which are developed directly by the environment. Of course an Eskimo can find his way about in the wilderness better than the city dweller or the sailor, but he is likely to fall behind the white man of experience in just about the proportion you would expect, from knowing the greater advantage of training in logical thinking which the white man has had." Similarly, writing of the Sea Dyaks of Borneo, Gomes says: "Allowing for differences in environment, and consequent difference of similes, the idea expressed in many Dyak proverbs is precisely similar to that of some well known among the English." "The radical fundamental thoughts and passions of mankind all over the world, in every age, are much the same."

Judgments such as these may be found in the reports of observers in every part of the world, and the general view expressed is widely accepted by anthropologists. It is entirely possible that the obvious physical differences between men may be accompanied by corresponding psychical differences, but even if it be admitted that there are congenital differences in 'races,' and that the influences of these differences may ultimately become an important study, in our present state of ignorance these differences are negligible quantities, and man may be treated as an unchanging quantity. The opinion of anthropologists coincides, in general, with that of psychologists like McDougall, who thinks that the primary innate tendencies, which are the essential springs or motive powers of all thought and action, are common to men of every race and of every age. So investigators widely separated in their immediate interests reach the same conclusion, namely, that we have every reason to think that the mind of the savage and the mind of the civilized are fundamentally alike. "There can be no doubt," Boas states, "that in the main the mental characteristics of man are the same all over the world." "The working of the human mind," Gomme believes, "is on the same plane wherever and whenever it operates or has operated."

It must be admitted, however, that even this unanimity does not remove all possibility of question or debate, and as a consequence we accept Morgan's axiom of "the specific identity of the brain of all the races of mankind," and Temple's "law of the constancy of human reasoning," not as self-evident or demonstrated truths, but as methodological assumptions set up for the purposes of a particular investigation. We delimit our field by taking man 'as given,' by assuming that all human groups have started from the same level, that in every group the same capacity for 'advancement' has been present, that man is, and has been, very much the same all the world over.

4) If, now, we turn to consider the processes manifested in fixity or stagnation, we may observe that the mental activity of any individual is conditioned at every step by the idea system of which he stands possessed. Assuredly, this conditioning body of ideas is not a product of the individual's own activity, but is imparted to him by the group into which he is born and in which he is brought up. Every individual comes into existence in association with some group, and is subjected from the commencement of his career to a discipline or drilling in the modes of thinking, feeling, and acting of the group. Thus at the foundation of his life there lies a great body of conclusions, motives, and customs for which he is in no manner responsible, but in accordance with which his behavior is unconsciously regulated. "He accepts from the group," as Brinton says, "the ideas, conclusions, and opinions common to it, and the motives of volition, such as customs and rules of conduct, which it collectively sanctions."

This normal condition of dependence is most easily discernible in primitive man, for the lower we descend in the scale of civilization the more strictly, to all appearance, is the individual controlled by the group of which he forms a part. Indeed, the savage is completely hedged about by conventions, at once minute and obligatory, the violation of which is attended by drastic penalties. Hence, as McDougall remarks, "in primitive societies the precision of the customary code and the exact coincidence of public opinion with the code, allow no occasion for deliberation upon conduct, no scope for individual judgment and choice." "We see the same result among all savage communities still existing on the earth, and among all peoples of whom we have any record at the dawn of civilization. Their actions, whether individual or collective, are hampered, controlled, or enforced at every step by custom." It is, unquestionably, because of this rigid enforcement of custom that the lower groups have remained for long periods of time in a fixed or stationary condition, that their manners, customs, and modes of life have continued almost unaltered for generations.

While, however, the discipline of the individual by the group may be more immediately apparent in groups less advanced than our own, the same process is visibly operative in modern life. For, indeed, what we mean by 'civilization' and 'culture' is neither more nor less than the store of ideas, beliefs, conventional opinions, and tastes which is transmitted from each generation to the next, and into which each member of the community is inducted by his elders. And while the modern teacher, but recently become self-conscious of his function, has much to say of the responsibility of the community for the 'education' of the child, there has been, as Cook remarks, a pretty successful education of the race from the days of primitive prehistoric man. It is but formulating the practice of the ages to say that the resources of government and law, religion and morality, must be enlisted to constrain the individual in order to procure a common likeness in impulses, habits, and ideas within the group.

It follows from this unsought initiation into the idea system of his ancestors that, even in the most backward group, the individual enters upon life at a relatively high stage of human advancement; he stands upon a platform which has been laboriously constructed by his unremembered predecessors. At the same time, it must be recognized that, even in the most advanced groups, this initiation imposes severe limitations. At best, the platform is narrow; and the individual acquires habits of thought and a fixity of ideas which render him unduly tenacious of what has been inculcated in him, and unduly suspicious and obstinate in the presence of what may appear to him to be different or new. While, then, the educative discipline tends to preserve what has been acquired, it presents a very real obstacle to further advance. In the face of this consideration, the theory commonly expressed, that "the inheritance of the permanent achievements of one generation by the next is the main factor of progress," that, in fact, human advancement has been due to the maintenance of tradition, to the drilling through which the individual has been put in possession of the acquisitions of the group, will be seen to express but a partial truth, for if this process had been the only one in operation, advancement would, manifestly, have been impossible. What, however, we have in this process of group discipline is the element which must be considered first in any attempt to show how man everywhere has come to be as he is today. This it is that produces that condition of sameness, stagnation, fixity, and persistence which has been dwelt upon by all who have had occasion to speak of backward peoples, lower classes, and illiterate individuals. The operation of this process tends to the maintenance of the idea system of the group or individual as it exists at any given moment, and the study of man involves, as its next step, an inquiry into the manner in which modifications and changes in idea systems have been, and still are, brought about.

5) Under actual conditions this fixity of ideas is never complete, and in all human groups there may be observed in operation certain processes through which idea systems are being slowly but continuously modified.

The processes of modification are of various types, and these are of varying degrees of influence. In the first place, we may readily see that, while the initial discipline of any two individuals may proceed along the same lines, and while their lives may be led in the same surroundings, their experiences in life will never be identical, and in maturity their responses to any given excitation will not be exactly the same. The difference of response will be all the greater if the lives of the two men have been passed in different circumstances. Again, while every member of a primitive group is drilled in its traditional ob- servances and customs, the performance of these obligatory acts cannot be identically transmitted from generation to genera- tion; unconsciously and unobserved, modifications will creep in. This is true even in respect to verbal formulas, the value of which is believed to reside in their exact repetition, for here, in addition to the possible treacheries of memory, the repro- duction will be affected by the unceasing modifications in the use of words. Language, indeed, provides in itself a perfect illustration of the fact that use entails wear, and it is in lan- guage that the processes of modification have been most care- fully observed.

Furthermore, while it is taken for granted that men are very much the same all the world over, this is not to be taken to mean that all men are identical. They are the same on the aver- age, which implies that with reference to any given characteris- tic or faculty a certain percentage of the individuals in a group will be above and below the mean. It follows, for example, that in any group there will be some individuals of greater personal initiative than the majority of their fellows. These undoubt- edly will have an influence, but what is frequently overlooked is that the mental equipment, the idea system, of such indi- viduals, however gifted they may be, is strictly that of the group to which they belong. For more than one reason, indeed, no 'genius' can make any great departure from the idea system of his people; the individual may influence the group, but such modifications as he may succeed in introducing will proceed along established lines, and so cannot be regarded as significant changes.

It is evident, then, that the idea systems of all groups are sub- ject to slow, continuous modification through the operation of processes which may be described as internal or self-contained. They are also modified in varying degrees by 'the contact of peoples.' This term has acquired a special significance in recent years as associated with the hypothesis—based upon the ethnographical study of the distribuiton of culture objects, designs, and practices—that the present status of any group is to be explained in terms of the transmission of culture elements from one group to another. It may at once be said that this hypothesis describes a process, practically universal in its application, which has been of the greatest importance in the gradual modification of idea systems, but one which, nevertheless, cannot be accepted as providing an explanation of the phenomenon of 'advance.'

To make this distinction clear, it is necessary to consider that the process of modification by exterior contact has many phases. A simple form may be instanced in the interchange of objects between contiguous groups, and by this means culture objects may be dispersed over great distances by a series of border exchanges, without the coincident transportation of individuals. An extension of this phase comes when the objects or practices are carried from one group to another by traders, missionaries, or other travelers; and one has but to consider the spread of the megalithic monuments to recognize the antiquity of this mode of influence. Another stage is reached when traders, like the Cretans, Phoenicians, and Greeks, establish themselves among alien peoples; and the farthest step is taken when backward groups are brought under subjection by others of superior culture, as when the inhabitants of Iberia and Gaul were conquered by the Romans, or those of Mexico and Peru by Spain. Now, without question, an influence is always exerted on the idea system of the recipient group, but this influence is by no means subversive of the idea system affected. The new elements enter into the old system, modifying and being in turn modified by it, but do not effect its disintegration; for, although any idea system is a coördinated whole, separate new ideas may be taken over gradually to an almost unlimited extent without affecting its predominant characteristics. This is notably so where material objects or mechanical inventions are concerned, and the introduction of the horse and gun no more revolutionized the American Indian's ways of thinking and acting than the telephone and aeroplane have upset our own conventionalized philosophy of life. A small body of immigrants may thus have an influence on the recipient group out of all proportion to their number, and it would be wholly impossible to understand the present condition of mankind without taking the process of modification by contact into consideration.

Nevertheless, when we turn to apply this process to the special problem of advancement—exemplified concretely in the European civilization of the present—it affords no direct explanatory assistance. The reason is not far to seek, for while the contact process may tend, theoretically, to bring all groups to the level of the highest, it cannot serve to place any one group far in advance of the rest. Even if we suppose that the intruding few, like the British in India, could raise the recipient many to a level with themselves (which may be regarded as an impossibility), this would not raise the status of the more advanced group to which the intruders belong. We may say, therefore, that, in the endeavor to discover how men everywhere have come to be as they are today, we must take into account the operation of a whole series of modifying processes, but we must admit further that these processes do not provide an explanation of the emergence of higher idea systems.

6) In approaching the problem of 'change,' it is above all things important that the investigator should be on his guard against the widely disseminated idea that human advancement has been due to human volition. We must beware of projecting ourselves and our modern intellectual interests into the past, and of imagining ourselves freed from the limitations under which, as we are quite ready to admit, our forefathers labored. The exercise of the will is not a recent acquirement, and today, as formerly, men are largely unconscious of the factors and processes that lie behind their most consciously determined

resolutions. No theory of advancement that is based upon a supposed desire for betterment can be accepted as explanatory of how man has come to be as he is. Primitive man is not engaged in a struggle to emancipate himself from tradition; his efforts are not directed to the inauguration of change, but to the maintenance of the existing status—and it takes some radical upheaval to disturb his confidence in his own ways. Again, in spite of the prepossessions we unconsciously absorb from an acquaintance with biological discussions, we must avoid the assumption that human history displays any such regular and even process of change as is postulated in the Darwinian conception of 'evolution.' This supposition leads inevitably to theories of slow, unbroken progress directed toward some determinable end, but the evidence before us provides no basis for optimistic philosophizing. What we find actually throughout the course of history is the unmistakable results of constant processes manifested in fixity or persistence, tempered by other processes which gradually effect a modification of this rigidity. In addition to these two sets of processes, however, there is abundant evidence of the fact that at different times and in different places certain events have led to significant changes in the groups affected, and that these changes stand in direct relation to the phenomenon of 'advance.'

Investigation in different fields of the study of man has led many scholars—Petrie, Haddon, Rivers, Mackinder, Hogarth, Myres, Temple, Balfour, Smith, Hall, Jastrow, Sollas, to name but a few—to observe that human advancement has followed upon the collision of different groups. Pieced together, the conclusions arrived at so far may be summarized in the statement that definite advance has taken place in the past when a group, forced from its habitat, supposedly by a change in climate, has been brought into collision with another differing from it considerably in culture, and has remained upon the invaded territory. It is probable that this statement as a whole would not receive unquestioned support from all those who have contributed to it in part; on the other hand, it is to be understood

that the palaeontologist, geographer, anthropologist, archae-
ologist, or historian, as the case may be, has arrived at his
conclusion, one may say, incidentally, and has not turned aside
from the matter in hand to give this generalization independent consideration. Thus in any given instance it might be
sufficient to say that "the dispossession by a newcomer of a race
already in occupation of the soil has marked an upward step
in the intellectual progress of mankind," without pursuing the
question further. As a consequence, the conclusions, even in
the abbreviated form here given, have not been carried to a
point at which they might constitute a hypothesis explanatory
of human advancement.

Indeed, it is only when we take a further step and come to
ask how conceivably usurpation of territory, or war, or ad-
mixture of peoples could affect intellectual advancement, that
the underlying problem is brought to light. It cannot well be
assumed that either the intermarriage of different stocks or the
struggle of battle will of itself bring about this result; and while
it is said that "if you would change a man's opinions—trans-
plant him," it does not follow that the change will be effected
by the scenery. In short, the 'change' that leads to advancement
is mental. What, then, is of importance to notice is that when
enforced migration is followed by collision, and this by the
alien occupation of territory, there ensues as a result of the
conflict the breaking down or subversion of the established
idea systems of the groups involved in the struggle. The breakdown of the old and unquestioned system of ideas, though it
may be felt as a public calamity and a personal loss, accomplishes the release of the individual mind from the set forms
in which it has been drilled, and leaves men opportunity to
build up a system for themselves anew. This new idea system
will certainly contain old elements, but it will not be like the
old, for the consolidated group, confronted with conflicting
bodies of knowledge, of observances, and of interpretations,
will experience a critical awakening, and open wondering eyes
upon a new world. Thus it is not the physical contact of men

that is of supreme importance in human advancement, but the overthrow of the dominance of the traditional system in which the individuals composing the group have been trained, and which they have unconditionally accepted; though advancement seems rarely to have been possible, in the past, save when diverse groups have been set face to face in desperate struggle.

Here, then, is a process which differs essentially from those previously described, for it is manifested only when some exterior disturbance or shock has, for the time being, weakened or overcome the influence or effect of the previously described processes. When manifested, however, this process is always the same. The hypothesis required may now be stated in the form that human advancement follows upon the mental release of the members of a group or of a single individual from the authority of an established system of ideas. This release has, in the past, been occasioned through the breaking down of previous idea systems by prolonged struggles between opposing groups which have been brought into conflict as a result of the involuntary movements of peoples. What follows is the building up of a new idea system, which is not a simple cumulation of the knowledge previously accepted, but the product of critical activity stirred by the perception of conflicting elements in the opposed idea systems.

7) The foregoing statement describes only in the most general terms the processes manifested in human history, and should be regarded merely as indicating directions in which investigation is required, for, as must be readily apparent, each of these sets of processes demands careful analysis. While this further analysis will not be continued here, it is of some importance for us to arrive at an understanding of the means which may be employed to verify the results obtained.

It was stated earlier that any theory of how man has come to be as he is must be applicable to all human groups, 'backward' as well as 'advanced'; must apply to the 'backward' and 'advanced' members of all groups, and hence must apply to the experience of the individual in the world today. It follows, therefore, that the processes indicated above are operative in our several individual lives, and, consequently, that the accuracy of the description may be tested by each investigator from the resources of his own personal observation. This, it must be clearly understood, does not mean that the individual is in a position to discover the processes manifested in history through introspection; it does mean that, when results have been arrived at through the scientific study of the past, these results may be verified by reference to what is going on within and around us in the present.

Thus, for example, if we consider the processes manifested in the fixity and persistence of idea systems and ways of doing things, no one can be at a loss to discern the influence upon himself of the community in which he has grown up. From the beginning of life each one of us has been subjected to a discipline by those surrounding us which has determined and defined the avenues open to us for self-assertion or individual purposive activity. Again, each one of us is conscious of explicit restrictions in mental activity due to the particular selection of information and ideas which has been imparted to him at the outset of his career; the mental equipment which each one receives represents only a limited selection from the whole body of knowledge at the command of the group, and yet this selection, which under any other circumstances whatever would have been different, has been, and must remain, a dominant factor in our lives.

Notwithstanding the tenacity with which we cling to mental habits once acquired, our ideas and ways of doing things are continually undergoing modification, the actuality of which we may also verify by direct observation. Indeed, this process is particularly noticeable in advanced groups, for in these, while group discipline is effective in maintaining a certain uniformity in external behavior, the idea systems of individuals vary within wide limits. This variability is due, primarily, to the vast extent of the intellectual heritage of modern groups. Among ourselves, the body of knowledge immediately available is so great that its complete transmission to any individual is wholly unthinkable. It follows that, in modern groups, the participation of the individual in the group idea system is irregular and incomplete, and that under actual conditions each member of a given community acquires a personal system of ideas which differs considerably from that of his fellows, though drawn from the same source. As a consequence, the contact of individuals, being accompanied by the interchange of differing personal views, leads to a continual criticism and modification of our outlook upon the world; and, indeed, the attitude which we regard as specifically characteristic of members of advanced groups is a wide tolerance of these differences in ideas, and a conscious admission of the merely tentative validity of our most cherished convictions.

Every individual, then, may verify from his own experience the actuality of the processes which are manifested, first, in the persistence, and, second, in the slow modification of ideas and ways of doing things, but the case is different when we come to consider the processes and factors of change and advance. As we have seen, change ensues upon a condition of relative fixity through the interposition of shock or disturbance induced by some exterior incident. Now, while, historically, advancement has been dependent upon the collision of groups, the resultant response has taken place in the minds of individuals, and so we are led to see that all transitional eras are alike in being periods of individual mental awakening, and of the release or emancipation of individual initiative in thought and action. This applies equally whether we consider the past or the present, and, consequently, since the antecedents of advance are realized only rarely, we are forced to rely, for the verification we are now discussing, upon the testimony of exceptional individuals. That the historical process of individualization of thought is also the form through which advancement proceeds today would best be shown by an extended examination of the biographies of notable men, but for the present we may accept the evidence adduced by psychologists and other investigators who have already directed attention to the facts.

In reality, there is nothing abstruse about the processes involved, for, primarily, as S. A. Cook has pointed out, we hold ideas simply because nothing has occurred to disturb them; the fact is, in the words of Sir Oliver Lodge, that unless we encounter flaw or jar or change, nothing in us responds. So Bateson, seeking for an alternative to the method of Darwin, has proposed to "consider how far we can get by the process of removal of what we may call 'epistatic' factors, in other words those that control, mask, or suppress underlying powers and faculties." "I have confidence," he says in the course of his inquiry, "that the artistic gifts of mankind will prove to be due not to something added to the make-up of an ordinary man, but to the absence of factors which in the ordinary person inhibit the development of those gifts. They are almost beyond doubt to be looked upon as *releases* of powers normally suppressed." It is, however, in the later writings of William James that the subject receives fullest consideration. Reviewing Herbert Spencer's *Autobiography*, he says, "Mr. Spencer himself is a great social force. The effects he exerts are of the nature of *releases*—his words pull triggers in certain kinds of brain." "In biology, psychology, and sociology," he continues, "the forces concerned are almost exclusively forces of release." Furthermore, at this point one might well incorporate entire his remarkable essay on "The Energies of Men." In this he points out that "as a rule men habitually use only a small part of the powers which they actually possess and which they might use under appropriate conditions." "We are all," he says, "to some degree oppressed, unfree. We don't come to our own. It is there, but we don't get at it." The inhibition is due to the influence of convention, and he remarks that "an intellect thus tied down by literality and decorum makes on one the same sort of impression that an able-bodied man would who should habituate himself to do his work with only one of his fingers, locking up the rest of his organism and leaving it unused." To what, then,

he asks, do men owe their escape? and to what are improvements due, when they occur? In general terms, he says, the
answer is plain: "Excitements, ideas, and efforts are what carry
us over the dam." Ideas, in particular, he regards as notable
stimuli for unlocking what would otherwise be unused reser-
voirs of individual initiative and energy. This effectiveness he
ascribes to the fact, first, that ideas contradict other ideas and
thus arouse critical activity, and, second, that the new ideas
which emerge as a result of this conflict unify us on a new plane
and bring to us a significant enlargement of individual power.
Thus, in complete unconsciousness of the historical aspect of
the subject, James has described, from the point of view of the
individual, what proves to be the essential element in the process through which human advancement has everywhere been
made.

8) We are now in a position to recognize the nature of the
processes which have been operative throughout human history, and to see how the actuality of these may be verified
under present conditions. It must be repeated, however, that
the statement here given is of the most general character, and
that continued research, entailing the minute examination and
comparison of eras of transition, will be required to determine
fully and completely the elements of history. Nevertheless, it
may be urged that the mode of procedure here outlined brings
into one connected view bodies of fact which have hitherto remained disparate and intractable, and that it opens up new
problems and new fields of inquiry for historical investigation.
Indeed, even to the student who regards the construction of
narratives as the sole and proper aim of history, it offers new
phases of interest, suggests new aspects of human activities, and
provides a basis for the treatment of 'general' history which
renders him independent of time-honored philosophies.

Nor is it to be overlooked, in considering the possibilities
of this approach to the study of how man has come to be as he
is, that, in addition to the stimulus it may afford to history, it
makes feasible a mutual understanding and coöperation be-

tween the different specialties of humanistic study. It must be admitted, I think, that the manner in which studies like anthropology, history, and geography, art, literature, and religion, philology, politics, and economics have been carried on in separate compartments has not been conducive in the highest degree to the advancement of knowledge. These subjects are not independent sciences; they are aspects of the study of man which have been pursued in comparative isolation because of the circumstances of their several origins, and because they have not been brought into relation by a common methodology. On the other hand, when it is seen that the undertaking in which they are one and all engaged is the attempt to determine how the idea systems of men have come to be as we find them today, the fundamental unity of these studies at once becomes apparent; and, indeed, as an illustration of this unity, one might well agree with the sentiment (though certainly not with the wording) of Ostwald's statement that the history of the sciences furnishes the best and most trustworthy materials for the study of the laws that govern the development of humanity.

Finally, the method herein described brings the study of history into direct relation with the problems of life. I have indicated that, throughout the past, human advancement has, to a marked degree, been dependent upon war. From this circumstance, many investigators have inferred that war is, in itself, a blessing—however greatly disguised. We may see, however, that this judgment is based upon observations which have not been pressed far enough to elicit a scientific explanation. War has been, times without number, the antecedent of advance, but at other times, as when Buddhism was introduced into China, the same result has followed upon the acceptance of new ideas without the introductory formality of bitter strife. As long, indeed, as we continue to hold tenaciously to customary ideas and ways of doing things, so long must we live in anticipation of the conflict which this persistence must inevitably induce.

It requires no lengthy exposition to demonstrate that the ideas which lead to strife, civil or international, are not the products of the highest knowledge available, are not the verified results of scientific inquiry, but are 'opinions' about matters which, at the moment, we do not fully understand. Among modern peoples, the most important of these opinions are concerned with the ordering of human affairs; and in this area all our 'settlements' of the problems which confront us must continue to be temporary and uncertain compromises until we shall have come to apply the method of science in their solution. Science is not a body of beliefs and opinions, but a way or method of dealing with problems. It has been said by a notable contemporary that men begin the search for truth with fancy, after that they argue, and at length they try to find out. Scientific method is the term we use for the orderly and systematic effort to find out. Hitherto, the most serious affairs of men have been decided upon the basis of argumentation, carried, not infrequently, to the utmost limits of destruction and death. It should be possible to apply in this domain the method of finding out, and it has been my hope to contribute, in however tentative a manner, to this end.

Related Publications by Frederick J. Teggart

"The Circumstance or the Substance of History," *American Historical Review*, 15(1910): 709–719.

Prolegomena to History: The Relations of History to Literature, Philosophy, and Science. Berkeley: University of California Press, 1916.

"The Approach to the Study of Man," *Journal of Philosophy*, 16(1919): 151–156.

"Geography as an Aid to Statecraft: An Appreciation of Mackinder's 'Democratic Ideals and Reality'," *Geographical Review*, 8(1919): 227–242.

"Anthropology and History," *Journal of Philosophy*, 16 (1919): 691–696.

"Clio," *University of California Chronicle*, 24(1922): 347–360.

"Turgot's Approach to the Study of Man," *ibid.*, 28(1926): 129–142.

"The Humanistic Study of Change in Time," *Journal of Philosophy*, 23(1926): 309–315.

"The Responsibility of the Historian," read before the American Historical Association, December 28, 1927, and privately printed in *Two Essays on History*, Berkeley, 1930.

"Notes on 'Timeless' Sociology," *Social Forces*, 7(1929): 362–365.

"Spengler," *Saturday Review of Literature*, 5(1929): 597–599. Reprinted in *Two Essays on History*, *op. cit.*

Rome and China: A Study of Correlations in Historical Events. Berkeley: University of California Press, 1939.

"A Problem in the History of Ideas," *Journal of the History of Ideas*, 1(1940): 494–503.

"World History," *Scientia*, 69(1941): 30–35.

"War and Civilization in the Future," *American Journal of Sociology*, 46(1941): 582–590.

"Causation in Historical Events," *Journal of the History of Ideas*, 3(1942): 3–11.

"The Argument of Hesiod's *Works and Days*," *Journal of the History of Ideas*, 8(1947): 45–77.

Index